THE STANDARD BOOK OF
Bidding

CHARLES H. GOREN

THE STANDARD BOOK

OF Bidding

INTRODUCTION BY W. SOMERSET MAUGHAM

NEW REVISED EDITION

GARDEN CITY, NEW YORK   1948

Doubleday & Company, Inc.

FOREWORD

ANY EXPOSITIONIST who seeks the attention of a large audience must, in the very nature of things, establish his claim to authority. I hope you will regard it as a pardonable lack of modesty on my part if I base my claim on the simple factor of success. Over a period of ten years it has been my good fortune to gather more National Championships than any other player in the country, and, during the same period, to have won more tournaments and gained more Master Points than any other player in history. And it is with no affectation of modesty that I ascribe this success not to any personal superiority, to which I lay no claim, but rather to the efficacy of the methods herein advocated.

Certain of my readers will refer to the principles set forth in this volume as the "Goren System." Whether or not they are so designated is of little consequence. What I desire to make very clear is that this is the way I bid and I think you can too.

Almost all bridge writers who actually compete have at one time or another been indicted under the charge, "He advises his readers to do one thing, but in his own play he does something entirely different," or "He doesn't play his own system." I can see the reason for it. These writers have seen fit to compromise between their own convictions and what they thought the public could absorb. This I have not chosen to do. I play as I write, or, perhaps more properly, I write as I play.

To this I have many witnesses. At no time have I ever denied kibitzing privileges to anyone who might have been interested. My game is therefore constantly open to inspection. One kibitzer I recall with special interest. Her name has long since escaped me, but I remember that she was a contract bridge teacher in Cleveland. She sat quietly through the entire final session of the Team-of-Four event at the National Championships one year when they were held in that city. Our Philadelphia team had just successfully defended its title and my partner and I felt gratified at having just delivered what we regarded as a dream game. It was, in my opinion, the finest performance of our careers. Few if any of the hands found their way into the public prints, for the game was not of the sensational variety; there were no psychics, no squeezes, no involved coups. But for thirty-six successive hands we made the correct decision in each case and not a single error was committed.

At the conclusion of the game, quite by chance, I overheard our kibitzer comment to one of her cronies, "I don't see where he's so wonderful. There wasn't a thing he did tonight that I couldn't have done." To an unsympathetic ear, her remark may have carried with it the barest suggestion of arrogance. In point of fact, she was quite right. There wasn't a thing we did that night that she couldn't have done.

A story this long should have a moral and it does. It's simply this: That the type of game played by the top flight experts is much simpler and far less involved than the average tea-and-crumpet bridge game.

The question of systems is not nearly as important as it was in the early days of contract. To be sure, there are a few bidding situations which are managed somewhat differently by various groups of players, but for all practical purposes contract bidding methods have become standardized. The differences are mainly in refinements, and I have pointed these out where it has been practical to do so. The methods I employ, and which I here recommend to your use, have been tested in the crucible of actual competition and represent, I believe, the best thought of the most successful players in the country today.

Throughout the book I have concerned myself not so much with the conventional aspects of the game as with the logic of cards. It is the reason rather than the rule that should be the primary object of your attention.

As usual, I wish to make a broad acknowledgment to those writers from whom I have borrowed both ideas and examples, and I am especially grateful to Lawrence Weiss for permission to use a number of illustrations from his very scholarly treatise on the subject.

To my friend Albert H. Morehead, I am indebted more than it is possible to estimate for his invaluable suggestions on many of the theoretical aspects of the game.

CHARLES H. GOREN

CONTENTS

INTRODUCTION

I AM NOT at all the proper person to write an introduction to this book, for I am an indifferent bridge player and my chief asset as a partner is that I have never thought myself anything else. I do not engage in post-mortems, for I think the players who habitually do so make a bore of the most entertaining game that the art of man has devised; the fact is that if you cannot see a mistake when you have made it no argument will convince you of your error and so the carping critic may just as well hold his peace and deal the next hand. When my partner blames me for having played the wrong card, I accept his reproof with humility, and when he has let me down fourteen hundred by grossly overcalling, I bid him cheerfully not to give it another thought. Of such, you will say, is the kingdom of heaven, and I modestly agree.

Charles Goren asked me to write a short piece to present his new book to the public and I accepted with alacrity; I thought it a great compliment that he paid me. I felt as proud as a lieutenant might feel if he were bidden by his admiral to lead the flagship into battle. But having a practical side to an otherwise idealistic nature I told him that I thought I had better let him know at once what my terms were. He blanched, but agreed to them. They were that he should dine and play bridge with me. Of course I knew I should lose my money, but I was convinced that the fun it would be must make whatever it cost well worth it. I have played only half a dozen times with the life masters and it is rash to generalize on such a slight experience, but it has seemed to me that they are easier to play with than players of the second or third class, for you know that they have a good reason for doing what they do, and when they speak they mean what they say. The chief difficulty the indifferent player playing with indifferent players has to contend with is that they will trust their hunches rather than their common sense and allow their wishes to influence their judgment. I was glad to be given the opportunity to write this introduction also because it will have enabled me to disembarrass my conscience of a sense of guilt.

Charles Goren is an amiable man, and I have aroused in the breasts of those with whom I habitually play bridge a cordial dislike of him. It came about by accident. I had been reading and rereading my author's *Better Bridge for Better Players* and I was playing a contract which I had little hope of making. A suit was led of which I had the ace and king in my hand with the jack in dummy, and as I put up the jack I murmured: Charles Goren does not recommend the lead from the queen. The jack held, and this innocent remark so disorganized the defense that I made my contract and won the rubber. Since then, when the occasion has presented itself, I have used Charles Goren's precepts as useful weapons in the war of nerves, and the effect has been highly satisfactory, but I am bound to admit that with my friends he has become a highly unpopular character. It is in vain that I ask them mildly: "But why don't you read his book?" They reply with an indignant snort.

For my own part I can say that I profited as much as it was in my sinful nature to do from *Better Bridge for Better Players,* and I hope I have profited by reading the book I now present to you. On a first reading, which is all I have so far been able to give it, I felt that I could never hope to remember all the rules it gives and that to try to do so would only confuse me, but as I thought it over, it occurred to me that very few of them, not more than half a dozen, perhaps, were obligatory—rules which must be followed as you follow those of any game; all the rest depended on common sense, and if you had common sense and were prepared to abide by it you need not clutter your brain with any great number of precepts. The moral I have gathered from reading Charles Goren's book is that if you have a cool head, the ability to put two and two together and get the right answer, and tell the exact truth about your hand when you bid, you will be a useful partner at the bridge table and a formidable opponent.

I should like to end this introduction with a warm appreciation of Charles Goren, but in his foreword he has himself so adequately said all I could possibly say about him that I can think of nothing to add. But everything he has said is fully justified. I will leave you, therefore, to profit by the excellent book he has written for your instruction. You can learn a great deal from it, but even then I doubt whether you will become as fine a bridge player as its author. For to be that, more than application and industry are needed. But you will certainly play bridge better than you did before.

W. Somerset Maugham

THE STANDARD BOOK OF
Bidding

CHAPTER I

OPENING BIDS

MANY READERS FEEL that an author is assuming a patronizing
attitude toward them when he devotes any considerable time
and space to the subject of the opening bid. They seem to think
that nothing more is required than to count up the hand and look
for a biddable suit. But it is not as simple as all that. First of all,
there are many close questions as to whether or not the hand
should be opened, and the use of good judgment is frequently required in finding the answer. Then again, so many hands present
a choice of opening bids that the proper selection at the start may
be vital to the success of the hand. It will pay the student, therefore, to examine some of the problems, starting from the Letter A.

First let us dispose of the problem of how to count. Are you
accustomed to the Culbertson Honor Trick Table, the Four Aces
Point Count, the Reith Point Count, the Point Count advocated
by the late Milton Work? For many years the bridge-playing
public has been confused by conflicting claims of accuracy on
the part of rival systems for their tables of card values or methods
of counting. I have a feeling that these claims have about as
much merit as those held forth by rival manufacturers of aspirin;
that in all but a few isolated cases the various methods lead to
the same conclusion. "Analysis of thousands of hands has shown,"
claims one author, "that my count is more accurate by .016."
This very argument is its own indictment. Cards do not behave
that way. No hand has ever been lost by a tenth of a trick.

In presenting my bidding technique I am in the happy position
of not having to insist upon any special table of valuation. My
students are at liberty to count their hands in any manner they
find most suitable to their tastes. I admire the technique of my
golf pro. He does not care very much how his pupils hold the golf
club, but he does insist that they be comfortable. Actually I do

not like counting too much and try to avoid it whenever possible, although I do recognize that a certain amount of counting is necessary, particularly where No Trump bids are involved. Since the majority of players prefer the honor trick measure, I most frequently speak in those terms. The reader should bear in mind that whenever I refer to an honor trick it represents approximately the equivalent of an Ace. Therefore if you are in the habit of using a table of point counts, substitute the figure representing the value of an Ace for the term "honor trick." In other words in most of my discussions herein an honor trick will be synonymous with 4 points.

TABLES OF VALUES

TABLE OF HONOR TRICKS

2 Honor Tricks	1½ Honor Tricks	1 Honor Trick	½ Honor Trick
A K	A Q	A	K x
		K Q	Q J x
		K J 10	

Jacks accompanied by other honors, and Queens not otherwise counted, are regarded as plus values. A plus value may be looked upon as about a quarter of a trick, so that two plus values are equal to ½ honor trick.

4-3-2-1 POINT COUNT

Ace	4
King	3
Queen	2
Jack	1

(For purposes of making up a one No Trump opening, two tens may be valued as the equal of a Jack.)

Average hand	10
Total of pack	40

Hands counting 14 (an Ace above average) are obligatory openings.

THE FOUR ACES POINT COUNT

Ace	3
King	2

Queen	1
Jack	1/2
Average hand	6½
Total of Pack	26

A hand counting 9½ or more must be opened.

A hand counting 7 to 9 may be opened with certain distributions, as will be illustrated later.

Wherever not otherwise designated throughout this text the point count used in valuing hands for No Trump will be the 4-3-2-1.

The Honor Trick Table is a table of defensive tricks, that is, tricks that you will probably win even if the adversaries play the hand. Therefore honor tricks generally include only those that are apt to win tricks on the first or second round of the suit. After that, it is probable that the opponents will ruff your high cards. As an illustration: Ace-King-Queen-Jack would count only 2-plus honor tricks because the third round of the suit will probably be ruffed by the opponents. Of course, when you play the hand yourself we assume that you will be able to draw trumps and that the Ace-King-Queen-Jack will take four tricks. So when you are calculating the number of tricks you can take if you play the hand, you employ the Table of Honor Winners, which follows.

TABLE OF HONOR WINNERS (*Playing Tricks*)

A K Q.........3	winners	K Q J.........2		winners
A K J.........2½	"	K Q 10.......1½		"
A Q J.........2-plus	"	K Q x.........1-plus		"
A Q 10........1½-plus	"	K J 10.........1-plus		"
A J 10........1½	"	K J x.........1		"
A J...........1-plus	"	Q J 10........1		"
K J...........½-plus	"	Q J x.........½-plus		"

Value solid or near-solid four-card combinations as follows:

A K Q J......4	winners	K Q J 10.....3	winners
A K J 10.....3½	"	K J 10 9......2-plus	"
A Q J 10.....3-plus	"	Q J 10 9......2	"
A J 10 9......2½	"	J 10 9 8.......1	"

Any other card held with one of the above 4-card combinations is valued as one full winner.

In addition to the tricks declarer will take with high cards, he will develop some tricks with his lower cards. The value of the low cards depends upon whether they are in trumps or in a side suit. The following is the:

TABLE OF LONG-SUIT WINNERS

In own trump suit (if supported)	Length of suit	In any side suit or in partner's suit
1 winner	4 cards	½ winner
2 winners	5 "	1 "
3 "	6 "	2 winners
4 "	7 "	4 "

WINNERS IN DUMMY HAND

(1) Honors and solid suits count at their full value. In addition count one winner for the Ace, the King or the Queen-Jack, and ½ winner for the Queen, of partner's suit.

(2) Long cards in partner's trump suit and in side suits count according to the table of long-suit winners. But you must remember not to give values for length in a side suit when partner has shown a two-suiter. In other words, when your partner is very short in your four-card side suit it is very evident that he will have no chance to develop that side suit.

(3) If your hand contains a singleton or a doubleton with three or more trumps, your partner will probably be able to ruff that suit in your hand. Therefore count short-suit values as follows:

RUFFING WINNERS

With two short suits, count only one—the shorter	With 3 trumps	With 4 or more trumps
Doubleton	½ trick	1 trick
Singleton	1 "	2 tricks
Void	2 tricks	3 "

The declarer should not count ruffing winners in his own hand, because that would be counting his trumps twice. Ruffing winners are counted only in the dummy hand. The declarer counts only his honor winners and long-suit winners.

HONOR TRICK REQUIREMENTS FOR OPENING SUIT-BIDS OF ONE

The honor trick requirements for an opening suit-bid of one are:

> 3 honor tricks with a non-rebiddable suit
> 2½ honor tricks with a rebiddable suit

In other words, 2½ honor tricks do not automatically produce an opening bid. In order to understand opening bids you must understand what constitutes a biddable suit.

BIDDABLE SUITS

In recent years the requirements for biddable suits have been reduced. A four-card suit is now biddable if it is headed by the Queen-ten. Any five-card suit is biddable.

For example, these are biddable suits:

> Q 10 x x   K x x x   A x x x

REBIDDABLE SUITS

A rebiddable suit is one which may be bid a second time without partner's having supported it. The first requirement is that it must contain at least five cards. A four-card suit should not be rebid if partner has not raised it. If partner supports your four-card suit you may rebid it as many times as your hand warrants. Not all five-card suits are rebiddable. Even a five-card suit should have solidity in order to be rebid. The following suits are rebiddable.

A K x x x	A J x x x	K Q x x x
K J 9 x x	Q J 9 x x	x x x x x x

It will be noted that any six-card suit, regardless of its top strength, is rebiddable.

DECIDING WHEN TO OPEN THE BIDDING

The first question to determine is whether to open the bidding.

The textbook requirements are stated above, but it is not contemplated that you will adhere to them slavishly. The table is your servant, not your master.

It is to be borne in mind that an opening bid is not an isolated event. It is the first step in a campaign and it is imperative to look one step ahead and contemplate what your partner is most likely to bid in response. You must then have a clear idea of what your second bid will be. If that second bid is going to cause you embarrassment you have made an error. Either you should not have opened, or you opened the bidding with the wrong suit. This, in plain language, sums up the principle of preparedness.

It is appropriate at this time to refer to the universally accepted convention known as the New Suit Forcing principle, which is:

If you open the bidding with one of a suit and partner responds with some other suit you are obliged to speak once more.

This is an obligation that rests only on the person who *opens* the bidding. It does not apply to anyone else at the table. (Nor does it apply when partner has previously passed.) This principle applies only to the showing of a new suit. If the opener bids 1 Spade, for example, and partner responds with 1 No Trump, the opener need not bid again, nor need the opener bid again if partner makes a simple raise from one to two in the same suit.

It has many times been suggested that no opening bid should be made unless the hand contains a rebid. That is essentially true, but let us see if we can clarify this rule. You deal and hold:

♠ A K J x   ♡ x x x   ◊ A x x   ♣ x x x   (12 points)

A reference to the table of opening bid requirements (page 5) will reveal that you have the essentials of an opening bid. You have 3-plus honor tricks, and a biddable suit. But look a minute into the future. If you bid 1 Spade partner might respond with 2 Hearts. What then? You are not in a position to raise the Hearts. You may not rebid a four-card Spade suit, and a rebid of 2 No Trump is unthinkable, because your hand is not strong enough. There is nothing left for you to do, yet you may not pass, since you are the opener and partner named a new suit. In a word, you are very uncomfortable. If that is true you have committed an error. You should have foreseen this possibility and consequently should not have opened the bidding.

Let us change this hand slightly, retaining exactly the same high card strength:

♠ A K x x   ♡ A J x x   ◇ x x   ♣ x x x   (12 points)

You open with 1 Spade. If partner responds with 2 Clubs or 2 Diamonds you are in a position to rebid by calling 2 Hearts, and partner may return to 2 Spades if he so desires. If partner responds with 2 Hearts you can raise. You will have discharged your obligation to rebid without causing yourself any discomfort.

♠ A K J x x   ♡ K x x   ◇ x x   ♣ x x x

You have 2½-plus honor tricks and a rebiddable suit. This meets the requirements. You open with 1 Spade. If partner bids two of any suit you may safely rebid 2 Spades.

♠ K 10 x x x   ♡ A K x   ◇ x x   ♣ x x x

This hand contains 2½ honor tricks but a suit that is not quite rebiddable. If partner should respond with two of a suit you would be obliged to rebid an unrebiddable Spade suit.

♠ K 10 x x x   ♡ A K x x   ◇ x x   ♣ x x

This hand possesses exactly the same high-card content as the preceding one, but an opening bid of 1 Spade is recommended because if partner responds with 2 Clubs or 2 Diamonds you can rebid 2 Hearts and give partner a cheap choice.

IN A NUTSHELL

In order to be prepared for his second bid the opener, in addition to the required strength, must have either a rebiddable suit or a rebiddable hand.

REBIDDABLE HANDS

What makes a hand rebiddable? Either another suit which can be shown without getting the bidding up too high, or an excess of strength. For example:

♠ A K J x   ♡ K J x   ◇ A x x   ♣ x x x

This hand contains no rebiddable suit and no second suit, but its excess strength makes a second bid convenient. If partner responds with 2 Clubs we are strong enough to bid 2 No Trump. If partner responds with two of anything else we are strong enough to raise.

Some players make a distinction between the requirements for vulnerable and non-vulnerable openings. Except in cases of preëmpts I do not subscribe to that view. If you think a hand calls for an opening bid, vulnerability should not deter you from opening. In fact, there is a distinct psychological advantage in being the first to speak, and it is just as improper to pass a hand that should be opened as it is to open a hand that falls short of the requirements.

There are certain hands on which an opening bid is mandatory, even though they are short of the count. This is because there are some values that do not appear in the cold mathematical figures of the honor trick table. Whenever there is something that you like especially well about a hand, add a plus value. You may be fond of a hand for any number of reasons:

a. *Length of suit.* A long, strong suit provides safety and convenience, because you can sign off by repeated rebids in the suit. This hand is a good 1 Spade bid:

♠ K Q 10 x x x   ♡ A x   ◇ Q x x   ♣ x x

b. *The possession of two five-card suits.* These hands are always better than their actual count. To a somewhat lesser degree this is true of 5-4 two-suiters.

♠ K Q 10 x x   ♡ K Q 10 x x   ◇ Q x   ♣ x

An opening bid of 1 Spade is recommended. It is an easy hand

IN A NUTSHELL

A hand should be opened in third position with a King less than the normal requirements, provided you have a fairly good suit.

THE SHORT CLUB BID

This is not a system. It is a convenience. I make this point because so many players are heard to inquire, "Partner, do you play the Short Club?" as though referring to some special convention. They explain that they open with a Club to show three tricks. And what, pray, do you bid with

♠ K x x   ♡ x x   ◇ x x x   ♣ A K Q 10 x,

a hand that contains only 2½ tricks? To which, of course, the answer is 1 Club.

The point of the Short Club is this: There are certain hands which must be opened because they contain too many high cards to be passed, but which contain no convenient opening bid because they would be difficult to rebid. In such cases an opening bid of 1 Club is recommended on a three-card suit, if it is headed by at least a Queen. For example:

♠ A K J x   ♡ J 10 x   ◇ x x x   ♣ A 10 x

This hand contains considerably more than 3 honor tricks (over 13 points) and therefore must not be passed. However, if you should make the normal opening bid of 1 Spade it is evident that you will have no convenient rebid should partner respond with two Diamonds. For your own personal convenience this hand should be opened with 1 Club. If partner's response is 1 Diamond or 1 Heart, the rebid is 1 Spade. If his response is 1 Spade, you raise to two. If the response is 1 No Trump, you pass, and if his response is 2 Clubs, you should also pass.

This bid of 1 Club is made not *because* your Club holding is short, but *in spite of it*. It is a practice devised strictly for the convenience of the opener, and it should be no concern of partner. He should treat all Club bids as though they were natural bids, being careful, however, not to raise Clubs without four good trumps. This subjects him to no hardship, since it is so easy to find some other bid at the level of one.

There is another type of hand which some players like to open with 1 Club:

♠ Q 10 x x   ♡ K x x x   ◇ 10 x   ♣ A K x

This meets the minimum requirements. It can be opened with 1 Spade, but then if partner responds with 2 Diamonds it will be necessary to rebid 2 Hearts. The weakness of the two suits and the border-line nature of the hand make one hesitant about adopting this bidding sequence. A Club opening may be conveniently employed in this case. If partner responds with a major, that suit is raised. If partner responds with 1 Diamond a rebid is available in one of the major suits.

When there is no occasion to worry about a rebid, a hand like this one, previously shown:

♠ A K J x   ♡ J 10 x   ◇ x x x   ♣ A 10 x

need not be opened with 1 Club.

When is there no occasion to worry about a rebid? When your partner has previously passed and, for that reason, you are persuaded that there is no more than a part score in the hand. In third position, for example, the proper opening with the above hand is 1 Spade, since you are trying for a part score and intend to pass any bid that partner makes.

IN A NUTSHELL

The "Short Club" is not a system. It is a convenience.

BIDDING WITH MORE THAN ONE SUIT

When a hand contains more than one biddable suit there is often a question as to the sequence in which they should be shown. While general principles may be laid down to cover the vast majority of hands, nevertheless there remain a considerable number of cases in which the exercise of sound judgment will be required. As is usual in such cases, the decision involves looking one step ahead in the bidding. Let us examine a few of the basic principles.

Length of suit is one of the prime considerations. When you hold two five-card suits the higher ranking (not necessarily the stronger) should be bid first.

♠ Q 10 x x x   ♡ A K x x x   ◊ K x   ♣ x

The proper opening bid is 1 Spade, not 1 Heart, although the Heart suit is stronger. When Hearts are shown on the next round partner will have the option of returning to the first suit without increasing the contract.

As a general rule, with two suits of unequal length the longer is bid first.

♠ A K Q x   ♡ A J x x x   ◊ K x x   ♣ x

The proper opening bid is 1 Heart. When you bid Spades on the next round partner will recognize that you have only four of them. There are certain exceptions to this principle, which will be discussed later.

Similarly, holding a 6-5 distribution, the six-card suit is shown first regardless of rank, but the subsequent bidding is developed in a somewhat different manner:

♠ x   ♡ A K x x x   ◊ A Q J x x x   ♣ x

You open the bidding with 1 Diamond. Partner responds with 1 Spade. You next bid 2 Hearts. At this point, partner is under the impression that you have five Diamonds and four Hearts, but that impression will soon be corrected. Over your 2 Heart bid let us assume that responder rebids his Spades. Now there may be a temptation to bid 3 Diamonds, but this should be stifled. The proper call is 3 Hearts. This will indicate that you have a five-card Heart suit, inasmuch as you have rebid it without support from partner. When your partner learns that you have five Hearts he will realize that you must have six Diamonds, since with two five-card suits you would have shown the higher ranking first.

CHOICE BETWEEN TWO FOUR-CARD SUITS

It is the hands that contain more than one four-card suit that seem to cause the average player most concern.

Perhaps the simplest and most effective guide is the following: Look for the shortest suit in your hand (either singleton or doubleton) and bid first that suit which ranks below your singleton or doubleton. If the suit below is not biddable select the next below that. To illustrate:

1. ♠ x x x   ♡ x x   ◇ A K x x   ♣ A Q J x

Here the shortest suit is Hearts. The suit ranking next below Hearts is Diamonds. The correct bid is 1 Diamond.

2. ♠ A K x x   ♡ x x x   ◇ x x   ♣ A Q J x

In this hand the shortest suit is Diamonds. The suit ranking next below is Clubs. The proper opening bid is 1 Club.

3. ♠ A K x x   ♡ A Q J x   ◇ x x x   ♣ x x

In this hand the shortest suit is Clubs. We must bid first the suit that ranks "next below" Clubs. Since there is no such suit we start over, and the correct bid is 1 Spade.

4. ♠ x x x   ♡ A K x x   ◇ A Q J x   ♣ x x

In this hand the shortest suit is Clubs. The next suit below (for the purpose of this rule) is Spades, but since the Spades are not biddable we go to the next suit below that and the proper bid is 1 Heart.

Let us take these four examples and see how conveniently this rule works out in practice.

In No. 1 the opening bid is 1 Diamond. If partner responds with 1 Heart or 1 Spade your rebid is 2 Clubs, permitting partner to return to 2 Diamonds. If partner responds with 2 Clubs you are in a position to raise that suit.

In No. 2 you open with 1 Club. If partner responds with either 1 Diamond or 1 Heart your rebid is 1 Spade.

In No. 3 the opening bid is 1 Spade. If partner bids 2 Hearts, you raise. If partner bids 2 Diamonds or 2 Clubs you bid 2 Hearts, permitting partner to return to 2 Spades.

In No. 4 the opening bid is 1 Heart. If partner bids either 1 Spade or 2 Clubs your rebid is 2 Diamonds, permitting partner to return to 2 Hearts.

It will be seen, therefore, that in each case the rebid was very convenient, inasmuch as the second suit could be shown at a reasonable level and partner was permitted to return to the first suit at a level no higher than two. That is the test.

Observe that if the wrong suit had been selected for the opening in any of these cases it would have been impossible for partner to return to your original suit at the level of two, and in case No. 2 it is quite apparent that if you open with 1 Spade partner will be obliged to bid two of a red suit, which will force you immediately into the three zone if you choose to show your second suit.

THE CHOICE WHEN HOLDING THREE FOUR-CARD SUITS

The same principle is followed when you have three four-card suits. Start with the suit immediately below your singleton.

The practical reason behind the rule is this: The probabilities favor partner's responding in your shortest suit and this method renders your second bid more convenient.

♠ A K x x   ♡ A J 10 x   ♢ x   ♣ K J x x

The correct opening bid is 1 Club, the suit below the singleton. If partner responds with 1 Diamond you rebid 1 Spade. If he then bids 2 Diamonds you may bid 2 Hearts.

♠ A 10 x x   ♡ A Q x x   ♢ A Q x x   ♣ x

The proper opening bid is 1 Spade. (Spades are considered to rank immediately below Clubs for the purpose of this rule.) If your partner responds with 2 Clubs your next bid will be 2 Hearts, and if necessary or convenient you may show the Diamonds later.

♠ A K J x   ♡ 10 x x   ◇ A Q J x   ♣ x x

Here the recommended bid is 1 Spade. Partner's most probable response is 2 Clubs and your rebid will be 2 Diamonds, which will permit partner to return to 2 Spades if he chooses.

♠ A K J x   ♡ x x   ◇ A Q J x   ♣ 10 x x

With this hand the recommended bid is 1 Diamond. Partner is most likely to respond with 1 Heart and you have the convenient rebid of 1 Spade, whereas had you opened with 1 Spade and partner responded with 2 Hearts you would have been in an awkward position.

What happens, you will naturally ask, when partner does not act according to specifications and responds in an unexpected suit?

I agree that an awkward situation develops and you must extricate yourself in the cheapest possible manner, even though it involves a little tampering with the truth.

Look at the last hand again. You open with 1 Diamond and partner responds, rudely enough, with 2 Clubs. You are sorry now that you did not open with 1 Spade, but it's too late to worry about that. What is the cheapest way to get out? Not by a bid of 2 Spades, because that makes it impossible for partner to return to 2 Diamonds. A raise to 3 Clubs is not desirable. The most practical solution is to tell a white lie about your Diamond suit. Rebid 2 Diamonds. At least partner will realize that you have not a strong opening bid. But, you will contend, a four-card suit is not rebiddable when unsupported by partner. You are quite right, and if you have a partner who is a stickler for technicalities do not admit that you rebid the four-card suit. Slyly place a little Heart among your Diamonds and blame it on the bad lighting in the room. "You were almost sure you had five Diamonds." It's better to lie about a suit than about the strength of your hand as a whole.

With the hand before that, you opened with 1 Spade. Suppose partner responds with 2 Hearts. You are faced with a similar embarrassment. You may, if you choose, stretch a point and bid

3 Hearts; or you may engage in the same type of chicanery suggested above, misread your hand to see five Spades, and rebid the suit.

In the majority of cases the recommended rule will work. One slight exception is suggested. Holding four Clubs and four Hearts, best results will as a rule be obtained by opening with 1 Club.

1.	♠ x x x	♡ A Q x x	◇ x x	♣ A K x x
2.	♠ x x	♡ A Q x x	◇ x x x	♣ A K x x

With No. 1 the rule applies. Open 1 Club, the suit below the doubleton.

With No. 2 the exception applies. The suit below the doubleton is Hearts, but it is better to open with 1 Club. If partner responds with 1 Diamond the rebid is 1 Heart. If partner responds with 1 Spade, a slightly unnatural rebid of 1 No Trump should be resorted to, for a rebid of 2 Hearts, which makes it impossible for partner to return to 2 Clubs, would require a stronger hand than this. The objection to opening with 1 Heart is that partner might respond with 2 Diamonds, which would leave you in an awkward position.

IN A NUTSHELL

With more than one four-card suit, bid first that suit which ranks below your shortest suit, except that with four Clubs and four Hearts, the hand should be opened with 1 Club, regardless of the shortest suit.

SOME EXCEPTIONS

We come now to a few cases which are handled somewhat exceptionally:

Opener	Responder
♠ A K J x	♠ x x
♡ A Q x x	♡ K J 10 x x
◇ K Q J x	◇ x x x
♣ x	♣ x x x

The recommended rule for hands containing three four-card suits is to begin with that suit which ranks below the singleton. Under this rule the opener's bid should be 1 Spade. But with a hand so rich in high cards there is a slight risk involved in opening with 1 Spade, since partner may find it difficult to keep the bidding open. He may fear to show his suit at the level of two. Observe how this works in the example shown. If the opening bid is 1 Spade responder is obliged to pass; whereas had the opening bid been 1 Diamond responder would have chanced a 1 Heart bid, whereupon the partnership would straightway have proceeded to game.

The exception to the rule may therefore be stated as follows: With 4-4-4-1 hands containing about 5 honor tricks, where the normal opening should be 1 Spade, it is sound strategy to open with a minor suit to afford partner the opportunity to respond at the level of one, since he probably has not a good hand.

Another type of hand which is managed exceptionally is the following:

♠ K x x x x   ♡ x   ◇ x x   ♣ A K J x x

The accepted rule is: With two five-card suits bid first the higher-ranking. Following the rule would lead to discomfort with this hand. If you open with 1 Spade, partner will very likely respond with two in a red suit. Quite obviously you cannot afford to bid 3 Clubs. Your hand is not good enough. You are therefore forced to rebid the rather feeble Spade suit. That is not comfortable.

The recommended procedure therefore is to open the bidding with 1 Club, as though your Spade suit were only four cards long. (For practical purposes the Spade suit is not much better than a decent four-card suit.) When partner responds with one of the red suits your rebid will be 1 Spade.

A slightly different example:

♠ A K J x x   ♡ x   ◇ x x   ♣ K x x x x

On hands of this type there is divided opinion. Some experts open this hand with 1 Club so that both suits may be shown.

Others prefer to open with 1 Spade and over a response of 2 Diamonds or 2 Hearts they rebid to 2 Spades. The latter group, it will be seen, favors opening with the Spade suit if it is soundly rebiddable. They feel that it is no hardship to conceal the five-card Club suit. With this view I concur.

REVERSING

It has been observed that with suits of unequal length you bid the longer first, regardless of rank. To this rule there are several exceptions, based entirely on expediency.

♠ A K J x   ♡ K J x x x   ◊ x x x   ♣ x

How should you open this hand? Some players would bid 1 Heart, following the orthodox rule. But suppose partner's response is 2 Clubs. What then? If you wish to show your other suit you must bid 2 Spades. This makes it impossible for your partner to return to 2 Hearts, and if he is forced to return to 3 Hearts you may well be in trouble. The alternative—to rebid this questionable Heart suit, deliberately suppressing the Spades—is almost equally undesirable. Expediency therefore dictates that you deliberately misdescribe your hand for the sake of safety. You will originally treat the Hearts as though they were a four-card suit. In that case the proper opening would be 1 Spade. If partner responds with 2 Clubs your rebid is 2 Hearts, which permits partner to return to 2 Spades if he chooses.

Let us examine a stronger hand:

♠ A Q 10 x   ♡ A K J x x   ◊ K x   ♣ x x

This is a very fine hand and naturally your opening bid is 1 Heart. There is no necessity to misdescribe this hand. If partner bids 2 Diamonds your rebid will be 2 Spades. It is true that this makes it impossible for your partner to return to 2 Hearts, but if partner is obliged to return to 3 Hearts you are well prepared to play there. Your hand is sufficiently strong.

This sequence of bids—that is, Hearts first and then Spades (always showing more Hearts than Spades)—is technically known as a "reverse." This is a confusing term and is really a misnomer. Actually it is better to avoid the use of the expression. You will frequently hear people say, "Partner, you reversed. You showed a powerful hand." A better way to put it is this: Whenever you make it impossible for partner to return to two of your original suit you should have a very good hand. Similarly, whenever you reach the level of three at your second bid you should have a very good hand. That's all there is to it. There isn't any more!

♠ A J x x   ♡ A K J x x   ◇ x x x   ♣ x

The recommended opening bid with this hand is 1 Heart. If partner responds with 2 Clubs you must not bid 2 Spades. That would make it impossible for partner to return to 2 Hearts, and might drive him to three, for which you are not prepared. However, this is no hardship upon you because you are in a position to make a very comfortable rebid of 2 Hearts.

Some players make it a practice to open hands like this with 1 Spade in order to be able to show both suits. I do not agree with them. If you open with 1 Heart there is only slight danger that the Spade suit will be lost, because if partner has four fairly good Spades he will be willing to show that suit. Another objection to opening with 1 Spade and later showing the Hearts is that partner will be under the impression that he is asked to choose between two more or less equal suits, in which case he may prefer Spades with approximately equal strength in Hearts.

To put the exception into the form of a rule: On hands of moderate strength with a five-card suit and a four-card suit which are next-door neighbors (Spades and Hearts, Hearts and Diamonds, Diamonds and Clubs), if the higher-ranking suit is a *good* four-card suit treat the second suit as though it were of equal length with the other. A few more illustrations:

♠ A K x x   ♡ Q J 10 x x   ◇ Q x   ♣ Q x

Bid 1 Spade, reserving 2 Hearts as a rebid.

♠ x x   ♡ A Q J x   ◇ K 10 9 x x   ♣ K x

Bid 1 Heart, reserving 2 Diamonds as a rebid.

♠ x x   ♡ x x   ◊ A K Q x   ♣ A 10 x x x

Bid 1 Diamond, reserving 2 Clubs as a rebid.

♠ A Q 10 x   ♡ x x   ◊ A Q J x x   ♣ x x

Players who have learned the above exception sometimes apply it improperly to a case such as this. I have seen them open this hand with 1 Spade. This is highly improper. If they get a 2 Heart response they are cornered. It is necessary for them to bid 3 Diamonds and the hand is not good enough to rebid at that level. The proper opening bid is 1 Diamond. If partner responds with 1 Heart the rebid will be 1 Spade. If partner instead responds with 2 Clubs it is not permissible to bid 2 Spades, because that makes it impossible for partner to return to 2 Diamonds; but the opener is not embarrassed, for he may conveniently rebid 2 Diamonds.

Let us take one or two more cases which involve looking ahead:

♠ A K x x   ♡ K J x   ◊ K 10 x x x   ♣ x

The orthodox opening bid is 1 Diamond. However, a brief glance into the future will warn of a possible 2 Club response. What would then be the rebid? Surely not 2 No Trump; and a rebid of 2 Spades would make it impossible for partner to return to 2 Diamonds. This hand is not strong enough to warrant such action. An exception should therefore be made in the interest of convenience, and the recommended opening bid is 1 Spade, which will take care of all responses. If partner bids 2 Hearts or 2 Diamonds you have a good raise. If partner bids 2 Clubs you will bid 2 Diamonds, permitting a return to 2 Spades if necessary.

If we transpose the Hearts and Clubs in the above hand:

♠ A K x x   ♡ x   ◊ K 10 x x x   ♣ K J x

Here again it is desirable to look into the future. We cannot open with 1 Spade because we will have no convenient rebid over 2 Hearts. The orthodox opening bid of 1 Diamond is therefore proper. If partner responds 1 Heart, we naturally rebid 1 Spade; if he responds 2 Clubs, our Club support gives us some assurance against immediate trouble whether we choose to raise the Clubs or stretch a point and bid 2 Spades.

As indicated above, the term "reverse" has been responsible for a great deal of confusion. A certain number of players make it a practice to go deliberately out of their way to "reverse" in order to show a good hand. I have seen the following strange phenomenon:

♠ K Q J x x   ♡ A K x x x   ◇ K x   ♣ x

Players holding this hand have actually been known to open with 1 Heart so that they could bid Spades later and "by reversing indicate a good hand." This borders on the absurd. There is no occasion to distort this hand. The opening bid should be 1 Spade and on the next round a jump is made in Hearts to show the overpowering strength.

To summarize: A poor hand must sometimes be bid abnormally to avoid reaching a dangerously high level. With good hands we need not fear high levels and such hands should be bid normally.

To repeat: All good hands should be bid naturally.

IN A NUTSHELL

When your second bid is made at such a level that it becomes impossible for partner to return to two of your first suit you must have a very good hand.

OPENING TWO—BIDS (IN A SUIT)

Occasionally a player will hold a hand so powerful that game can be scored even though partner has little or nothing. He cannot afford to open with a game bid because he may desire partner's cooperation in an effort to discover the hand's possibilities, yet he cannot risk opening with a bid of one lest partner pass the hand out. The opening bid of two in a suit is employed in these cases to demand an eventual game contract. Partner is forced to respond and to *keep responding* until a game contract has been reached, no matter how empty a hand he may hold.

What are the requirements for a two-bid? First, it must be supported by a certain number of high cards, never less than 4 honor tricks. At this point it may be well to dispose of a very popular misconception. That is, that a two-bid requires the holding of 5½ honor tricks, or that hands containing 5½ honor tricks and a biddable suit must be opened with two of a suit. This notion develops out of confusion with the opening bid of 2 No Trump, which is based on 5½ honor tricks.

In opening a two-bid in a suit the prime requirement is that you have a virtual game in your own hand. You may stretch a point by about one playing trick, but not more than that. A hand with as many as 6½ honor tricks may not qualify as an original bid of two in a suit, if it has too many losing tricks. Other hands which are so rich in playing strength as to be absolute lay-down games, may not qualify as two-bids if they have not the necessary 4 honor tricks. A combination of the two is required.

Let us examine a few illustrations:

♠ A K Q J x x x   ♡ A x x   ◊ A x   ♣ x

Bid 2 Spades. You have nine certain winners. In other words, you have within a trick of a lay-down game in your own hand. You have also the required 4 honor tricks. Partner might not respond to a bid of 1 Spade and yet an odd King or even an odd Queen might produce your tenth trick.

♠ A K J   ♡ A K J x x   ◊ A   ♣ K Q 10 x

Bid 2 Hearts. Unless you run into extremely hard luck you should not lose more than four tricks on this hand, which places you within a trick of game-in-hand.

♠ A K x x   ♡ A K x x   ◊ x   ♣ A K x x

Bid 1 Club. This hand contains 6 honor tricks, but is nowhere near an opening two-bid. There are too many losing tricks. The correct opening is 1 Club. If partner is unable to respond then be quite sure that no game will be missed.

♠ K Q J x x x   ♡ A Q J x x x   ◇ x   ♣ None

Bid 1 Spade. This hand is a lay-down game in one of the major suits, yet it lacks the required minimum of 4 honor tricks. There is no necessity to open with a bid of 2 Spades and run the risk that partner will misjudge the high-card content of your hand. With so many high cards outstanding it is inconceivable that no one of the other three players at the table will find a bid. When it is next your turn to call you will, of course, make a jump bid in Hearts and eventually reach at least a game contract.

If you have any doubt that the bidding will be kept open by someone when you hold such a hand, it is suggested that you try an experiment with a deck of cards. Lay out these thirteen cards. Shuffle the remaining thirty-nine. Deal them out and see if the final contract will ever be 1 Spade.

IN A NUTSHELL

An opening bid of two in a suit does not require 5½ honor tricks. Four honor tricks is the minimum, but opener must be able to take within one trick of game in his own hand.

RESPONSES TO TWO-BIDS (SUIT)

The opening bid of two in a suit is unconditionally forcing to game. Responder must bid even with a blank hand and must keep on bidding, no matter how many calls it takes, until a final game contract is reached (or the opponents have been doubled).

With a weak hand the conventional response is 2 No Trump, regardless of distribution. Here is a 2 No Trump response to an opening 2 Diamond bid:

♠ 10 x x x x x   ♡ x   ◇ x x x   ♣ 10 x x

With adequate trump support and at least 1 honor trick an immediate single raise is given. You would raise 2 Spades to three with this:

♠ J x x x   ♡ x x   ◇ K J 10   ♣ x x x x

If you have 1-plus honor trick and a biddable suit, it should be shown. Avoid showing very weak suits if some other bid is available. As a rule a suit should be headed by at least Queen-Jack. If you lack trump support for partner and have no biddable suit, but your hand contains 1½ honor tricks, the response is 3 No Trump. Any hand containing more than that will surely develop a slam and you should maneuver around in order to determine the best contract, never forgetting that the eventual contract will be at least six.

My policy is to make the natural response first and show Aces individually at a later stage in the bidding, after the eventual trump suit has been determined.

When the opening two-bidder rebids his suit, that must be accepted as the final trump, and the responder must not thereafter experiment with some new suit of his own.

For example: Partner opens with 2 Hearts and you hold:

1. ♠ K J x x x
    ♡ x x x
    ◇ K x x
    ♣ x x

Bid 2 Spades; you have 1-plus honor trick.

2. ♠ x x
    ♡ J x x
    ◇ K Q x
    ♣ J x x x x

Bid 3 Hearts; the Club suit is too weak to bid.

3. ♠ Q x x
    ♡ x x
    ◇ A J x
    ♣ x x x x x

Bid 3 No Trump; this hand is too strong for a 2 No Trump response.

4. ♠ A Q x x
    ♡ x x x
    ◇ K J x x
    ♣ x x

Bid 2 Spades; you will eventually play at a slam, but there is no hurry.

THE DOUBLE RAISE

The double raise is a special bid. It denies a strong hand. It describes one that contains good trump support, either Q x x x or five small, but no Ace, no King, and no singleton. It warns partner not to bid a slam unless all he needs is plenty of trump support. For example:

♠ J x x x x   ♡ x x   ◇ Q x x   ♣ x x x

Raise partner's 2 Spades to 4 Spades.

The development of the bidding after an opening two-bid will be more fully discussed in the chapter on slam bidding.

OPENING NO TRUMP BIDS

THE 1 NO TRUMP BID

No Trump openings are made as a rule on hands that are distributed 4-3-3-3, although 4-4-3-2 and 5-3-3-2 hands are also acceptable if they contain the precise high-card requirement.

The high-card requirement for an opening bid of 1 No Trump is about 4 honor tricks. It may be a little less if your hand contains some fillers in the way of Jacks and tens; and a little bit, but not much, more if you have no fillers. The absolute maximum for 1 No Trump is 4½ honor tricks and even such a hand is too big for 1 No Trump if it contains any additional strength in intermediate cards.

There is the further requirement that at least three of the suits must be safely protected.

The opening bid of 1 No Trump differs distinctly from opening bids of one in a suit, both in its nature and in the way it is responded to. An opening bid of one in a suit is an ambiguous bid. It can mean anything from a minimum to a hand that is almost a two-bid, and the opener's second bid must clear up the doubt. In other words, it takes at least two bids to describe a hand that is opened with one of a suit. That is why the responder must strain to keep it alive; he cannot tell at first how strong the opening bid may be. But with the 1 No Trump opening a complete and exact description of the strength of the hand is given in one bid. It can never be ambiguous.

REQUIREMENTS FOR 1 NO TRUMP BID

Four Aces count 11 to 12½. Hands counting 13 and 13½ are too big for 1 No Trump and must be opened with one of a suit.

4-3-2-1 POINT COUNT

Requirements for 1 No Trump opening 16 to 19. Hands counting 20 to 21 are too big for 1 No Trump and must be opened with one of a suit.

1. ♠ Q J 10   ♡ K x x   ◇ A x x   ♣ A K J x
2. ♠ K J x   ♡ K Q x   ◇ A J 10   ♣ A K J x

No. 1 is a proper opening bid of 1 No Trump (point count of 18), but it would be absurd to open No. 2 with 1 No Trump. In fact it meets the requirements of a 2 No Trump bid (point count of 22), and should be so opened.

There are certain hands which come in between these two.

♠ K x x   ♡ K Q x   ◇ A x x   ♣ A K J x

This hand is stronger than No. 1 above, and not as strong as No. 2. In other words, it is bigger than a 1 No Trump bid and not strong enough for a 2 No Trump bid (point count of 20). It is an "in-between" hand, and since an exact description of it cannot be given in one bid it must not be opened with 1 No Trump. The proper bid is 1 Club. A jump in No Trump should be made on the next round if partner responds.

A common error of many players is their lack of exactness in opening with 1 No Trump. The following examples will show how few liberties you may take with this bid.

♠ A Q	♠ K x x
♡ K x x x	♡ A K x
◇ Q 10 x x	◇ 10 x x x
♣ A Q x	♣ A x x
A proper 1 No Trump bid (17 points)—3½-plus honor tricks, strength in every suit, and 4-4-3-2 distribution (which is not ideal, as is 4-3-3-3, but is acceptable).	Not strong enough for 1 No Trump (14 points)—only 3½ honor tricks. Some bid 1 No Trump on this because they "have no suit." This is wrong. Bid 1 Club.

2 NO TRUMP BIDS

An opening bid of 2 No Trump must not be confused with an opening bid of two in a suit. The 2 No Trump bid is not forcing.

It is an exact measurement bid, announcing 5½ to 6 honor tricks with all suits safely stopped, and asking partner to raise to three if he has ½ honor trick. If partner has nothing he should pass. Thus 2 No Trump differs from the bid of two in a suit, which is absolutely forcing to game regardless of partner's hand.

REQUIREMENTS
FOR 2 NO TRUMP OPENING:
FOUR ACES COUNT

Opening bid of 2 No Trump requires 14 to 16 points.

4-3-2-1 COUNT

Opening bid of 2 No Trump requires 22 to 24 points.

The following are illustrations of typical 2 No Trump openings:

♠ A K J ♡ K Q x ◇ A J x ♣ K Q x x (23 points)
♠ A K Q ♡ A J ◇ A Q J x ♣ Q 10 x x (23 points)

3 NO TRUMP BIDS
FOUR ACES COUNT

Opening bid of 3 No Trump requires 16½ to 18 points.

4-3-2-1 COUNT

Opening bid of 3 No Trump requires 25 to 27 points.

The opening 3 No Trump bid is the same type hand as the opening 2 No Trump bid except that it contains 1 honor trick more. In other words, between 6½ and 7 honor tricks. Bid 3 No Trump on this:

♠ A K J ♡ K Q x ◇ A K J ♣ K Q J x (point count 27)

Hands stronger than this should be opened with a bid of two in a suit. Or if they contain ten reasonably sure winners with a bid of 4 No Trump (this, of course, is not a Blackwood bid).

IN A NUTSHELL

An opening No Trump bid can never be ambiguous. Make an opening No Trump bid only if you have the exact type and strength of hand for it.

RESPONSES TO NO TRUMP BIDS

In No Trump bidding Queens, Jacks and tens assume a more prominent position than in other phases of bidding, and greater accuracy will consequently be attained by resorting to point counts in estimating the value of a hand. I have here provided the requirements in terms of the more popular methods:

	Honor Tricks	*Work*	*Four Aces*
Raise 1 No Trump to 2 with	1½-plus	8	5½
Raise 1 No Trump to 3 with	2½-plus	10	8

When partner opens with 1 No Trump you need not strain a point to keep the bidding alive. There is no real danger of missing anything, since partner's hand is limited to a little over four tricks. He cannot have any more if he is bidding properly.

If you have only 1 honor trick or less you should pass unless you have a freak hand.

A response of two in Clubs or Diamonds always denotes a hand on which you have not the high-card requirement for a raise to 2 No Trump. It may be a freak hand; or it may be a hand that is just short of a raise and a little too good to pass, a hand, for example, with a little over 1 honor trick and a five-card suit. The opening No Trump bidder won't be expected to speak again unless he has a maximum No Trump.

A response of 2 Spades or 2 Hearts is in a slightly different category. There are many hands on which the responder has the high-card ingredients of a raise to 2 No Trump, but the hand contains a five-card major and perhaps a short suit, and the responder feels there is a chance that the hand might possibly play better in a suit. In order to give partner a choice responder bids 2 Spades or 2 Hearts and opener is expected to bid again unless he has a rock-bottom opener. If he supports the suit responder will go to four. If opener rebids 2 No Trump responder expects to take him to three.

With a very long suit, or with unbalanced distribution and major-suit strength, it is good policy to count your winners to decide whether or not game is probable. The opener can be relied upon to develop four tricks in the play. If your hand has the value of 5½ playing tricks the total is 9½, sufficient to justify a gamble for game. In such a case you should bid four of your major suit directly, even though your hand is poor in high cards.

If, with that much playing strength, your hand contains more than 2 honor tricks, the proper procedure is a jump to three of your major suit, forcing to game.

Suppose partner opens with 1 No Trump and you hold:

1. ♠ x x ♡ J x x ◇ K x x x ♣ A 10 x x

Raise to 2 No Trump. You have 1½ honor tricks, plus a Jack and a ten (point count of 8).

2. ♠ A Q J x x ♡ x x x x ◇ J x x ♣ x

Bid 2 Spades. You have the essentials of a raise to 2 No Trump but the hand might possibly play better at Spades and opener should be given the choice (8 points).

3. ♠ J x ♡ J x x ◇ Q x x x ♣ A J x x

Raise to 2 No Trump. You have the proper count (9 points).

4. ♠ A x x ♡ Q x ◇ Q J x x ♣ K J x x

Raise to 3 No Trump. The hand has a point count equivalent to almost 3 honor tricks (13 points).

5. ♠ Q x x x x x ♡ x x ◇ K x x ♣ x x

Bid 2 Spades. The six-card suit justifies this action. With one less Spade the recommendation would be a pass.

6. ♠ Q J x x x ♡ x ◇ A J x ♣ x x x x

Bid 2 Spades. You have the ingredients of a raise, but a major-suit game may be better.

7. ♠ x x x ♡ x x ◇ K x x ♣ A Q x x x

Raise to 2 No Trump. You have 2 honor tricks (9 points). *Don't bid 2 Clubs.*

8. ♠ A Q x x x ♡ x x ◇ K x x ♣ x x x

Bid 2 Spades, intending to go to 3 No Trump if partner rebids 2 No Trump. Note the distinction between this and No. 7.

9.   ♠ Q 10 x x x   ♡ x x   ◇ Q x x   ♣ x x x

Pass. A rescue of the No Trump to 2 Spades is not recommended. If partner is doubled at 1 No Trump you may then bid your Spade suit.

10.   ♠ A x x x   ♡ K x x   ◇ x x x   ♣ x x x

Pass. You have a skeleton 1½ tricks with insufficient point count (only 7 points). If one of your suits were a five-carder a raise to 2 No Trump would be recommended.

11.   ♠ x x   ♡ x x x   ◇ K 10 9 x x   ♣ K 9 x

This is an "in-between" hand. It is not quite good enough for a raise to 2 No Trump and yet perhaps a little too good to pass, because of the five-card diamond suit. A 2 Diamond take-out is therefore recommended, with the intention of gambling it out at 3 No Trump if partner raises to 3 Diamonds or even if he rebids 2 No Trump in the face of the mild warning. A minor suit take-out warns opener that responder's hand is not worth a raise.

12.   ♠ x   ♡ K Q 10 x x x   ◇ K x x   ♣ x x x

Bid 4 Hearts. You have about 5½ winners.

13.   ♠ x   ♡ K Q J x x x   ◇ A J x   ♣ x x x

Bid 3 Hearts. You have six winners and more than 2 honor tricks. A slam may be possible.

14.   ♠ x   ♡ A Q J x x   ◇ K x x x x   ♣ x x

Bid 3 Hearts. You have more than six winners and over 2 honor tricks. You wish to insist upon a game but prefer to play at a suit.

IN A NUTSHELL

There is no reason to strain to keep the bidding alive over a 1 No Trump bid.

RESPONSES TO 2 NO TRUMP BIDS

The opening bid of 2 No Trump, unlike the bid of two in a suit, is not forcing. Responder may pass if he has nothing.

	Honor Tricks	Work	Four Aces
Raise 2 No Trump to 3 with	½-plus	4	3
Raise 2 No Trump to 4 with	1½-plus	9	6½

Any six-card suit should be shown in response. Any five-card major suit should be shown if your hand contains ½ honor trick.

Let us take a few examples in which partner has opened 2 No Trump and you hold:

    1.   ♠ Q J x   ♡ Q x x   ◇ x x x x   ♣ x x x

Bid 3 No Trump. You have a little over ½ honor trick (point count of 5).

    2.   ♠ x x   ♡ K 10 9 x x   ◇ x x x   ♣ x x x

Bid 3 Hearts. You have a 5-card major suit with ½ honor trick.

    3.   ♠ x x   ♡ x x x   ◇ K J x x x   ♣ x x x

Bid 3 No Trump. It is pointless to bid 3 Diamonds, since there is no desire to play for game in the minor suit.

    4.   ♠ x x   ♡ K Q x x x x   ◇ Q x x   ♣ x x

Bid 4 Hearts. This is not a shut-out but announces the full strength of the hand. It should be made on a hand that does not have much honor strength but can win five tricks in the play. You have 7 points, partner might have 24. A total of 31 with a 6-card suit suggests slam possibilities.

RESPONSES TO 3 NO TRUMP BIDS

Since an opening bid of 3 No Trump shows close to 7 honor tricks, very little is required to produce a slam. Raise an opening 3 No Trump bid to 4 with a point count of 7.

With a five-card biddable suit and ½ honor trick, show the suit. Raise to 4 No Trump with a little over 1 honor trick.

    ♠ x x   ♡ K J x x x   ◇ x x x   ♣ x x x

Bid 4 Hearts. You have a five-card suit headed by ½ honor trick.

♠ K x x   ♡ Q x x   ◇ x x x x   ♣ Q x x

Bid 4 No Trump. You have more than 1 honor trick and the combined partnership assets should be about eight tricks, or almost the deck. The deck contains 40 points. You can count the minimum number which your partner has by the size of his opening bid. Add these to your own total. If they reach 33 or 34 you ought to be willing to try a slam because that will mean that the adversaries have between them no more than 6 or 7 points, which is less than 2 tricks. When slam is in contemplation, tens should not be valued. In the above case you have 7 points, partner has at least 25—the total of 32 places you on the threshold of a slam. If partner's opening was based on 26 or 27, he should chance a slam bid.

Where the partnership count reaches a total of 37 or 38 you should be willing to risk a grand slam.

OPENING PREËMPTIVE BIDS

A preëmptive bid is an opening of three, four or five in a suit. Such bids denote hands that are relatively weak in high cards. They are made in fear that the opponents have a better holding, and in an effort to destroy their lines of communication. They are naturally based on a very long trump suit.

A hand should not be opened with a preëmptive bid merely because it has a long suit; holding 2½ or more honor tricks, don't preëmpt. With that much defensive strength an orthodox opening bid of one in a suit should be made.

To put it in another way: Experienced players never preëmpt unless the future of the hand appears to be hopeless.

In making a preëmptive bid you must have a reasonable amount of safety. You should be prepared, if you are doubled, to lose no more than 500 points. That is to say, if you are not vulnerable you may overbid by three tricks. If you are vulnerable you should restrict the overbid to only two tricks. For example:

♠ K Q J x x x x x   ♡ x   ◇ x x   ♣ x x

If not vulnerable you may bid 4 Spades. This is an overbid of three tricks. Even if doubled you will be down no more than 500 points. If you are set that many tricks the opponents unquestionably have a game and conceivably even a slam. But if you are vulnerable you may chance a bid of only 3 Spades, an overbid of two tricks, which if doubled will risk a set of 500 points.

Since preëmptive bids are not made with good hands, if your partner preëmpts you should not raise unless you have an unusual amount of strength. You can expect your partner to have overbid by three tricks if you are not vulnerable, and by two tricks if you are, so you know how many tricks he can win. You must provide the rest.

A preëmptive bid of four in a major suit may sometimes be made on a good hand for strategic purposes when partner has already passed. For example:

♠ x ♡ A K Q 10 x x x ◊ A J 10 x ♣ x

If partner has previously passed the chances of reaching a slam are so remote that they may for practical purposes be dismissed. A preëmptive bid of 4 Hearts may therefore be good strategy. First of all, you expect to make it. Secondly, it minimizes the danger of the disquieting competition in Spades that may be expected from the opposition.

I have seen players make the preëmptive bid of 3 Spades on a hand like the following:

♠ A K Q J 10 x ♡ x x ◊ Q x x ♣ x x

This practice I heartily disapprove. The hand is too good for a preëmptive bid. It is by no means hopeless. In fact, it has distinct possibilities. I prefer an opening bid of 1 Spade, despite the questionable defensive strength. If you do not choose to open with 1 Spade it is best to pass and enter the bidding later.

IN A NUTSHELL

An opening preëmptive bid should not be made on any hand that has the high-card strength for an opening bid (2½ honor tricks).

OPENING BID QUIZ

(ANSWERS BEGIN ON PAGE 36)

You are dealer. Holding each of the following hands, what is your opening bid?

1. ♠ A J x
   ♡ A 9 x
   ◇ A 9 x x
   ♣ Q x x

2. ♠ A x x
   ♡ J x x x
   ◇ A x x
   ♣ A J x

3. ♠ A 10 x x
   ♡ A K Q x
   ◇ x x x
   ♣ x x

4. ♠ A Q x x
   ♡ J x x
   ◇ A K x x
   ♣ x x

5. ♠ x x x
   ♡ Q J x x
   ◇ A Q J x
   ♣ A x

6. ♠ A K
   ♡ K J 10
   ◇ K Q J x
   ♣ A J x x

7. ♠ K Q J x
   ♡ A K x x x
   ◇ x x
   ♣ x x

8. ♠ x x x
   ♡ A K x x
   ◇ A x x
   ♣ x x x

9. ♠ J x x
   ♡ K Q 10 x
   ◇ A Q x
   ♣ A J x

10. ♠ K J 10 x x
    ♡ A x
    ◇ Q x x
    ♣ J 10 x

11. ♠ A J x x
    ♡ K Q x x
    ◇ A Q x x
    ♣ x

12. ♠ K 10 9 x x
    ♡ A J x x
    ◇ Q J x
    ♣ x

13. ♠ A K x x
    ♡ x x
    ◇ A J x x x
    ♣ x x

14. ♠ A Q 10 x
    ♡ A J x
    ◇ K x x x x
    ♣ x

15. ♠ A 10 x
    ♡ K Q x
    ◇ Q x x
    ♣ A 9 x x

16. ♠ K Q x
    ♡ Q J x
    ◇ A x x
    ♣ Q 10 x x

17. ♠ A x x
    ♡ Q J x
    ◇ K 10 x
    ♣ Q J 10 x

18. ♠ A x x
    ♡ K x
    ◇ A K J x x
    ♣ Q x x

19. ♠ K x x
    ♡ A J 9 x x
    ◇ A 10 x x
    ♣ x

20. ♠ A x x x
    ♡ A K Q x
    ◇ A Q x
    ♣ Q x x

21. ♠ A J 10 x x
    ♡ x
    ◇ A K J x x x
    ♣ x

22. ♠ ——
    ♡ A K Q 10 x
    ◊ A Q J x x x
    ♣ K Q

23. ♠ A K J 10 x x x
    ♡ A Q
    ◊ x x
    ♣ x x

24. ♠ J 10 x x
    ♡ A Q x
    ◊ A Q x
    ♣ A K x

25. ♠ A K Q x x x
    ♡ Q x x
    ◊ x x
    ♣ x x

26. ♠ Q 10 x x
    ♡ K 10 x x
    ◊ x
    ♣ A Q x x

27. ♠ A Q x x x
    ♡ A K x
    ◊ A K x
    ♣ x x

28. ♠ J 10 x x x
    ♡ A K
    ◊ K 10 x
    ♣ x x x

29. ♠ A K x
    ♡ A Q 10
    ◊ A K J x
    ♣ K Q 10

30. ♠ ——
    ♡ Q J 10 9 x x x x
    ◊ x
    ♣ Q J 10 9

31. ♠ A Q
    ♡ K 10 9
    ◊ A 10 x x
    ♣ K Q x x

32. ♠ x x
    ♡ A K Q J 10 x
    ◊ K Q J 10 x
    ♣ ——

33. ♠ A K 10 x
    ♡ A Q x x
    ◊ A 10 9 x
    ♣ A

34. ♠ A 9 x x x
    ♡ K x x x x x
    ◊ A
    ♣ x

35. ♠ A J x
    ♡ A K x
    ◊ A K J x
    ♣ A J x

You are in third position, after two passes, and you hold:

36. ♠ A x x x
    ♡ A Q x
    ◊ Q x x
    ♣ x x x

37. ♠ A Q x x x
    ♡ x x
    ◊ x x x
    ♣ A x x

38. ♠ A K 10 x
    ♡ J x x
    ◊ x x x
    ♣ A J x

OPENING BID QUIZ ANSWERS

1. 1 Diamond. Just barely short of an opening 1 No Trump bid (point count 15).

2. 1 Club. Too much to pass. Not enough for 1 No Trump (point count 14). An example of bidding a three-card minor when no other satisfactory bid is available. Your rebid will be convenient. If partner calls 1 Heart you raise. If he bids one of any other suit you rebid 1 No Trump.

3. 1 Spade, the suit "below" the doubleton. A Heart bid is improper. It affords no convenient rebid if partner responds with two of a minor suit.

4. 1 Spade, the suit below the doubleton. Over 2 Clubs the rebid is 2 Diamonds. Over 2 Hearts the rebid must be 3 Hearts.

5. 1 Heart, not 1 Diamond. The suit below the doubleton.

6. 2 No Trump is the best bid. 1 Diamond is acceptable. 2 Diamonds would be improper despite the 5½ honor tricks (point count of 22).

7. 1 Spade, rather than 1 Heart, to show both suits economically.

8. Pass. No rebid is available if partner responds with 2 Clubs or 2 Diamonds.

9. 1 No Trump. Three suits are stopped, there are exactly 4 honor tricks (counting the plus values) and the 4-3-3-3 distribution is ideal (point count 17).

10. 1 Spade. Although this hand is technically short of 2½ honor tricks, plus values should be added for the possession of seven honor cards and the holding of an honor in each suit. The rebid, if necessary, is 2 Spades.

11. 1 Spade, the suit below the singleton.

12. 1 Spade. The hand contains only 2-plus honor tricks but plus values are added for the possession of six honor cards, and for the holding of nine cards in the majors. The rebid will be 2 Hearts.

13. 1 Diamond. Over 2 Clubs the rebid is 2 Diamonds. A Spade bid would be wrong because no convenient rebid would be available over a 2 Heart response.

14. 1 Spade. Over 2 Clubs the rebid is 2 Diamonds. Over 2 Hearts the rebid is 3 Hearts. A Diamond opening is undesirable because it provides for no convenient rebid over 2 Clubs.

15. 1 Club. Not strong enough for 1 No Trump. (15 points)

16. 1 Club. Not quite 3 honor tricks but the hand contains seven honor cards and a high card in each suit. The rebid is convenient, 1 No Trump.

17. 1 Club. Only 2½ honor tricks but eight honor cards and the convenient rebid of 1 No Trump. (14 points)

18. 1 No Trump. The 5-3-3-2 distribution is acceptable, all suits are stopped, and there are *about* 4 honor tricks. If you bid 1 Diamond, over a 1 Heart response you would be a bit too weak for a rebid of 2 No Trump but too strong to rebid 2 Diamonds or 1 No Trump. (17 points)

19. 1 Heart.

20. 1 Heart. Too big for 1 No Trump. Not quite big enough for 2 No Trump (point count 21).

21. 1 Diamond.

22. 2 Diamonds. Game in hand, with 4½ honor tricks.

23. 1 Spade. A preëmptive bid is improper because you have too much honor strength.

24. 1 Club. This hand is too big for 1 No Trump and not big enough for 2 No Trump (point count 20).

25. 1 Spade. Don't preëmpt with this hand.

26. 1 Club. Add a plus value for six honor cards. Add a plus value for the possession of eight major suit cards and for convenience of rebid.

27. 1 Spade. Not a two-bid. Too many losers. If partner has nothing there is no game.

28. Pass. No convenient rebid is available if you open with 1 Spade.

29. 3 No Trump. A better bid than 2 Diamonds. Don't err by opening with only 2 No Trump (point count 26).

30. 4 Hearts. Eight sure winners and no defense.

31. 1 No Trump (point count 18). This is preferable to 1 Diamond because it gives a more accurate description. If you open with 1 Diamond and partner responds with 1 Heart you will be a little uncertain about your rebid, not being quite strong enough for a rebid of 2 No Trump.

32. 1 Heart. Though you have game in hand you have not the required 4 honor tricks for a 2 Heart bid. Don't fear that the 1 Heart bid will be passed out.

33. 1 Diamond. Exceptional. The hand is so big partner may find it difficult to respond to a Spade bid, but might risk a weak one-over-one response if you open with 1 Diamond.

34. 1 Spade. For sake of economy of bidding space, treat the Hearts as though they were the same length as the Spades.

35. 3 No Trump. Just the right count. (25 points)

36. Pass. You have a little over 2½ honor tricks but the hand has defensive rather than offensive strength and no good suit to bid.

37. 1 Spade. Just enough to justify a third-hand bid.

38. 1 Spade, trying for a part score and intending to pass any response by partner. It is unnecessary to open with a Club in third position, since you need not prepare for a rebid.

CHAPTER 2

RESPONSES

WHEN YOUR PARTNER makes an opening bid, it is your duty (if
your hand is strong enough) to make some bid which will show
what kind of hand you have. Depending on your strength and
distribution, you may raise partner's suit, or bid No Trump, or bid
a suit of your own. Any such bid is called a response.

If you raise or bid No Trump, you give precise information,
for these responses are kept within very strict limits. If you bid a
suit of your own, your response is highly ambiguous, because a
suit response may range from a hand of moderate strength to a
very strong holding. Because a suit take-out is so ambiguous, it is
made forcing for one round so that you will have an opportunity
to rebid and describe the limits of your hand more exactly.

In general you should try to choose a response which is *natural*.
For example:

♠ A J x x x   ♥ x   ♦ J x x x   ♣ x x x

I have seen players bid 1 No Trump over partner's Heart bid on
this hand, explaining, "I didn't think the hand was strong enough
to force with." That is not the question. A 1 No Trump response
on this hand is unnatural, because you do not want to play such a
hand at No Trump; if you play it at all, you would rather play
it in Spades.

But take a similar hand:

♠ x x x   ♥ x x   ♦ A J x x x   ♣ Q x x

Over partner's Heart it would be more natural to bid 1 No Trump
than to bid 2 Diamonds on this hand, simply because you would
rather play such a weak hand at a contract of one than at a contract of two.

RESPONDING TO BIDS OF ONE IN A SUIT

KEEPING THE BIDDING OPEN WITH WEAK HANDS

When your partner has opened the bidding with one of a suit and your hand contains some slight trick-taking power you should strive to keep the bidding alive. This provides the opener with another chance to bid should he have another suit, at which the hand might play better, or should he have a very powerful opening, one that is just short of a demand bid.

If you have little or nothing, of course you may pass. Sometimes you may pass with as much as one skeleton trick, provided the hand is barren in all other respects. The bidding may be kept open with a moderate hand, in one of three ways:

I. By bidding 1 No Trump. (1 Heart by partner, 1 No Trump by you)

II. By raising your partner from one to two in his suit. (1 Heart by partner, 2 Hearts by you)

III. By bidding some other suit *at the level of one*. (1 Heart by partner, 1 Spade by you)

I. KEEPING THE BIDDING OPEN BY A BID OF 1 NO TRUMP

This is regarded as the weakest of all responses. When you desire to keep the bidding alive with a moderate hand but are unable to give partner a raise, and have no suit that you can show at the level of one, the practice is to respond with 1 No Trump. The minimum requirement for this response is approximately 1 honor trick (provided that the honor trick is divided between two suits). Responder must have at least 6 points for a response of 1 No Trump.

In each of the following cases partner opened with 1 Spade. You hold:

1. ♠ x x x　　♡ A x x x　　◇ x x x　　♣ x x x　　(4 points)

Pass. You have one bare trick but not in two suits.

2. ♠ x x x   ♡ K 10 x x   ◊ Q 10 x   ♣ J x x   (6 points)

Bid 1 No Trump. You have about 1 honor trick in two suits.

3. ♠ x x   ♡ Q x x   ◊ K J x x x   ♣ x x x   (6 points)

Bid 1 No Trump. You have a little over a trick and no suit that you can show at the level of one.

4. ♠ x x x   ♡ A x x   ◊ A J x   ♣ x x x x   (9 points)

Bid 1 No Trump. This is a maximum. No other bid is available.

FREE BIDS OF 1 NO TRUMP

When partner opens with one of a suit and the next opponent inserts a bid (known as an overcall) you are no longer under pressure to keep the bidding alive; the opposition has already done so, and partner is automatically afforded another chance to speak. Any action you may take at this point is purely voluntary and shows a desire to bid, which naturally must be supported by a good hand. For example:

♠ K 10 x   ♡ x x x   ◊ A x x   ♣ J x x x

Partner opens with 1 Heart. If the next hand passes, you respond with 1 No Trump to give your partner another chance. But if the adversary ahead of you overcalls with 1 Spade, it would be improper for you to bid 1 No Trump, merely because you have a Spade stopper. That would denote a good hand and a desire to go places. You should pass it around to partner. If you learn, from subsequent action on his part, that he holds a good hand you may try No Trump later. Holding:

♠ K 10 x   ♡ x x x   ◊ A Q x   ♣ J x x x

on the same sequence of bids you may make a free bid of 1 No Trump. This is the minimum strength on which such action may be based. In other words, a free bid of 1 No Trump indicates a hand that is only slightly short of an ordinary 2 No Trump response. Such a bid should be supported by a point count of approximately 10.

II. THE RAISE TO TWO IN THE SAME SUIT

This response is, generally speaking, a little more encouraging than the response of 1 No Trump. The first requirement is that you be mildly satisfied with partner's suit, which means that you must have what is considered normal trump support, that is, at least x x x x or Q x x or J 10 x. Until you learn otherwise you must act on the assumption that your partner holds a four-card suit. If you determine, on subsequent rounds of bidding, that your partner holds a rebiddable (a good five-card) suit, then you may be satisfied with that suit as trump with less than normal support. If the hand is satisfactory in other respects you may now raise with three small trumps or Q x. And if your partner has bid the suit a third time without support from you in that suit, you may presume that he has six, and may raise with two small trumps.

In other words, if partner bids a suit once, assume a four-card suit. If he bids the suit twice, assume a five-card suit. If he bids it a third time assume a six-card suit. Generally speaking, for the trump suit to be acceptable the partnership should possess eight cards of the suit.

In addition to trump support your hand must possess some trick-taking qualities to justify the raise. Generally speaking, the requirements for a courtesy raise (one made merely for the purpose of keeping the bidding open) are normal trump support, a short suit and a high card.

The following is an example of a minimum courtesy raise from 1 Spade to 2 Spades:

♠ 10 x x x   ♥ x x   ♦ K x x x   ♣ x x x

But if you hold:

♠ 10 9 x   ♥ x x   ♦ K x x x   ♣ x x x x

you have a short suit and a high card and a little bit less than normal trump support. This does not justify a raise to 2 Spades and the hand should be passed.

When you hold a singleton slightly greater liberty may be taken in giving a raise. For example, holding:

♠ Q x x x   ♡ x   ◇ Q 10 x x   ♣ x x x x

you may raise to 2 Spades.

In some cases you may give partner a single raise with slightly less than normal trump support, if no other suitable bid is available. Suppose partner opens with 1 Spade, and you hold:

♠ 10 9 x   ♡ x   ◇ K x x x x   ♣ Q x x x

You should bid 2 Spades. The hand is not strong enough to bid 2 Diamonds, and 1 No Trump is not to be considered with a singleton Heart.

THE FREE RAISE

The raises discussed above have assumed cases in which the opponent on your right has passed. When the adversary on your right inserts a bid you should not raise with any of the hands previously shown. In such a position you do not strain a point to act, because the bidding is already kept open for your partner. Any action by you at this time denotes a sound raise.

The question arises, what strength is required to justify a free raise? Perhaps the most accurate test is to measure the playing-trick strength. To justify a free raise you must hold a minimum of 3½ playing tricks. Stated in a less technical way, such a hand must contain the equivalent of three quick winners. For the specific purpose of this estimate you may regard a singleton as the equivalent of an Ace, and a doubleton as the equivalent of a King. You may also regard adequate (four-card) trump support as being equivalent to an Ace. Let us examine a few illustrations:

1. ♠ J 10 x x   ♡ x   ◇ Q 10 x x   ♣ x x x x
2. ♠ J 10 x x   ♡ x   ◇ A 10 x x   ♣ x x x x
3. ♠ J 10 x x   ♡ x x   ◇ A Q x x   ♣ x x x

Your partner has opened with 1 Spade and the next hand bids 2 Clubs.

With Hand 1 you should not raise to 2 Spades, although you would have kept the bidding alive had second hand passed.

With Hand 2 you may make a free raise. The hand possesses 4½ playing tricks according to the table of Winners in Dummy (on page 4). Estimating the hand according to our special rule, we have one quick winner in the Ace of Diamonds. The single-ton Heart is regarded as equivalent to an Ace, and adequate trump support is also regarded as equivalent to an Ace, which gives us three quick winners.

With Hand 3 you may make a free raise to 2 Spades. The hand contains 4 playing tricks, according to the Table of Winners. You have 1½ high-card tricks in Diamonds; the doubleton Heart is regarded as the equivalent of a King, and the trump support is the equivalent of an Ace, giving you three quick winners and justifying a voluntary raise.

III. KEEPING THE BIDDING OPEN BY A BID OF ONE IN A SUIT

When your partner opens the bidding with one of a suit you may keep the bidding alive on certain mediocre hands by bidding another suit, provided you are able to do so at the level of one. Such a response does not promise any more strength than does the response of 1 No Trump. This is an important observation. A one-over-one response may be made on a relatively weak hand. (Where it is necessary to increase the contract to show your suit more strength is required.) With weak hands the wisest pro-cedure is to make the cheapest response, and one of a suit is cheaper than 1 No Trump.

♠ J x x   ♡ K J x x   ◇ x x   ♣ Q 10 x x

Partner opened with 1 Diamond. You have more than 1 honor trick and should keep the bidding open. It is the practice of many players to respond with 1 No Trump. This is unsound. Your proper response is 1 Heart. Remember that a bid of 1 Heart does not promise any more strength than does a bid of 1 No Trump. Furthermore, the one-over-one response makes partner's rebid easier in any case in which his second suit happens to be Spades. By bidding 1 Heart you permit him to rebid by showing his Spade suit at the level of one, whereas a 1 No Trump response would have forced him to the level of two in order to show the suit. This he may fear to do.

Avoid responding 1 No Trump when you can bid one of a suit.

FREE ONE-OVER-ONE BIDS

The foregoing discussion has contemplated an opening bid by partner and a pass by second hand. When second hand bids, you are no longer under pressure to keep the bidding alive and should not speak even at the level of one unless you have definite values. Let us take an example:

♠ K x x x x ♡ x x x ◇ Q x x ♣ x x

Your partner opens with 1 Club. If the next hand passes, you should respond with 1 Spade; but if the opponent overcalls partner's Club bid, with 1 Heart for example, you must not make a free bid of 1 Spade. You should pass. Partner will have another opportunity, and your hand is too weak for a free bid.

To make a free bid at the level of one you should have a minimum of 1½ honor tricks, unless you have very favorable distribution, in which case a little less will do. Let us take a hand:

♠ A Q J x ♡ x x ◇ J x x x ♣ J x x

Partner opens the bidding with 1 Club and second hand overcalls with 1 Heart. With this hand you have just about enough to warrant a free bid of 1 Spade. But with the following hand:

♠ x x x ♡ x x x ◇ A Q J x ♣ J x x

Your partner opens the bidding with 1 Club and second hand bids 1 Heart. It would require a bid of two to show your suit and your hand is too weak for this. You should pass.

IN A NUTSHELL

With a mediocre hand you may keep your partner's bid alive

a. By bidding 1 No Trump (with a little over 1 honor trick —6 to 9 points).

b. By bidding one of a suit (with the same requirements, or even a little less, than it takes to respond with 1 No Trump).

c. By raising to two of your partner's suit (with 2½ to 4 playing tricks).

RESPONSES OF TWO IN A SUIT

When it is necessary for you to increase the level to name your suit, naturally more strength is required. To respond at the level of two with a normal hand, you generally need a minimum of 2 honor tricks with a five-card suit. Holding:

♠ 10 x x   ♡ x x   ◇ K x x   ♣ A x x x x

Partner opened with 1 Heart. You are in duty bound to keep the bidding alive but your hand is not strong enough for a 2 Club response. You must therefore respond with 1 No Trump.

Greater liberties may be taken when you possess a five-card major suit:

♠ x x   ♡ A Q J x x   ◇ J x x   ♣ x x x

Partner opens with 1 Spade. You may respond with 2 Hearts although you have not 2 honor tricks. Had your suit been Diamonds or Clubs a No Trump response would have been preferred.

Slightly less is required in honor tricks when you have a six-card suit.

♠ x   ♡ x x x   ◇ A Q 10 x x x   ♣ x x x

Your partner opens with 1 Spade and second hand passes. You may respond with 2 Diamonds, though with one less Diamond such action would not be permissible. But if second hand over-calls with 2 Clubs, a free bid of 2 Diamonds would not be advisable, even with the six-card suit. Remember that it forces your partner to speak once more, and whether he rebids 2 Spades or 2 No Trump you will find yourself in an uncomfortable position.

FREE RESPONSES OF TWO IN A SUIT

Generally speaking, you may make a free response of two in a suit on about the same strength you would require for the bid if second hand had passed, provided your suit is lower-ranking than partner's suit.

♠ x x x   ♡ x x   ◇ A Q 10 x x   ♣ K J x

Partner bids 1 Heart. Second hand overcalls with 1 Spade. You have 2 honor tricks (slightly more) and you are within a King of an opening bid. Bid 2 Diamonds.

With the minimum of 2 honor tricks, no plus values to speak of, and only a five-card suit, do not make a free response of two in a suit, even if your suit is lower in rank than partner's.

♠ x x x   ♡ x x   ◇ x x x   ♣ A K x x x

Partner opens with 1 Heart, second hand bids 1 Spade. Despite your five-card suit and 2 honor tricks there is no bid that you can safely make and you are obliged to pass.

Great caution is indicated when a free bid is made by responder in a suit higher in rank than his partner's suit.

♠ x x x   ♡ K Q 10 x x   ◇ Q J x x   ♣ x

Your partner opens with 1 Club and an opponent overcalls with 1 Spade. It would be extremely impolitic for you to bid 2 Hearts. Such action forces partner to speak again, and if his rebid is 3 Clubs, which is not at all unlikely, you will find yourself in a mess brought on by your own conduct. Had your partner's opening bid been 1 Spade and the overcall been 2 Clubs, a 2 Heart bid by you would not be attended by nearly so much danger, since it permits partner to rebid his suit, if necessary, at the level of two. Similarly:

♠ K Q x x x   ♡ 10 x x   ◇ A x x   ♣ x x

Partner opens with 1 Heart and an opponent overcalls with 2 Clubs. You cannot afford to bid 2 Spades, for your partner may not be prepared to rebid safely at the level of three, and unless he happens to have strength in Clubs he cannot safely bid No Trump. In this case, however, you may stretch a point and raise your partner to 2 Hearts, even though you have slightly less than normal trump support. By raising you show that your hand is not hopeless, but you do not force your partner to bid again unless he has additional strength. If you unfortunately had only two small Hearts it would be dangerous to raise and you would have to pass.

Another illustration; as South you hold:

♠ x x x   ♡ A 10 x x x x   ◇ Q x x   ♣ x

The bidding has proceeded:

North	East	South	West
1 ♣	1 ♠	?	

Despite the six-card suit, you dare not bid 2 Hearts, since this may force your partner to bid 3 Clubs, or possibly 2 No Trump, neither of which you will find very comfortable. You should pass.

Again, as South you hold:

♠ K J x   ♡ A Q x x x   ◇ x x x   ♣ x x

The bidding has proceeded:

North	East	South	West
1 ♣	1 ♠	?	

There may be a contemplation on your part to bid 2 Hearts, but this is not good strategy. If partner is obliged to bid 3 Clubs you will hardly know what to do; to try 3 No Trump over 3 Clubs may be very disastrous, because you have not yet learned whether your partner has a good hand. However, some action by you must be taken and the recommended call is a free bid of 1 No Trump. This will denote a good hand but will give partner the option of passing if he has a minimum. If he rebids 2 Clubs or 2 Diamonds you will have the opportunity to bid Hearts on the next round.

IN A NUTSHELL

Don't make a free response of two in a suit unless you are prepared to bid again over partner's forced rebid.

RESPONDING WITH GOOD HANDS

THE JUMP RAISE FROM ONE TO THREE

When the responder jumps from one to three in the opener's suit it is a demand for game.

The opener is obligated to go to game regardless of the fact that he may have opened an absolute minimum. There is one exception: if the responder has previously passed, the opener may use his own judgment even after a double raise.

There are fairly distinct requirements for the double raise.

1. Responder must have more than just normal trump support. The minimum requirement is J x x x. A raise from one to three should rarely be made with only three trumps. In such cases some temporary bid in another suit is usually better.

2. A double raise requires a certain high card holding. This raise is never given on distribution only.

The technical high card requirements for a double raise are:

With a singleton	2-plus honor tricks
With a doubleton	2½ honor tricks
With no short suit	3-plus honor tricks

(The honor tricks must not be concentrated principally in the trump suit. At least 1-plus honor trick must be on the side.)

To put it another way: To justify a double raise the responder, in addition to adequate trump support, must have, roughly speaking, the equivalent of an opening bid. For the purpose of this rule a singleton may be regarded as an Ace and a doubleton as a King.

A few illustrations; in each case partner has opened with 1 Spade, and your proper response is 3 Spades.

1.	♠ K J 10 9	♡ x	◇ x x x x x	♣ A J 10
2.	♠ K Q x x	♡ x x	◇ A x x x	♣ K x x
3.	♠ K x x x	♡ J x x	◇ A K x	♣ K 10 x

In No. 1, regarding the singleton as the equivalent of an Ace, you have the equal of an opening bid—one trick in Spades, one trick in Hearts, and better than one trick in Clubs.

In No. 2, again you have the equivalent of an opening bid (regarding the doubleton Heart as equivalent to a King gives you 3 honor tricks and a four-card suit).

In No. 3, you have adequate trump support and the equivalent of an opening bid.

It must be pointed out that a raise from one to three is not an indefinite bid. It should be confined within specific limits. It should approximate the strength of a minimum opening bid, and may possess a little bit more, but not much more. Many players make a practice of responding with a double raise on almost all big hands, regardless of their strength. This is an error. The double raise should not be vague. If the strength of your hand approximates a full trick more than an opening bid, slam possibilities are present and the hand is too strong for a double raise. In those cases exploratory bids are made; these will be discussed in the chapter on slam bidding.

A jump from 1 Spade to 3 Spades, or from 1 Heart to 3 Hearts, simply announces that if partner has a minimum opening there should be a very fine play for game, but at the time the bid is made a slam is not in contemplation, although subsequent developments may make the responder change his mind.

A double raise in a minor suit—from 1 Club to 3 Clubs, or from 1 Diamond to 3 Diamonds—is a bid to avoid, if you can possibly respond by showing a new suit or if you can respond with a jump to 2 No Trump. Only when you have no alternative strength-showing bid should you give partner's minor a double raise.

♠ A K x   ♡ x   ◇ K Q x x x   ♣ x x x x

This hand justifies raising partner's 1 Diamond bid to 3 Diamonds.

THE JUMP FROM ONE TO FOUR IN A MAJOR SUIT

The raise from one to four in a major suit is a specialized bid. It describes a hand that is very rich in trump support and in distribution (it must contain a singleton or void) but is not rich in high cards. It is made on hands on which responder believes he has a fairly good chance to fulfill the contract, and also is desirous of preventing any adverse bid. This preëmptive raise must never contain more than 1½ honor tricks. If it does contain more it qualifies as a jump from one to three.

To summarize: A jump from one to three indicates good trump support and good high card strength. A jump from one to four indicates better trump support but less high card strength.

1. ♠ Q J x x x   ♡ x   ◇ K J x x x   ♣ x x
2. ♠ K x x x x x   ♡ x   ◇ x x   ♣ Q J x x

Partner has opened with 1 Spade. Holding either of these hands you should bid 4 Spades.

It is common practice to refer to this preëmptive raise as a shut-out bid. This is an unfortunate expression. Actually there is no such thing as a shut-out bid. Since the responder does not know the nature of his partner's hand it would be quite arrogant of him to insist upon silence from his partner. It is simply the responder's duty to describe his own hand. He has done so by announcing great trump length and distribution. He has denied high cards. If the opener has most of the high cards and all he needs is great trump support and distribution to produce a slam, certainly he should be at perfect liberty to proceed. I advise strongly against the use of the term "shut-out bid." It is much better to describe this raise from one to four as a bid with plenty of trumps but no high cards.

An exception should be noted here. The raise from one to four does not deny high cards when responder has previously passed. A jump from 1 Spade to 4 Spades, or from 1 Heart to 4 Hearts, then becomes stronger than a jump to three, simply because the opener might decide to pass a raise to three if he has opened a light hand in an attempt to steal a part score.

THE JUMP TAKE-OUT IN NO TRUMP

A jump response of 2 No Trump is forcing to game, just as is a jump from one to three in a suit. In fact, it may be broadly stated that whenever a responder (who has not previously passed) makes a single jump, the partnership is committed to a game contract.

As in all cases where responder guarantees game, HIS HAND MUST AT LEAST EQUAL AN OPENING BID FOR HIM TO JUMP TO 2 NO TRUMP (13 points). Many players have formed the habit of regarding the 2 No Trump response as a hand containing 2½ honor tricks. This is an unsound practice.

In addition to the high card requirements, a 2 No Trump responder should have at least two cards of his partner's suit, and all other suits protected. In other words, this response describes not only the high card strength of the hand but also indicates its type.

Examples, partner having opened with 1 Spade:

1. ♠ 10 x   ♡ K J x x   ◇ K J 10   ♣ A 10 x x

Respond with 2 No Trump. Your hand is just about the equal of an opening bid when plus values are added to your 2½ honor tricks. The hand contains eight honor cards, two cards in partner's suit, and protection in all the unbid suits (point count 13).

2. ♠ x x   ♡ A x x x   ◇ A x x   ♣ K x x x

It would be improper to respond with 2 No Trump because you are not strong enough to insist upon a game contract. The hand contains 2½ honor tricks but is not equal to an opening bid. With this type hand one must make haste slowly by making a temporary response, preferably in Clubs. Now if partner rebids 2 Diamonds the responder may try 2 No Trump. This invites partner to proceed but does not force him to do so, as would be the case had responder chosen to make a jump to 2 No Trump.

3. ♠ Q x   ♡ A Q x   ◇ x x x x x   ♣ K Q J

You may respond with 2 No Trump. Your hand is the equivalent of an opening bid, and the Diamond suit, with five cards, may be considered protected. (14 points)

4. ♠ Q x x   ♡ x x x   ◇ K J x x   ♣ A K x

This hand contains the equivalent of an opening bid and has the proper distribution, but a 2 No Trump response is not recommended because an unbid suit, Hearts, is not protected. A temporary bid of 2 Diamonds is the proper procedure, and whether or not No Trump will be tried later will depend upon developments.

Another illustration of a hand in which No Trump should be avoided, although sufficient high card strength is held, is the following:

♠ Q J x x   ♡ A Q x   ◇ x x x   ♣ K J x

Your partner has opened with 1 Club. Because of the lack of protection in the Diamond suit a 2 No Trump bid is not recommended. You have a perfectly satisfactory response of 1 Spade, which does not by any manner of means preclude a subsequent No Trump contract. You may find that partner has four Spades and is short in Diamonds, in which case a game at No Trump will be out of the question, and the prospects for a game in Spades will be very bright. There is the additional advantage that partner may have some holding in Diamonds which he would rather have led up to.

Occasionally a 2 No Trump response is better than revealing a good minor suit. For example, your partner has opened the bidding with 1 Spade and you hold:

♠ x x x   ♡ A Q x   ◇ K x   ♣ K J 10 x x

Your response is 2 No Trump rather than 2 Clubs. It is quite apparent that you desire to become declarer on this hand, to gain the advantage of having the lead come up to you in Diamonds and Hearts. Had your partner's opening bid been 1 Diamond the 2 No Trump response should not be regarded as proper, because of the unguarded Spade suit.

One more thought in connection with the 2 No Trump response. It is a precise bid, and is definitely limited in strength. It must never contain more than $3\frac{1}{2}$ honor tricks. In other words, it may be a little stronger than an opening bid, but not much. If the hand is of the No Trump type and contains more than $3\frac{1}{2}$ honor tricks a response of 3 No Trump is in order.

THE JUMP TAKE-OUT TO 3 NO TRUMP

It has been seen above that the take-out of an opening bid of one of a suit to 2 No Trump requires about 3 to $3\frac{1}{2}$ honor tricks, *but no more.* With greater strength it is obligatory to make a stronger bid. Holding from 3½ to 4 honor tricks and 4-3-3-3 distribution, responder should bid 3 No Trump. This gives an exact picture of his hand and enables the opener to judge immediately the probable trick-taking capacity of the partnership. A jump from one of a suit to 3 No Trump requires a point count of 16, or to put it in another way, in order to make a jump response of 3 No Trump, your hand must be equal to an opening 1 No Trump bid itself.

An illustration: Partner opened with 1 Spade. You should respond 3 No Trump on this hand, which has more than 3½ honor tricks:

♠ Q x x   ♡ A Q x   ♢ K x x x   ♣ A Q x   (17 points)

When the responder holds more than 4 honor tricks his hand is too strong even for a 3 No Trump response, and he must make a more positive slam try, in the form of a jump in a new suit.

IN A NUTSHELL

A jump to 2 No Trump by responder shows approximately the strength of an ordinary opening bid. (13 to 15 points)

A jump to 3 No Trump by responder shows approximately the strength of an opening 1 No Trump bid. (16 to 18 points)

Where responder's hand is stronger than a 1 No Trump bid, he should make a jump shift.

THE JUMP TAKE-OUT IN A NEW SUIT

A jump shift, that is, a jump take-out into a new suit, is the method employed by the responder to make an immediate announcement that he is interested in a slam.

Where only game is in contemplation, there is no necessity for an immediate jump shift. The mere naming of a new suit insures another chance to bid, when the game strength can be shown.

The textbook requirement for a jump shift is about 3½ honor tricks and a good suit. Sometimes, however, possession of even more than 3½ honor tricks does not justify a jump shift. The hand should be so composed that a slam can be visualized at once, else the big guns should be held up till the next round. Responder, too, should have a fairly good idea of where the hand can safely play.

There is a popular misconception to the effect that you are not permitted to make a jump take-out in a new suit unless you have support for your partner's suit. Where there is danger of a misfit, naturally one must proceed with caution, but responder may jump shift if his hand is self-sustaining, i.e., he holds a solid suit of his own that requires no support, or where partner's suit is not relied upon. Responder does promise by his jump shift that there is a contract at which the hand can play conveniently.

♠ A K Q 10 x   ♡ x   ◇ A K J x x   ♣ x x

Partner opens with 1 Heart. You have no support in partner's suit, but this has all the earmarks of a slam in one of your two suits. You should therefore respond with 2 Spades, a jump shift.

♠ x   ♡ A Q 10 x   ◇ A K J x x   ♣ x x x

Partner opens with 1 Spade. You have more than 3½ honor tricks and a good suit, but it would be unwise to bid 3 Diamonds. You can hardly say that you are interested in a slam at this point. You are not even sure as to where the hand will play. You must proceed slowly until you determine the best contract. There is no question but what you will eventually reach game. Your proper response is 2 Diamonds. If partner rebids his Spades you have plenty of bidding space in which to bid 3 Hearts, leaving the door open to any of a number of different contracts.

♠ x   ♡ A K 10 x   ◇ A Q x x   ♣ Q 10 9 x

Partner opens with 1 Club. A 2 Heart response is acceptable since the strong trump support makes slam prospects bright.

♠ A Q 10 x   ♡ x   ◇ A K J x   ♣ Q 10 x x

Partner opens with 1 Spade. Respond 3 Diamonds. There is a slam aroma about this hand. It is far too strong for a jump raise.

♠ A K x x x   ♡ A Q x   ◇ Q J   ♣ K x x

Partner opens with 1 Diamond. Respond 2 Spades, though you have neither a powerful suit of your own nor strong support for partner's suit. If partner has no long trump suit then his opening bid values, like yours, must be general and you can safely play in No Trump.

To put it more definitely: In order to justify a jump shift the responder must have at least a full trick more than the equivalent of an opening bid, and must have in prospect a safe place to play the hand.

DOUBLE JUMP TAKE-OUTS

The jump shift which is forcing to game and highly suggestive of a slam is a single jump—a bid of one trick more than necessary. When the responder jumps two or more levels above the opener's bid, he is not showing strength:

OPENER	RESPONDER		OPENER	RESPONDER
1 ◇	3 ♠		1 ♣	4 ♡

Both the 3 Spade response and the 4 Heart response are preëmptive take-outs, showing (as does an opening preëmptive bid) a long suit but little or no high-card strength.

The double jump take-out to three of a suit is not recommended. For one thing, the opener is far too likely to misread it as an ordinary jump shift and think he should go slamming. For another thing, such hands are usually better shown by a one-over-one response, which does not crowd the bidding.

A jump to four may occasionally be made on a hand like this:

♠ x   ♡ K Q 10 x x x x x   ◇ x x   ♣ x x

Partner opens with 1 Diamond. Next hand passes. A jump to 4 Hearts is proper, though I would not criticize a bid of 1 Heart. However, fourth hand *may* have Spades which he would bid over 1 Heart but which will be shut out by the jump to 4 Hearts.

IN A NUTSHELL

A raise from one to three shows trump support and high-card tricks.

A jump from one to four shows plenty of trumps but not much in high cards.

A jump from one of a suit to 2 No Trump shows a balanced hand with about the equal of an opening bid (13 to 15 points).

A jump from one of a suit to 3 No Trump shows that the responder's hand is the equivalent of an opening 1 No Trump bid (16 to 18 points).

A jump take-out in a new suit is made only on hands that look like a slam. If only game is in prospect the mere naming of a new suit by the responder is sufficient.

CHOICE OF RESPONSES

On a great many hands there is a choice of responses; that is, any of several bids may be technically correct. It is incumbent upon the responder in those cases to make the best of the choices.

CHOICE BETWEEN A SINGLE RAISE AND A 1 NO TRUMP RESPONSE

This is, so to speak, a choice of rotten apples, inasmuch as these two responses are regarded as less favored children. Where the choice between raising your partner to two of his suit and bidding 1 No Trump is very close, the distribution of the hand will usually determine the choice. With a 4-3-3-3 distribution you should prefer to bid 1 No Trump. With any other distribution you should prefer to raise your partner's suit.

♠ K x x   ♡ x x x   ◇ A x x x   ♣ x x x

Partner opens with 1 Spade. You have a choice of responding with 1 No Trump or 2 Spades. Because of the even distribution this hand has very little playing strength in support of Spades— to be exact, 2½ playing tricks. A No Trump response is therefore preferable. If, however, one of the small Hearts were converted into a Club, you would prefer to bid 2 Spades, because the doubleton Heart would add a ruffing value and promote the hand to 3 playing tricks.

Even with a balanced hand a single raise should occasionally be preferred to a 1 No Trump response. Such a hand contains about 2 honor tricks and the responder does not wish to sound too depressing.

♠ K x x   ♡ Q x x x   ◇ A x x   ♣ J x x

Partner opens with 1 Spade. This hand is average in high cards. A single raise is preferred to a 1 No Trump response, because of the desire to sound just the least bit encouraging.

CHOICE BETWEEN RAISING YOUR PARTNER AND BIDDING YOUR OWN SUIT

THE RULE OF FOUR PLUS

This phase of bidding provides a stumbling block to even the more experienced players. One frequently is presented with a choice between giving partner a single raise in his major suit and naming some other suit. Since it is usually more important to support your partner's major suit than to show your own, the question first to be answered is, "Can I afford to do both?"

If your hand is good enough to justify two bids you should show your suit first and support partner's suit later. If you feel that your hand is not strong enough to do both you should confine yourself to a single raise of partner's suit, hoping he can take further action.

The question arises, "How is one to determine whether or not the hand is worth two bids?"

The surest test is to be found in the table of playing tricks. If the responder's hand is worth 4 playing tricks or less in support of partner, the hand should be regarded as worth only one bid, in which case a single raise is given. However, if the responder's hand is worth more than 4 playing tricks the hand can support two bids, and in that case the responder's suit is first shown. For example:

♠ K x x   ♡ x x   ◇ A J x x x   ♣ x x x

Your partner opens with 1 Spade. The question is whether to raise to 2 Spades or to bid 2 Diamonds. Is this hand worth two bids? Your instinct probably tells you that it is not. You are right. The hand counts up to a little over 3½ playing tricks. Since more than four are required to justify making two bids, the proper response is 2 Spades and not 2 Diamonds. The objection to bidding 2 Diamonds becomes apparent. Let us suppose that partner, under compulsion to bid again, calls 2 Spades. What would you do? If you raise the Spades to three you are certainly doing a lot of bidding, and if you pass your partner will never know that you had Spade support and a game might conceivably be missed.

Let us change the above hand slightly, converting one of the Hearts into a Spade. We now have:

♠ K x x x   ♡ x   ◇ A J x x x   ♣ x x x

Again the question is whether to raise the Spades or to show the Diamonds. Is this hand worth two bids? A reference to the playing trick table will reveal that it contains 5½ playing tricks. Therefore the hand is worth more than one bid, yet it is not strong enough in high cards for a jump to 3 Spades. In other words, this is the type of hand on which the most comfortable bid would be a response of 2½ Spades. In all such cases you make a temporary bid first (2 Diamonds in this case), intending to raise partner's suit on the next round. You are sure to have another chance because the 2 Diamond bid is a one-round force on the opener.

In applying this Rule of Four Plus you will frequently find it necessary to bid two in a very weak suit, as a waiting bid. For example:

♠ K x x x   ♡ x x   ◇ K 10 x x   ♣ A x x

Your partner opens with 1 Spade. This hand is too good for a single raise and not good enough for a jump raise. It contains 4½ playing tricks. This is another one of those hands which best could be described by a raise to 2½ Spades—a bid unfortunately not permitted by law. You must therefore arrange to bid some other suit. You have no good suit but there is no objection to taking out with 2 Diamonds, as a temporary measure, since it is your full intention to raise Spades on the next round. Here again it should be pointed out that if you must tell an untruth it is much better to lie about the strength of your suit than to tell a falsehood about the strength of your hand.

On a few occasions it is necessary to resort to a three-card minor suit for a take-out. Suppose, for example, partner opens with 1 Spade and you hold:

♠ Q x x x x   ♡ x x   ◇ K x x   ♣ A 10 x

This hand is not good enough for a jump to 3 Spades, which would guarantee a game, but it is obviously too good for a mere single raise. The suggested response is 2 Clubs. This should not shock even the most squeamish, for there is not the remotest danger that the hand will ever play in Clubs.

In cases such as are illustrated by the four previous examples the responder's task is simplified if the opponent overcalls the opening bid. In each of these cases the responder should bid 2 Spades, a free bid denoting a good hand. It is not now necessary to make indirect bids in the side suits, since the voluntary action on the part of responder indicates a good hand.

CHOICE BETWEEN GIVING A DOUBLE RAISE AND NAMING A NEW SUIT

Here you have a choice between two good bids, either of which may be correct. Tactics may suggest that one is to be preferred on certain types of hands. Observe the following case:

♠ J x x x x   ♡ x   ◇ A Q x x   ♣ K x x

Partner opens the bidding with 1 Spade. This hand qualifies as a jump to 3 Spades. Note that it contains adequate trump support, with 2 honor tricks and a singleton; regarding the Heart singleton as an Ace, the hand is equivalent to an opening bid and game may be promised.

The responder, if he chooses, may make a temporary bid of 2 Diamonds, intending to raise Spades later. I do not regard this as the best strategy, however, since little is to be gained by making an indirect bid in this case. *Where there is a direct bid which precisely describes your hand, such a bid is much preferable to in-*

direct action. A jump to 3 Spades exactly fits this hand and is a direct bid. An indirect bid in such a case may lead to confusion on subsequent rounds of bidding.

♠ J x x x x   ♡ x   ◇ A K Q x   ♣ K x x

Here again partner has opened with 1 Spade. This hand contains a little bit more than would be required for a jump to 3 Spades, so we cannot give a completely accurate description of its strength in one bid. It is preferable, therefore, to respond with 2 Diamonds (so good a suit provides possible discards) with the full intention of contracting for game in Spades on the next round, even if partner makes a minimum rebid.

In certain cases a Diamond response on a hand like the foregoing one may induce partner to investigate slam possibilities. If he has three small Diamonds, for example, your response may relieve him of one possible source of worry.

♠ A Q x x   ♡ K x x   ◇ A x x x   ♣ x x

Partner opens with 1 Heart. You have sufficient honor strength for a jump to 3 Hearts, but such action would be improper since you have only three trumps. It is your full intention to contract for game eventually, but if partner has an indifferent four-card Heart suit you may want to play this hand at some other declaration, probably No Trump, possibly Spades. The waiting bid of 1 Spade is recommended. Partner is not permitted to pass, of course. If Hearts are rebid you should jump to four in that suit. If partner's rebid is of an aggressive type, your fancy may turn to thoughts of a slam.

RESPONDING WITH TWO-SUITERS

When the responder has two suits, both of which he intends to show, they should usually be bid in the orthodox sequence. That is, with suits of equal length he bids the higher-ranking first, whether they are four-carders or five-carders; with suits of unequal length he bids the longer first. But remember the proviso that *he intends to show both.*

Your hand must be strong to allow such action. If your hand is not of sufficient strength to justify the naming of both suits, common sense and economy will dictate the choice. Here is an illustration:

♠ A K J x   ♡ x x   ◇ x x   ♣ K 10 x x x

Partner opens with 1 Heart. With this hand you are prepared to show both suits and you should bid them in the normal sequence, that is, the Clubs first. The proper response is 2 Clubs. If partner rebids 2 Hearts you intend to bid 2 Spades and partner will have a photographic description of your hand.

Some players engage in the unsound practice of responding with 1 Spade on the foregoing hand, explaining that they wish to keep the bidding low. But, in the first place, there is no necessity for keeping the bidding low with a hand that has game prospects. You have virtually an opening bid yourself, so that the outlook for game is bright. Secondly, you actually get the bidding up higher by first responding with 1 Spade. If partner rebids 2 Hearts, you no doubt intend to bid 3 Clubs. You are now up higher than you would have been on proper bidding and your partner has no exact information as to the length of your suits.

Let us reduce the hand slightly:

♠ A J x x   ♡ x x   ◇ x x   ♣ K x x x x

Partner opens with 1 Heart. At first blush the natural response would be 2 Clubs. But your hand is not quite strong enough to justify a take-out to the two level. Rather than respond with 1 No Trump, bid 1 Spade. If partner rebids 2 Hearts, we recognize that there is no game and we pass. We had no intention of bidding both suits.

Another exception:

♠ A J x x   ♡ K 10 x x   ◇ x x x   ♣ x x

Partner opens with 1 Club. You can afford to make only one response (unless partner subsequently gets very excited). The orthodox response would be 1 Spade, but there is a certain practical objection to this bid. If partner happens to have a hand of moderate strength containing a four-card Heart suit he will now be unable to show his suit at the level of one, and may be too weak to show it at the level of two, and the Heart suit may be lost. The best practice, therefore, is to respond with 1 Heart. If partner has Hearts he will have a pleasant raise. If partner's second suit is Spades he is able to show it at the level of one.

But if the hand is strong enough to warrant the showing of both suits the normal sequence is followed.

♠ A Q J x   ♡ K Q 10 x   ◇ x x x   ♣ x x

Partner opens with 1 Club. This hand has fairly good game-going prospects. You can afford to show both suits. The proper response is 1 Spade, with the intention of bidding Hearts on the next round.

Occasionally a responder will desire to show two suits on a hand of moderate strength. It may be impossible to name them both at a reasonable level if they are bid in normal order. A departure from normal will be found expedient in a hand such as the following:

♠ A K x x   ♡ Q x x x x   ◇ x x x   ♣ x

Your partner opens with 1 Club. You desire to show both suits in this hand, but if you respond with 1 Heart and partner rebids 2 Clubs it will become rather expensive to bid 2 Spades, since partner cannot then return to 2 Hearts. It is good policy, therefore, to respond with 1 Spade and if partner rebids 2 Clubs you may at a reasonable level rebid 2 Hearts.

A FEW SPECIALIZED SITUATIONS IN RESPONDING

RESPONDING WHEN YOU HAVE PREVIOUSLY PASSED

It is of paramount importance to bear in mind that almost any response made by you under these conditions can be dropped by the opener. He recalls your previous pass and may have said to himself as he opened the bidding, "I know, from my partner's pass, that we have no game in this hand, but I am opening simply for a part score and I am going to drop any response he makes." It follows, therefore, that a player who has previously passed cannot make a temporary bid because it might turn out to be permanent. He must be prepared to play the hand at anything he bids. To illustrate:

♠ Q 10 x x ♡ x x ♢ Q J 10 x ♣ A x x

Your partner deals and opens with 1 Spade. You consider your hand just a shade too strong for a mere single raise to 2 Spades, so you make a temporary bid of 2 Diamonds. This forces partner to bid again and you intend to raise Spades on the next round.

But if you have previously passed and partner opens with 1 Spade you are not in a position to bid 2 Diamonds, because partner might pass and let you play it there. In this position you should bid 2 Spades, to be quite sure the hand is played in the proper suit.

Let us examine a hand we have discussed before:

♠ K x x x ♡ x x ♢ K 10 x x ♣ A x x

Your partner deals and bids 1 Spade. Your hand is too good for a single raise and not quite good enough for a jump to three, so you temporize by bidding 2 Diamonds. But if you have previously passed and partner opens with 1 Spade in third or fourth position you dare not bid 2 Diamonds. Since the hand is still too good for a single raise, under these conditions you may jump to 3 Spades. Had you not previously passed, such a bid would be forcing to game. But not so now. If partner so chooses he may pass. You are announcing a hand that is just short of a regulation jump to 3 Spades.

What if, after passing, you feel convinced there is a game in the hand? You ought to bid it. You have:

♠ K Q x x ♡ Q 10 x x ♢ K Q x x ♣ x

You pass and partner opens with 1 Spade. You should gamble it out to 4 Spades yourself. If you jump to 3 Spades partner might pass.

A jump in a new suit, even after previously passing, is regarded as forcing.

♠ K Q J 10 x   ♡ K x x x   ◇ Q J x   ♣ x

You have passed originally, and partner opens with 1 Heart. With this hand you surely wish to reach game, and even a slam is not beyond reach if partner holds three Aces. The proper response is 2 Spades, a jump shift which is forcing even though you previously passed.

THE RESPONSE OF 1 NO TRUMP TO PARTNER'S 1 CLUB

When the opening bid is 1 Club the response of 1 No Trump is very rare. If responder decides to keep the bidding open on a light hand he has available to him a choice of 1 Diamond, 1 Heart or 1 Spade, even though the suit may be very weak.

A certain school of players has therefore adopted the policy of responding 1 No Trump to partner's 1 Club to indicate a rather fair hand, one that contains approximately 2 honor tricks and is evenly balanced. Take a hand such as the following:

♠ K x x   ♡ K x x   ◇ A x x x   ♣ x x x

Partner opens with 1 Club. If you respond with 1 Diamond and his rebid is 1 No Trump you are a little reluctant to pass, and yet have not sufficient to raise to 2 No Trump. The dilemma is solved in this case by responding with 1 No Trump.

Holding the following hand:

♠ K x x   ♡ J x x x   ◇ A J x x   ♣ x x

In response to a 1 Club bid the proper procedure is to bid 1 Diamond, not 1 No Trump, because partner may have a four-card Heart suit which he can show at the level of one and which you can very readily support. Holding:

♠ K x x   ♡ x x x   ◇ A x x x   ♣ x x x

In response to the Club bid the proper procedure is to bid 1 Diamond. Since you are not anxious to take any further action, you may as well make the cheapest possible bid.

RESPONSES QUIZ

(ANSWERS BEGIN ON PAGE 70)

What do you bid on each of the following, in the conditions stated?

Your partner opens with 1 Spade. Next hand passes.

1. ♠ x x x x
   ♡ A x x
   ◇ x x x
   ♣ x x x

2. ♠ x x x x
   ♡ A x x x
   ◇ x x
   ♣ x x x

3. ♠ K Q x x x x
   ♡ x
   ◇ K x x x
   ♣ x x

4. ♠ A 10 x x x
   ♡ x
   ◇ K Q 10 x x
   ♣ x x

5. ♠ K J x x x
   ♡ x x x
   ◇ x x
   ♣ K x x

6. ♠ K x x
   ♡ K x x
   ◇ x x x x
   ♣ x x x

7. ♠ x x
   ♡ K Q x x x
   ◇ K x x
   ♣ x x x

8. ♠ x x
   ♡ K x x
   ◇ K Q x x x
   ♣ x x x

9. ♠ 10 9 x
   ♡ x
   ◇ K J x x x
   ♣ Q x x x

10. ♠ K x x
    ♡ K x x x x x
    ◇ x x
    ♣ x x

11. ♠ J 10 x
    ♡ x x
    ◇ K Q J x x
    ♣ x x x

12. ♠ 10 9 x x x
    ♡ x
    ◇ Q x
    ♣ K Q 10 x x

13. ♠ 10 x x x
    ♡ K J x x
    ◇ x
    ♣ K J x x

14. ♠ x
    ♡ K J x x
    ◇ K x x x
    ♣ A K J x

15. ♠ x x
    ♡ A Q J 10 9 x
    ◇ A Q x
    ♣ K 10

16. ♠ A 10 x
    ♡ Q x x x
    ◇ A K x
    ♣ K Q x

17. ♠ x x x
    ♡ K Q x
    ◇ K x x
    ♣ A Q 9 x

18. ♠ A Q x x x
    ♡ K x x
    ◇ x x
    ♣ A K Q

Your partner opens with 1 Club. Next hand passes.

19. ♠ A x x
    ♡ K J 9 x
    ◊ A x x x
    ♣ x x

20. ♠ x x
    ♡ A J x x
    ◊ x x x x
    ♣ x x x

21. ♠ K J x
    ♡ K Q x
    ◊ A 10 x x
    ♣ A x x

22. ♠ A J x x
    ♡ K Q x x
    ◊ A Q J x
    ♣ x

23. ♠ A Q x x
    ♡ A x x x
    ◊ A x
    ♣ J 10 x

24. ♠ K x x x
    ♡ Q x x x
    ◊ Q x x x
    ♣ x

25. ♠ A 9 x
    ♡ Q x x
    ◊ A x x
    ♣ x x x x

26. ♠ K x x x
    ♡ Q J x x
    ◊ J x
    ♣ 10 x x

27. ♠ A x x
    ♡ K x x
    ◊ x x
    ♣ Q x x x x

28. ♠ K 10 x
    ♡ A 10 x
    ◊ A J x x
    ♣ Q x x

29. ♠ A K J x x x x x
    ♡ A
    ◊ Q J 10 x
    ♣ ——

30. ♠ J 9 x x
    ♡ J x x x
    ◊ Q x x x
    ♣ x

Your partner opens with 1 Heart. Next hand passes.

31. ♠ K J x
    ♡ J x x
    ◊ A Q x x
    ♣ A Q x

32. ♠ K 10 9 x
    ♡ K Q 9 x
    ◊ x
    ♣ A 10 x x

33. ♠ x x
    ♡ K x x x
    ◊ K Q J x
    ♣ J 10 x

34. ♠ x x
    ♡ K J x x
    ◊ K Q J x
    ♣ K x x

35. ♠ K J x x
    ♡ Q J
    ◊ A J 9 x x
    ♣ x x

36. ♠ A J 10 x
    ♡ J x x x
    ◊ x x
    ♣ x x x

37. ♠ K J 10 x
    ♡ Q 9 x
    ◊ x x x x
    ♣ x x

38. ♠ J 10 x x
    ♡ x x x
    ◊ A Q x
    ♣ Q J 10

39. ♠ J 10 9 x
    ♡ K J x x x x
    ◊ A
    ♣ A K

40. ♠ K 10 x x   ♡ ——   ◊ A J 10 x   ♣ Q 9 x x x

Your partner opens with 1 Spade. Next hand bids 2 Hearts.

41. ♠ 10 x x
    ♡ x x x
    ◇ A J 9 x x
    ♣ K x

42. ♠ x x
    ♡ x x
    ◇ A K x x x
    ♣ x x x x

43. ♠ 10 x x x
    ♡ x x
    ◇ A Q J x x
    ♣ x x

Partner opens with 1 Heart. Next hand bids 1 Spade.

44. ♠ A Q x   ♡ x x x   ◇ x x x x   ♣ J x x

Partner opens with 1 Diamond. Next hand passes.

45. ♠ A K x x   ♡ A K x x   ◇ x   ♣ Q x x x.

46. ♠ J x x x   ♡ A x   ◇ Q x x x   ♣ x x x

Partner opens with 1 Club. Next hand bids 1 Spade.

47. ♠ K J x   ♡ 10 x x   ◇ A 10 x x   ♣ K x x

48. ♠ J x x   ♡ K J x x x   ◇ K x x x   ♣ x

Partner opens with 1 Spade. Next hand bids 2 Hearts.

49. ♠ K J x   ♡ x x   ◇ A Q 10 x x   ♣ x x x

Partner has opened with (a) 1 Spade; (b) 1 Club. Next hand passes.

50. ♠ x x x
    ♡ K x
    ◇ A Q 9 x
    ♣ x x x x

51. ♠ x x x
    ♡ A Q x x
    ◇ K 10 x
    ♣ A x x

52. ♠ ——
    ♡ K J x
    ◇ A Q 10 9 x
    ♣ A x x x x

Partner has opened with 1 No Trump. Next hand passes. (Responses to No Trump bids were discussed in Chapter 1.)

53. ♠ J x x
    ♡ K Q x x x
    ◇ x x
    ♣ x x x

54. ♠ A x x
    ♡ x x x
    ◇ K Q x x x
    ♣ x x

55. ♠ Q J x x x x x
    ♡ x
    ◇ Q x x x
    ♣ x

Partner has opened with 2 No Trump. Next hand passes.

56.	♠ Q x x	57.	♠ J 10 x x x x	58.	♠ Q x x x
	♡ x x x		♡ x x		♡ Q x x
	◇ 10 9 x x		◇ Q x x		◇ x x x x
	♣ x x x		♣ x x		♣ x x

Partner has opened with 3 No Trump. Next hand passes.

59. ♠ x x   ♡ x x x   ◇ x x   ♣ K x x x x x

You are South in the following cases. The bidding is indicated. What is your response?

60.	♠ x		61.	♠ A 10 9 x
	♡ J 10 x x x			♡ K x x x x
	◇ A x x x			◇ x
	♣ K Q x			♣ Q J x

SOUTH	WEST	NORTH	EAST	SOUTH	WEST	NORTH	EAST
Pass	Pass	1 ♡	Pass	Pass	Pass	1 ♡	Pass
?				?			

62.	♠ K Q 9 x x		63.	♠ A Q x
	♡ x			♡ x x x
	◇ K x x x x			◇ K 9 x x x
	♣ K x			♣ K x

SOUTH	WEST	NORTH	EAST	SOUTH	WEST	NORTH	EAST
Pass	Pass	1 ◇	Pass	Pass	Pass	1 ♠	Pass
?				?			

64.	♠ A J x		65.	♠ K Q x x
	♡ K x x			♡ A x x
	◇ K x x x x			◇ Q J x
	♣ x x			♣ x x x

NORTH	EAST	SOUTH	WEST	NORTH	EAST	SOUTH	WEST
1 ♣	1 ♠	?		1 ♡	2 ♣	?	

RESPONSES QUIZ — ANSWERS

1. Pass. You have only one skeleton honor trick in one suit. (3 points)

2. Bid 2 Spades. The doubleton Diamond makes the difference between this and No. 1. The hand now possesses normal trumps, a high card, and a short suit; or, to put it another way, 2½ playing tricks.

3. Bid 4 Spades, saying, "Partner, I am rich in trumps but not in high cards."

4. Bid either 2 Diamonds or 3 Spades, but not 4 Spades because your hand contains 2 honor tricks and you must not preëmpt.

5. Bid 2 Spades. Do not get excited because of that fifth trump. The hand would be almost as good without it.

6. Bid 1 No Trump. Not enough playing tricks to raise to 2 Spades.

7. Bid 2 Hearts.

8. Bid 1 No Trump rather than 2 Diamonds. Note in the preceding example, the increased level was risked because of the possession of a major suit.

9. Bid 2 Spades, despite the questionable trump support. No other response is satisfactory.

10. Bid 2 Spades under the Rule of Four Plus. You cannot afford to make two constructive bids—that is, to bid 2 Hearts and later raise to 3 Spades—on this hand. Therefore you raise partner's major suit.

11. Bid 2 Spades. The hand is not strong enough for 2 Diamonds.

12. Bid 4 Spades. You should have a reasonable chance to make it. You are not interested in a slam and are desirous of preventing the opposition from getting together in one of the red suits.

13. Bid 2 Clubs. The hand has too much playing strength for a mere raise to 2 Spades. It is better to explore with the four-card minor than with the four-card major, inasmuch as you intend to return to Spades in any event.

14. Bid 2 Clubs. This is the best temporary bid. No doubt a game contract will eventually be reached. Over your 2 Club bid if partner has a four-card Heart suit he may show it conveniently. If he has not, you can forget about Hearts and concentrate on No Trump.

15. Bid 3 Hearts. Support for partner's suit is not required for a jump shift if your suit can stand on its own legs, and a slam is probable.

16. Bid 3 No Trump. An exact descriptive bid. This, however, is a maximum for such a response. Even here a jump shift to 3 Diamonds would be accepted as the correct answer (point count 18).

17. Bid 2 No Trump (point count 14). An exact descriptive bid. Nothing is to be gained by temporizing with a 2 Club take-out.

18. Bid 3 Clubs. A slam try. It would not be good policy to respond with 3 Spades.

19. Bid 1 Heart. This is to be preferred to a 2 No Trump response. The No Trump can wait for later.

20. Bid 1 Heart, not 1 No Trump. Had partner opened with 1 Spade you could choose between passing and responding with 1 No Trump.

21. Bid 3 No Trump (point count 17). An exact descriptive bid which is preferable to a temporary bid of 1 Diamond.

22. Bid 1 Spade (not 2 Spades). You intend to show all three suits and should allow yourself as much bidding space as possible.

23. Bid 1 Spade. A 2 No Trump response would be plausible but is not recommended, both because of the doubleton Diamond and because the hand might play better in one of the majors.

24. Bid 1 Diamond. This allows partner to rebid at the level of one in either major suit if he has one.

25. Bid 1 Diamond. This is not an attempt to be fancy. There is just no other satisfactory bid.

26. Bid 1 Heart. You intend to make only one bid and this allows partner to rebid at the level of one if he has a four-card Spade suit. A Spade response would make it difficult for partner to show Hearts.

27. Bid 2 Clubs. This does justice to the hand. If partner cannot bid again no game will be missed. Avoid the error of bidding 3 Clubs, which would commit you to a game. This is not equal to an opening bid.

28. Bid 2 No Trump (point count 14). An exact descriptive bid. Nothing is to be gained by the waiting bid of 1 Diamond.

29. Bid 2 Spades. A jump shift, suggesting a slam. Support for partner's suit is not prerequisite if your suit is self-sustaining.

30. Bid 1 Diamond. A sporting bid in an effort to find a better "spot." This affords partner the opportunity to rebid 1 Heart or 1 Spade, which you will drop like a hot potato.

31. Bid 3 No Trump (point count 17). Just the right distribution and honor strength. A 2 No Trump response would be improper.

32. Bid 3 Hearts. This is preferable to a temporary bid of 1 Spade, since it is more or less an exact descriptive bid.

33. Bid 2 Diamonds. An indirect bid is necessary because the hand is too good for a single raise and not good enough for a raise to 3 Hearts. Hearts will be supported next round.

34. Bid 3 Hearts, in preference to the indirect bid of 2 Diamonds. This just about describes your hand.

35. Bid 2 Diamonds. A response of 1 Spade would be improper. You can afford to show both suits and should do so in the logical order.

36. Bid 2 Hearts, not 1 Spade. You cannot afford to do both and you should make the more important bid.

37. Bid 2 Hearts in preference to 1 Spade.

38. Bid 1 Spade, reluctantly and as a temporary measure. The suit is not biddable but no other call is available. The hand is too good for 1 No Trump and not good enough for 2 No Trump.

39. Bid 3 Clubs, a slam suggestion. A 3 Heart bid must not be made on this strong a hand.

40. Bid 2 Clubs. You must anticipate a probable rebid of 2 Hearts, which will make it convenient for you to bid 2 Spades. A response of 1 Spade would make it necessary for you to bid three of some suit on the next round.

41. Bid 2 Spades. You should take some action and cannot afford to bid 3 Diamonds.

42. Pass. You cannot afford to bid 3 Diamonds.

43. Bid 2 Spades. A free raise does justice to your holding and it is improper to bid 3 Diamonds. Partner may be forced to rebid 3 Spades and you won't know whether or not the hand can make four.

44. Pass. You have not sufficient values for a free bid of 1 No Trump.

45. Bid 1 Spade. Despite your 4-plus honor tricks, a 2 Spade bid is improper because no slam is yet in sight.

46. Bid 2 Diamonds. This just about describes your hand. Don't make the error of responding with 1 Spade. If partner has a good hand containing four Spades he may show them over your 2 Diamond bid.

47. Bid 1 No Trump. This free bid indicates a good hand. Don't bid 2 No Trump, which would absolutely guarantee game.

48. Pass. You cannot afford to bid 2 Hearts because it might force partner into 3 Clubs, which you wouldn't like.

49. Bid 2 Spades. The free bid will denote a good hand. Had the opponent passed you could properly respond 2 Diamonds, intending to support Spades later.

50. (a) Bid 1 No Trump; (b) bid 1 Diamond.

51. (a) Bid 2 No Trump (point count 13). An exact descriptive bid, much preferable to the temporary bid of 2 Hearts. (b) Bid 1 Heart. 2 No Trump should not be bid, because of the unguarded Spade suit.

52. (a) Bid 2 Diamonds. Make haste slowly because of a possible misfit. (b) Bid 2 Diamonds, a jump shift suggesting slam possibilities, suggested by your good fit with Clubs and control of every suit.

53. Pass. There should be no game, when partner can have no more than 4 honor tricks. (6 points)

54. Bid 2 No Trump. There should be a game, and if you bid only 2 Diamonds partner might pass. (9 points)

55. Bid 4 Spades. Game is sure, but slam is out of the question.

56. Pass (point count of only 2). 2 No Trump is not forcing. ½ honor trick is required to raise.

57. Bid 3 Spades.

58. Bid 3 No Trump (point count 4). Even two Queens should produce game opposite partner's powerful hand.

59. Bid 4 Clubs. This is a slam try—and your hand, when combined with partner's 6½ or 7 honor tricks, is well worth it.

60. Bid 4 Hearts. You should be willing to gamble this hand out for game. A jump to 3 Hearts would not be forcing, since you previously passed. Even if partner has a light third-hand opening you should have a fair chance for game.

61. Bid 4 Hearts, for the same reasons as in the previous case. Don't bid 1 Spade; partner can pass it.

62. Bid 2 Spades. In view of your previous pass a 1 Spade response would not be forcing. With the splendid fit you should be willing to take your chances on a game contract.

63. Bid 3 Spades. This is exceptional, since you hold but three trumps. However, the alternate bid of 2 Diamonds is not acceptable. Because of your previous pass partner might not rebid. The 3 Spade bid is not forcing unless partner has a sound opening bid.

64. Bid 1 No Trump. This free bid just about describes the strength of your hand. A 2 Diamond bid would be poor strategy; for if partner then rebid 3 Clubs, you would have no idea of what to do.

65. Bid 2 Hearts. The free bid denotes a good hand. A bid of 2 Spades would be improper. Had second hand passed, a mere raise to 2 Hearts would have been too weak to do justice to the hand, and a temporary bid of 1 Spade would have been in order.

CHAPTER 3

REBIDS

THE OPENER'S SECOND BID is his most important by far. An opening one-bid in a suit is highly ambiguous. It does not put any precise limits on either the strength of the hand or the type (distribution) of the hand. The opener's second bid must tell what kind of hand the first bid was made on.

Sometimes it is possible to do both:

♠ x x   ♥ A Q J x   ♦ A Q 10 x   ♣ J x x

You bid 1 Heart. Suppose your partner responds 2 Clubs. Your rebid of 2 Diamonds shows a hand of minimum, or little more than minimum, strength, in which there are Heart and Diamond suits. Or suppose partner responds 1 Spade. Now you rebid 1 No Trump, again showing a hand of approximately minimum strength with balanced distribution. In either case, you have described your hand by your rebid.

Sometimes it is impossible to show both the strength and the type of hand by a single rebid. When you are in this situation the principle controlling your rebid should be this: *It is far more important to indicate the strength of your hand as a whole than to indicate the location or the distribution of this strength.* For example:

♠ A K J x x   ♥ J x   ♦ K Q x   ♣ A 10 x

You open with 1 Spade. Partner responds 2 Hearts. You would like to show that you have a rebiddable Spade suit; but you cannot do so by a jump to 3 Spades, for which your hand is not strong enough, and if you bid only 2 Spades it will indicate a much weaker hand than you have. So you rebid 2 No Trump, which shows a strong hand, and—since it shows distributed strength—does at least give a general idea of the type of hand.

REBID BY OPENER WHEN PARTNER HAS GIVEN A
SINGLE RAISE

When you open with one of a suit, next hand passes, and partner raises to two of the same suit, you are not expected to feel encouraged. Responder may have kept the bidding open on very moderate values. Unless you have considerably more than an opening bid there will be no chance for game, and you should pass even though your hand contains another suit.

But if you have definite excess values there is a chance for game, provided partner's raise was a fairly good one and not a questionable or "courtesy" raise. In such cases you test the nature of your partner's response. This you may do in one of several ways. The usual method is to bid three of your suit, which states, in effect, "Partner, I cannot tell how good your raise was. If you had a sketchy raise and were just keeping the bidding open for me I'll expect you to pass, but if your raise was good, please go on to game."

It is important for the opener to assess his values accurately when partner gives a single raise, before he decides whether to pass, to bid again, or to contract for game. If the opening bidder's hand is of a more or less balanced type there will be little hope for game unless he has about 1½ honor tricks in excess of his opening bid, in which case he may coax partner to go on. With 2 honor tricks in excess of his bid he should bid game himself.

Additional playing strength may take the place of excess honor values. To put it into a formula: If the opener has no more than 5½ playing tricks game is highly improbable. Opener should pass. If the opener has 6 playing tricks there is a chance for game if partner's raise was sound. If the opener has 7 playing tricks he should contract for game himself.

Let us examine a few cases, in each of which you have opened with 1 Spade and partner has responded 2 Spades, both opponents passing.

♠ A K x x x   ♡ A x x   ◇ Q x x   ♣ x x

You should pass. You have slightly more than a minimum. Your hand contains only 5-plus playing tricks. There is no game.

♠ A Q x x x ♡ K x x ◇ x x x ♣ A Q

This hand contains 5½ playing tricks. A game in Spades is highly improbable. There might conceivably be a play for nine tricks, and a rebid of 2 No Trump might attain satisfactory results, though it is doubtful.

♠ A K x x x ♡ A J x ◇ K J x ♣ x x

You have about 6 playing tricks and about 1½ honor tricks in excess of your opening bid values. There is a chance for game if partner's raise was sound. You determine this by bidding 3 Spades. If he had a good raise he should go on to game. If his raise was indifferent he should pass.

♠ A J 9 x x x ♡ A K ◇ Q J 10 ♣ x x

Your hand contains 7 playing tricks and you should contract for game yourself, relying on the responder to take care of three of your losers.

Your rebid need not be in the same suit. You may test out partner's raise by showing another suit or by bidding 2 No Trump, depending on the type of your hand.

♠ A K x x ♡ x x x ◇ A Q 10 x ♣ A x

You open with 1 Spade and your partner raises to two. You have 6 playing tricks; 1½ honor tricks in excess of your opening bid. You cannot promise a game but you should make a mild try to get there. You may bid 3 Diamonds, hoping that partner will now be able to contract for game in either Spades or No Trump on your display of additional strength. If he merely returns to 3 Spades you had better pass. That would mean that he had only a courtesy raise and probably no more than 3 playing tricks, which, added to your six, would produce only nine.

♠ A K x x ♡ A Q x ◇ K x x x ♣ Q x

You open with 1 Spade and partner raises to two. You have a little over 1½ honor tricks in excess of your opening and a hand that is well suited for No Trump play. You may try for game by bidding 2 No Trump, leaving the decision to your partner.

Do not make the mistake of bidding 2 No Trump, when your partner has given a single raise, merely because you have only a four-card suit. Such a rebid of 2 No Trump shows a very good hand, one which contains at least 1½ honor tricks in excess of the original requirements.

IN A NUTSHELL

When partner makes a single raise of your opening bid (in the absence of competition) don't continue the bidding with a normal hand unless you have 1½ honor tricks in excess values.

If you have 2 honor tricks in excess of your bid, go to game.

If you have 6 winners, try once more.

If you have 7 winners, go to game yourself.

REBID BY OPENER AFTER A 1 NO TRUMP RESPONSE

When partner responds to your opening bid by calling 1 No Trump you may expect to find in his hand very little to enthuse over. In the majority of cases game will be impossible. If you reach that conclusion you should make no further bid unless your hand is of a type that is not suitable for No Trump play. The mere fact that you have an unguarded suit does not render the hand unsuitable for play at No Trump, nor is the possession of a five-card suit a bar to No Trump play.

There are, generally speaking, three types of hand that belong to the No Trump family. They are distributed 4-3-3-3, 4-4-3-2, or 5-3-3-2. If your hand contains a singleton or two doubletons you may look for an excuse to play in a suit, but even then it is not obligatory to do so.

The first thing to do when partner responds with 1 No Trump is to try to judge the possibility of making game. The following table may serve as a practical guide:

If you have, in excess of your opening bid,

1 honor trick: Game is hopeless. Pass unless you hold a freakish hand.

1½ honor tricks: There is a chance for game if partner's 1 No Trump was a little on the sturdy side. Try for game by bidding 2 No Trump.

2 honor tricks: Sure game. Bid it yourself.

In these cases a survey of the combined point count will be helpful. The player who responds with 1 No Trump should have between 6 and 9 points. If on the assumption that responder has 9, you find that you still lack the total of 26 normally required to produce 3 No Trump, then you should quit. If 6 is all you need to reach the required total, you know that he has it and should contract for game yourself. Where you will make game provided he has a better No Trump, say of 7, 8, or 9, but not if he has a minimum, then raise to 2 No Trump and if he has only 6, he should not carry on.

When you come to the conclusion that there is no game you should pass, unless you have an unbalanced hand. Let us take a few examples. In each of the following cases you have opened with 1 Spade and partner has responded with 1 No Trump, both opponents passing.

♠ A K J x x	♠ A K x x
♡ x x	♡ 10 x x
◇ K J x	◇ A Q x x
♣ J x x	♣ x x

Pass. Game is out of the question. While you have a rebiddable suit, your balanced hand is suitable for play at 1 No Trump. The important consideration is not to get too high. Your 13 plus partner's maximum of 9 equals only 22.

Pass. Do not bid 2 Diamonds. Game is not to be contemplated and you should try to buy the hand as cheaply as possible. *The best place to play an indifferent hand is 1 No Trump.*

♠ A Q x x x x
♡ A x x
◇ x x x
♣ x

Bid 2 Spades. Although your hand is minimum in high cards it is unsuitable for play at No Trump and your six-card major suit should be rebid.

♠ A K x x x
♡ A Q J x
◇ x x
♣ Q x

Bid 2 Hearts. You have some excess values and with two doubletons you prefer to play at one of your suits rather than at 1 No Trump.

♠ A K J x
♡ A x x
◇ A 10 x x
♣ K x

Bid 2 No Trump. You have 1½ honor tricks in excess of your opening bid and if partner has a fairly good No Trump response he should proceed to game. You have 19. If partner's No Trump was not a minimum you should have game.

♠ A K 10 x
♡ A Q x
◇ A x x x
♣ K x

Bid 3 No Trump. You have slightly more than 2 honor tricks in excess of your opening bid and there should be a good play for game. You have 20. Partner has at least 6.

IN A NUTSHELL

When partner responds to your opening bid with 1 No Trump don't continue bidding with a normal hand unless you have 1½ honor tricks in excess values. In that case bid 2 No Trump. If you have 2 honor tricks in excess, go to 3 No Trump.

Don't rebid merely because you have a five-card major suit. The best place to play a mediocre hand is at 1 No Trump.

REBID BY OPENER AFTER TAKE-OUT TO ONE OF A SUIT

When you open with one of a suit and partner responds with one of another suit it is, of course, your duty to speak once more. It is at this point that you should clarify the nature of your opening bid, both as to type and as to strength. If your opening bid was of approximately minimum strength this is the time to make the announcement. The message is conveyed to partner in one of two ways, either by a rebid of 1 No Trump or by a rebid of two

of your suit, whichever best describes your hand. Such a rebid
sends the following message: "Partner, be on your guard. My
opening may be an absolute minimum, and in any case I have not
much more than an opening bid." For example:

♠ x x　♡ A K J x　◇ K J x　♣ K x x x

You open with 1 Heart and partner responds with 1 Spade. You
have practically a minimum hand and indicate it by rebidding
1 No Trump.

♠ x x　♡ A K 10 x x　◇ K x x x　♣ x x

You open with 1 Heart. Partner responds with 1 Spade. Here
again you have a minimum, but it is of the suit type, and you best
describe it by the rebid of 2 Hearts.

These minimum rebids are commonly referred to as "sign-
offs," but a sign-off by the opener should not send a cold chill
down partner's back. Responder must not accuse the opener of
having a bad hand, for after all he did open the bidding. His
opening bid has not disappeared.

The rebid of 1 No Trump by the opener designates a minimum
hand of the balanced type, but not necessarily a hand which has
no rebiddable suit. For example:

♠ A J x　♡ Q x　◇ K J 10 x x　♣ K x x

You open with 1 Diamond and partner responds 1 Heart. Your
best rebid is 1 No Trump, indicating a balanced hand of minimum strength.

Nor does the 1 No Trump rebid always deny a fit with partner's suit.

♠ J 10 x　♡ A K x x　◇ A 10 x x　♣ x x

You open with 1 Heart and partner responds 1 Spade. Your best
rebid is 1 No Trump, indicating a balanced hand of minimum
strength. Fear of Clubs should not be harbored. The important
consideration is not to get too high if partner has a moderate
hand.

♠ x x   ♡ A K x x x x   ◊ K x x   ♣ x x

You open with 1 Heart and partner responds 1 Spade. Your rebid is 2 Hearts. Partner now bids 2 No Trump, denoting a desire to go game. The suggested action by you at this time is a 3 Heart bid. This is a warning bid which says, "Partner, be very cautious. I still have my opening bid, but it was based on only 2½ honor tricks. I have bid my suit three times to show extra length but no additional high-card strength. Use your own judgment."

♠ A Q 10 x   ♡ x x   ◊ x x x   ♣ A Q x x

You open with 1 Club and partner responds with 1 Diamond. Your proper rebid is 1 Spade. *The naming of a second suit at the level of one requires no additional strength.*

♠ x x   ♡ A Q 10 x x   ◊ K Q J x   ♣ x x

You open with 1 Heart and partner responds 1 Spade. You have a minimum hand which is not suitable to No Trump, because of the two worthless doubletons, and apparently you should rebid to 2 Hearts. However, since a 2 Diamond rebid is just as cheap and permits partner to return to 2 Hearts, it is the recommended action. This will be particularly helpful when partner is very short in Hearts and has some length in Diamonds. Partner must realize that this is the cheapest possible level at which you could have shown this suit.

When you make it impossible for partner to return to two of your first suit you advertise a very good hand. For example:

♠ x x   ♡ A Q 10 x   ◊ A K J x x   ♣ A x

You open with 1 Diamond and partner responds with 1 Spade. Your rebid should be 2 Hearts. To be sure, this makes it impossible for partner to return to 2 Diamonds but if he is obliged to return to 3 Diamonds you are in no danger, for you have a very good hand. Partner should realize that you have great strength when you choose this sequence of bids.

♠ A Q 10 x   ♡ x x   ◊ A Q 10 x x   ♣ x x

You open with 1 Diamond. If partner responds 1 Heart you

naturally rebid 1 Spade, but if in response to your Diamond opening partner bids 2 Clubs you dare not bid 2 Spades because this makes it impossible for partner to return to 2 Diamonds and your hand is not strong enough to relish a 3 Diamond contract. You must content yourself therefore with a rebid of 2 Diamonds, with the intention of showing Spades only if partner takes further aggressive action.

RAISING PARTNER'S ONE-OVER-ONE RESPONSE TO TWO

When your partner responds with one in a suit for which you have support you must decide whether or not to offer partner an immediate raise. Such action by you at this point indicates a hand a little above the minimum requirements. This is a mildly encouraging rebid and offers partner an inducement to proceed if he has a fairly good take-out.

If your hand contains a singleton you may take the liberty of raising with very slight additional strength. If you have a doubleton you should have at least a King in excess of your opening bid to justify an immediate raise, unless you have four trumps for your partner. Let us examine a few cases:

♠ A x x   ♡ x x   ◇ A K J x x   ♣ x x x

You open with 1 Diamond and partner responds with 1 Spade. A raise to 2 Spades is not recommended because you have very close to a minimum hand. Merely rebid to 2 Diamonds. However, if you hold:

♠ A x x   ♡ x   ◇ A K J x x   ♣ x x x x

a raise to 2 Spades is indicated. The singleton makes that much difference.

♠ A x x x   ♡ x x   ◇ A K J x   ♣ x x x

In this case you have no additional honor strength but the possession of four Spades makes it best to give an immediate raise.

♠ A x x   ♡ x x   ◇ A K x x   ♣ K x x x

In this case you have only three trumps and a doubleton but you have a King in excess of your opening bid and a raise to 2 Spades is therefore justified.

To summarize: When you have opened the bidding you are justified in raising your partner's take-out to two only if you have additional values in honor tricks or in distribution.

When the opening bidder raises his partner's take-out from one to three he indicates a hand with substantial values in excess of the opening. Roughly speaking, to justify such a raise the opener must have 1½ honor tricks in excess of his bid, and for the purpose of this rule a singleton may be regarded as an Ace and a doubleton as a King. There is the added proviso that the opener must hold four of partner's trumps. To illustrate:

♠ A J 10 x   ♡ A K J x   ◇ x   ♣ Q J x x

You open with 1 Club and partner responds with 1 Spade. You have more than adequate trump support, and, regarding the singleton Diamond as an Ace, you have 1½ honor tricks in excess of your bid. You are justified in jumping to 3 Spades.

This is not a forcing bid. Partner is permitted to pass if his 1 Spade response was of a shaded nature. If, for example, partner holds

♠ Q x x x x   ♡ x x x   ◇ K x x   ♣ x x

he need not go on.

A RAISE FROM ONE TO FOUR

A raise from one to four by the opening bidder is stronger than the raise from one to three. There is a logical reason for this. If opener jumps to three and responder has a very weak hand he may not go on. If, however, the opener is strong enough to insist upon a game contract he should assume the entire responsibility himself. This requires about a trick more than is needed to jump from one to three. For example:

♠ A J x x   ♡ x x   ◇ A K J x   ♣ A Q x

You open with 1 Diamond and partner responds with 1 Spade. Regarding the doubleton Heart as a King, you have almost 2½ honor tricks in excess of your opening bid. You should therefore assume responsibility for a game contract by going to 4 Spades. Partner might have nothing but five Spades to the King and would still have a play for game, yet he certainly would not bid it if you jumped to only 3 Spades.

THE JUMP REBID TO 2 NO TRUMP

This rebid by the opener indicates a hand that is well suited to No Trump play and contains about 1½ honor tricks in excess of the opening. This is a very important requirement to bear in mind. There is a tendency on the part of a great many players to jump to 2 No Trump whenever they have slightly more than an opening bid. "Slightly more" is not sufficient. In fact, a full trick more is not enough. The opener must have the equivalent of 1½ honor tricks over and above his opening bid to justify a jump rebid. This may be shaded somewhat if the opener has a good suit. For example:

♠ Q x   ♡ K J x   ◇ A K J x x   ♣ A x x

You open with 1 Diamond and partner responds with 1 Spade. Regarding the Queen of Spades as promoted in value by reason of partner's bid, you have just about 1½ honor tricks in excess of your opening bid. This is the barest minimum on which you are permitted to make a jump rebid. Some players commit the error of making a jump rebid on hands of the following type:

♠ x x   ♡ A x x   ◇ A K x x   ♣ A x x x

They open with 1 Diamond and when partner responds with 1 Spade they fear to rebid only 1 No Trump lest partner will think they have a weak hand. Avoid this unsound practice. Partner will know you have not a weak hand by the very fact that you opened. If he is unable to bid again over 1 No Trump you may be quite sure that no game will be lost.

To repeat: A jump rebid to 2 No Trump requires 1½ honor tricks over and above the opening bid. This rebid is not forcing. If partner has made a very weak one-over-one take-out he is at liberty to pass.

THE JUMP REBID TO 3 NO TRUMP

It has been seen that when the opener's hand is suited for No Trump and contains 1½ honor tricks in excess values he should jump to 2 No Trump. When his hand contains even more than this—when it contains a little over 2 honor tricks in excess of the opening bid—he should take the full responsibility for a game contract himself by rebidding 3 No Trump. For example:

♠ A x ♡ A Q 10 ◇ A K Q x ♣ K J x x

You open with 1 Diamond and partner responds with 1 Spade. You have over two tricks in excess of your opening bid and should take the chance of a game contract yourself by jumping to 3 No Trump. Partner might pass a rebid of only 2 No Trump.

IN A NUTSHELL

A jump rebid to 2 No Trump by the opening bidder shows about 1½ honor tricks in excess of the opening bid.

A jump rebid to 3 No Trump by the opening bidder shows about 2-plus honor tricks in excess of the opening bid.

THE JUMP REBID IN OPENER'S SUIT

When the opening bidder has a good six-card (or longer) suit and a hand that will produce about seven tricks in the play, he may make a jump rebid to three of that suit, provided the hand contains at least 1½ honor tricks in excess of the opening:

♠ A x ♡ A K x x x x ◇ A x x x ♣ x

You open with 1 Heart and partner responds with 1 Spade. The proper rebid is 3 Hearts. This is not forcing. If partner has a very weak Spade response he is at liberty to pass the 3 Heart bid.

If he can win about eight tricks in his own hand, the opener needs only 1 honor trick above his bid:

♠ K x ♡ K J 10 x x x x ◇ A Q x ♣ x

You open with 1 Heart, partner responds 1 Spade, and you should rebid 3 Hearts.

The reader is cautioned not to make a jump rebid merely because he has a solid suit. Remember that additional high-card values also are required. For example, holding:

♠ x   ♡ A K Q x x x   ◊ K x x   ♣ x x x

You open with 1 Heart and partner bids 1 Spade. It would be improper for you to jump to 3 Hearts merely because of the length and solidity of your suit. You have little more than 2½ honor tricks and the proper rebid is only 2 Hearts.

Never make a jump rebid when your only excuse for doing so is the length of your suit.

THE JUMP REBID TO GAME

Suppose you hold:

♠ K Q x   ♡ A K Q J 10 x   ◊ A x x   ♣ x

You open with 1 Heart and partner responds 1 Spade. No matter how weak a response partner has made, you should be unwilling to play this hand for less than game and your proper rebid is 4 Hearts—not 3 Hearts, which partner might pass.

There are players who raise an objection to such a rebid. "It sounds too much like a shut-out," they contend. That is rather silly. What does shut-out mean? Usually it means a great many trumps but not much in high cards. Well, that cannot possibly be the case here, because the opener announced high cards by opening with 1 Heart. A subsequent jump to four does not announce a lack of high cards. It must on the contrary say, "Partner, I am afraid to take a chance on you. My hand is so good that I fear you won't go on, so I am taking full responsibility myself."

IN A NUTSHELL

A jump rebid to four of his suit (game) by the opening bidder denotes a very strong hand (about 8½ or 9 winners). It is stronger than a jump rebid to three, which is not forcing and shows 7 to 8 winners.

There is no such thing as a "shut-out" rebid.

THE JUMP SHIFT BY OPENING BIDDER

When the opening bidder wishes to insist upon a game he may do so in one of two ways: By jumping to game on the next round, as we have seen above; and by making a jump *in a new suit*. This, incidentally, is the only way the opening bidder can force the responder to speak again. A responder may pass if he hears a new suit mentioned. A responder may pass if he hears a jump in the same suit, or a jump in No Trump. But he has no option if partner jumps in a new suit. For example:

♠ K x x x ♡ A K J x ◇ A K J x ♣ x

You open 1 Heart and partner responds 1 Spade. This hand has great possibilities. A jump bid of 3 Spades would be grossly inadequate. Partner might have nothing more than five Spades to the Queen-Jack, in which case he would pass, and a game in Spades might be missed.

A jump to 4 Spades might be acceptable, but even that does not do complete justice to your holding.

The recommended rebid is 3 Diamonds, a jump shift. *This forces partner to speak again, regardless of the nature of his hand.* It is your intention to contract for game in Spades on the next round. If partner has a good hand the obligation to carry on (to a slam) will then be his.

Another case:

♠ J x ♡ A K Q 10 x ◇ x ♣ A K Q x x

You open with 1 Heart and partner responds with 1 Spade. Surely you are unwilling to play this hand for less than a game, but you are not quite certain as to the exact contract. In order to be sure that partner does not pass and that game will eventually be reached you must jump in a new suit, and your proper rebid is 3 Clubs.

IN A NUTSHELL

A jump in a new suit, even by the opener, is absolutely forcing to game, and suggests slam possibilities.

REBID BY OPENER AFTER TAKE-OUT TO TWO OF A SUIT

If you chose your opening one-bid properly, you will already have planned the rebid you will make if partner takes you out into two of his suit.

The principal things to remember are:

A rebid in the same suit you bid before, or a suit rebid which permits partner to return to your first suit at the level of two, warns partner that you may have bid originally on a minimum.

A bid of 2 No Trump, a raise of partner's suit to three, a bid of three in a new suit, or any bid which makes it impossible for partner to return to two of your first suit, *shows at least 1 honor-trick (or the equivalent) in excess of your opening bid.*

The following hand was previously shown:

♠ J 10 x   ♡ A K x x   ◇ A 10 x x   ♣ x x

You bid 1 Heart. When partner responded 1 Spade your rebid was 1 No Trump. But if partner should respond 2 Clubs, you must not bid 2 No Trump. You lack the 1 honor trick above your opening bid. You must bid 2 Diamonds, which permits partner —if his hand so indicates—to return to 2 Hearts.

♠ x x   ♡ A K x x x   ◇ Q x x   ♣ K J x

You bid 1 Heart; partner responds 2 Clubs. Rebid 2 Hearts. Your trump support is good enough to raise Clubs, but your hand as a whole is not strong enough.

When you have No Trump distribution and the required trick in excess values, 2 No Trump is a better rebid than two in a rebiddable suit, for the suit rebid might discourage partner.

♠ A x   ♡ A Q J x x   ◇ K J x   ♣ Q x x

You bid 1 Heart. Over partner's response of 2 Clubs or 2 Diamonds bid 2 No Trump, even though this prevents your telling immediately about your Heart suit. Remember, it is more important to describe the strength of your hand as a whole than to describe a particular suit.

CHOICE BETWEEN REBIDDING YOUR OWN SUIT AND
RAISING PARTNER'S SUIT

The opener is frequently faced with the question, "Should I rebid my suit or support my partner?" Generally speaking, the test is, "Do I wish to sound aggressive or do I wish to sound mild?"

If the opener wishes to display distinct additional values he should raise his partner. If, however, his hand is of the near-minimum type he should prefer to rebid his own suit as a mild warning to partner that prospects for game do not seem bright to him. To illustrate:

1. ♠ A K J x x ♡ K x x ◇ Q x x ♣ x x
2. ♠ A K Q x x ♡ K x x ◇ K x x ♣ x x

You open 1 Spade; partner responds 2 Hearts. With No. 1 rebid 2 Spades; a raise to 3 Hearts would be slightly too aggressive. But with No. 2, even though the Spades are better they should not be rebid because such action would be mildly discouraging. It is preferable to raise the Hearts, offering responder an inducement to go on.

Another form of this problem is presented when the opener has the choice of rebidding another suit or raising his partner. This is frequently a delicate question. Let us examine a few cases:

♠ K J x x ♡ K J x ◇ x x ♣ A Q J x

You open with 1 Club and partner responds with 1 Heart. You have a choice of bidding 1 Spade or supporting your partner with 2 Hearts. Which is preferable? The hand is of moderate strength and it would be doubtful strategy to bid both your suits and also support Hearts. Your partner would expect more strength. It is better therefore to raise to 2 Hearts, after doing which you may feel that you have done your full duty on the hand. However, if you had slightly more strength, as with:

♠ K J x x ♡ K J x ◇ K x ♣ A Q J x

a mere raise to 2 Hearts would not do complete justice to the hand and you have not quite sufficient strength for a jump to

2 No Trump. It is better tactics, therefore, to rebid 1 Spade, with the hope that partner will bid again (which he probably will), after which you will also support Hearts. In this case, by naming two suits and supporting your partner's suit you will have fully described the strength of your hand.

When your partner's suit is a minor it is not nearly so important to support it. For example, you hold:

♠ A J x x   ♡ x   ◊ J x x x   ♣ A K x x

You open with 1 Club; partner responds with 1 Diamond. You may raise the Diamonds if you choose, or you may show your four-card major. The latter bid is far more desirable. If over 1 Spade partner bids 1 No Trump, you intend to bid 2 Diamonds. If over 1 Spade partner bids 2 Diamonds, you intend to raise to 3 Diamonds and partner will realize that you are short in Hearts.

RAISING MINOR-SUIT TAKE-OUTS

When the responder takes out into 2 Clubs or 2 Diamonds, the opener may find himself in possession of such good support for his partner that he is tempted to raise to four of that suit. In many cases this impulse should be suppressed in favor of a single raise, to allow partner the opportunity to bid 3 No Trump should he desire to do so. Eleven-trick game contracts should be avoided if there is a reasonable chance to bring in nine tricks at No Trump.

Suppose you open with 1 Heart and partner responds 2 Diamonds.

♠ Q x   ♡ A Q J x x   ◊ A Q J x   ♣ K x

A jump to 4 Diamonds is not recommended. A raise to three affords partner the opportunity to try for 3 No Trump.

It is not nearly so desirable to raise a minor suit as to show other important features of the hand. For positional reasons you may elect to bid No Trump, concealing entirely your support for partner's minor, as in this case:

♠ K x   ♡ Q J x   ◊ A J 9 x   ♣ A Q x x

You open with 1 Diamond and partner responds 2 Clubs. The best rebid is 2 No Trump. It is vital for you to be declarer at No Trump, to safeguard the King of Spades against attack on the opening lead. Partner may have no stopper in Spades and still chance a No Trump bid if you raise his Clubs, and an opening lead through your King might then be disastrous to you.

Similarly:

♠ K x   ♡ A K x x   ◇ K 9 x x   ♣ K x x

You open 1 Heart and partner responds 2 Diamonds. Your rebid is 2 No Trump rather than 3 Diamonds.

REBID OF 2 NO TRUMP WITHOUT THE USUAL STRENGTH

It has been pointed out that when the opener's rebid is 2 No Trump, even though not a jump, a strong hand is indicated. However, an exception is to be noted in the case where your left hand opponent has overcalled first and your partner has made a free bid at the level of two, depriving you of some bidding space. In such a case a rebid of 2 No Trump need not be quite so strong as usual, since partner by his free bid has deliberately placed you in this awkward position. For example, as South you hold:

♠ Q x   ♡ A K x x   ◇ A 10 x x   ♣ x x x

The bidding has proceeded:

South	West	North	East
1 ♡	2 ◇	2 ♠	Pass
?			

You are forced to rebid and cannot support Spades or rebid Hearts. You are therefore obliged to rebid 2 No Trump. Partner must take into consideration the fact that his free bid at so high a level may have forced you to do so. When you opened the bidding you could not have foreseen that he was going to bid 2 Spades. You were prepared to rebid if his response were the expected 1 Spade or 2 Clubs, in which cases you could have rebid 1 No Trump or 2 Diamonds, respectively.

THIRD-ROUND REBID WITH A TWO-SUITER

It was observed in the chapter on opening bids that when two five-card suits are held the normal procedure is to open with the higher-ranking and show the lower-ranking suit on the next round if it is convenient to do so. When both suits have thus been shown and it becomes the opener's third time to bid, assuming that he must insist upon one of his own suits, the proper procedure is to rebid the lower-ranking suit in order to permit the return to his first suit at the same level. For example, as South you hold:

♠ A J x x x   ♡ K Q 9 x x   ◇ K x   ♣ x

The bidding has proceeded:

SOUTH	WEST	NORTH	EAST
1 ♠	Pass	2 ◇	Pass
2 ♡	Pass	2 N T	Pass
?			

At this point you wish to elicit from partner a choice between Spades and Hearts, since you are not enthusiastic about No Trump. The rebid of 3 Spades would be improper because it makes it impossible for partner to return to 3 Hearts. It would therefore by inference deny that the Hearts are five cards long. The correct bid is 3 Hearts. This permits partner to return to 3 Spades, to pass 3 Hearts if he chooses, or to insist upon 3 No Trump if he must.

REBIDS AFTER FORCING RESPONSES

When you have opened the bidding and your partner makes a jump response of any type—a double raise, a 2 No Trump response, or the more powerful jump shift—you can relax as far as game is concerned, but this does not make your choice of a rebid any less important.

Your guiding principle in rebidding over a forcing response should be this: Your rebid should show where, from your hand, you prefer that the hand should be played. For example:

♠ A J x x   ♡ A K 10 x   ◇ J x x x   ♣ x

You open with 1 Spade. Partner raises to 3 Spades. Rebid 4 Spades, despite the four-card suit. You do not want to play this hand at No Trump, with the singleton in Clubs. To bid 4 Hearts would be a slam try, and you do not have the extra honor tricks. But if partner responded 2 No Trump, your rebid would be 3 Hearts, again because you do not like a No Trump contract if a good suit contract can be found.

♠ J x   ♡ x x   ◇ A K x x x   ♣ A J x x

You open with 1 Diamond. Partner responds 2 No Trump. Bid 3 No Trump. You do not want to play the hand in either Diamonds or Clubs, because your hand is too weak to relish the eleven-trick contract necessary for game in a minor.

♠ A 10 x x x   ♡ x   ◇ A K x x   ♣ x x x

You open with 1 Spade. Partner responds 3 Hearts. Bid 3 Spades. You do not want to play this hand, with its singleton Heart and wide-open Club suit, at No Trump. *A rebid of 3 No Trump in this position is not necessarily any more of a sign-off than the rebid of 3 Spades.* Do not bid 4 Diamonds, which would imply additional strength.

REBID WHEN PARTNER HAS REFUSED TO KEEP THE BIDDING OPEN

Courage is an essential ingredient in the composition of the successful player, but this attribute is not to be confused with stubbornness. One must learn to accept fate, and staunch adherence to a lost cause is not to be admired in a bridge player.

You may recall a story Sidney Lenz used to tell about the headstrong cow that refused to let an oncoming freight train dislodge her from what she considered her rightful place on the railroad tracks. The engineer slowed up once or twice to give the animal a chance, but at last he ploughed through and blasted mankind's foster mother into eternity. A spectator commented to his companion on the outstanding courage of the animal. "Great courage," was the reply, "but darn poor judgment."

When you open with one of a suit and partner fails to keep your bid alive, you are to assume that he has nothing. It is pointless to carry on the fight unless you can pretty nearly fulfill the contract in your own hand.

You are South (vulnerable) and hold:

♠ A K 10 x x x   ♥ K x   ♦ x x   ♣ J x x

The bidding has proceeded:

SOUTH	WEST	NORTH	EAST
1 ♠	Pass	Pass	2 ♥
?			

What should you do? It is foolhardy to contest the auction when you know your partner has nothing. You are not even close to fulfilling a 2 Spade contract unassisted. When I saw this hand played the actual South stubbornly rebid 2 Spades, was doubled and set 800 points. The complete hand:

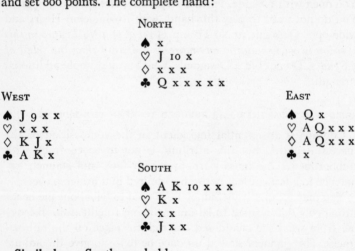

NORTH
♠ x
♥ J 10 x
♦ x x x
♣ Q x x x x x

WEST
♠ J 9 x x
♥ x x x
♦ K J x
♣ A K x

EAST
♠ Q x
♥ A Q x x x
♦ A Q x x x
♣ x

SOUTH
♠ A K 10 x x x
♥ K x
♦ x x
♣ J x x

Similarly, as South you hold:

♠ A Q x x   ♥ A Q x x   ♦ x x   ♣ A Q x

The bidding has proceeded:

SOUTH	WEST	NORTH	EAST
1 ♠	Pass	Pass	2 ◊
?			

True, you have 4½ honor tricks, but since partner has announced a worthless hand you will have to lead everything out of your own hand and may wind up taking no more than four tricks. You cannot reasonably expect to go places and should give up the fight. Any further action by you will result in a loss of 800 to 1,100 points, depending upon developments. The complete hand:

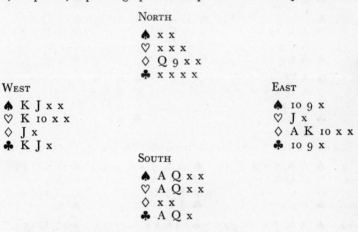

NORTH
♠ x x
♡ x x x
◊ Q 9 x x
♣ x x x x

WEST
♠ K J x x
♡ K 10 x x
◊ J x
♣ K J x

EAST
♠ 10 9 x
♡ J x
◊ A K 10 x x
♣ 10 9 x

SOUTH
♠ A Q x x
♡ A Q x x
◊ x x
♣ A Q x

When, however, you hold a hand like this:

♠ A K x x x   ♡ A K J x x   ◊ x   ♣ x x

and the bidding has proceeded:

SOUTH	WEST	NORTH	EAST
1 ♠	Pass	Pass	2 ◊
?			

Here you should bid 2 Hearts, because even though partner has no high card strength he may have some length in Hearts, in which case even a game in Hearts might not be beyond hope, and a contract of eight tricks should not be risky.

QUIZ ON REBIDS BY OPENER

(ANSWERS BEGIN ON PAGE 101)

What is your rebid on each of the following hands?

You open with 1 Heart. Partner raises to 2 Hearts. Opponents pass.

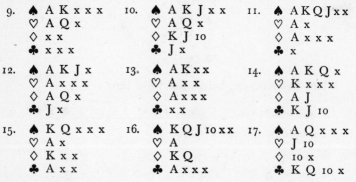

1. ♠ A x x
    ♡ A K x x x
    ◊ x x x
    ♣ Q x

2. ♠ A x x
    ♡ A K x x x
    ◊ K Q x
    ♣ x x

3. ♠ A K x
    ♡ A K Q J x
    ◊ x x x x
    ♣ x

4. ♠ x
    ♡ A K 10 x
    ◊ A x x x
    ♣ A x x x

5. ♠ Q x
    ♡ A K x x
    ◊ A Q x
    ♣ K x x x

6. ♠ A Q x
    ♡ A K x x x x
    ◊ x x
    ♣ x x

7. ♠ A Q
    ♡ A Q x x x
    ◊ x x x
    ♣ K x x

8. ♠ K x x
    ♡ A K x x
    ◊ A Q x x
    ♣ x x

You open with 1 Spade. Partner responds 1 No Trump. Opponents pass.

9. ♠ A K x x x
    ♡ A Q x
    ◊ x x
    ♣ x x x

10. ♠ A K J x x
    ♡ A Q x
    ◊ K J 10
    ♣ J x

11. ♠ A K Q J x x
    ♡ A x
    ◊ A x x x
    ♣ x

12. ♠ A K J x
    ♡ A x x x
    ◊ A Q x
    ♣ J x

13. ♠ A K x x
    ♡ A x x
    ◊ A x x x
    ♣ x x

14. ♠ A K Q x
    ♡ K x x x
    ◊ A J
    ♣ K J 10

15. ♠ K Q x x x
    ♡ A x
    ◊ K x x
    ♣ A x x

16. ♠ K Q J 10 x x
    ♡ A
    ◊ K Q
    ♣ A x x x

17. ♠ A Q x x x
    ♡ J 10
    ◊ 10 x
    ♣ K Q 10 x

You open with 1 Heart. Partner responds with 1 Spade. Opponents pass.

18. ♠ Q
    ♡ A Q x x
    ◊ A Q x x
    ♣ J x x x

19. ♠ A Q x
    ♡ A Q 10 9 x
    ◊ Q x
    ♣ x x x

20. ♠ Q x
    ♡ A Q x x x
    ◊ A J 10 x
    ♣ x x

21. ♠ x
    ♡ A K J x x
    ◇ A Q x
    ♣ K 10 x x

22. ♠ x
    ♡ A K x x x
    ◇ A 10 9 x
    ♣ J x x

23. ♠ A x x
    ♡ A Q 9 x
    ◇ K x
    ♣ 10 x x x

24. ♠ K 10 x x
    ♡ A K J x x
    ◇ A K x
    ♣ x

25. ♠ Q J 9 x
    ♡ A K Q 9 x
    ◇ A Q x
    ♣ K

26. ♠ Q x x
    ♡ A K 10 x x
    ◇ K J
    ♣ Q x x

27. ♠ x x
    ♡ A K J x x
    ◇ A Q J x
    ♣ x x

28. ♠ J x
    ♡ A K x x
    ◇ A 10 x x
    ♣ A Q x

29. ♠ Q x
    ♡ A K J x x
    ◇ K 10 x
    ♣ A 10 x

30. ♠ x x
    ♡ A K J 10 x
    ◇ A K x
    ♣ K x x

31. ♠ Q x
    ♡ A K x x x
    ◇ A K Q x x
    ♣ x

32. ♠ K x
    ♡ A K 10 x x
    ◇ A x x
    ♣ x x x

You open with 1 Spade. Partner responds 2 Hearts. Opponents pass.

33. ♠ A 10 9 x x
    ♡ x x
    ◇ A J x
    ♣ A x x

34. ♠ A K Q 10 x
    ♡ x x
    ◇ A J x
    ♣ Q J x

35. ♠ A K Q x
    ♡ Q x
    ◇ A 10 x x
    ♣ K Q x

36. ♠ A K x x x
    ♡ x
    ◇ x x x
    ♣ K Q 10 x

37. ♠ K J x x x x
    ♡ ——
    ◇ K x x x
    ♣ A K x

You open with 1 Spade. Partner responds with 2 Clubs. Opponents pass.

38. ♠ A K Q x x x x
    ♡ K x
    ◇ x x
    ♣ A x

39. ♠ A Q J x x
    ♡ x
    ◇ A J 10
    ♣ A Q J x

40. ♠ A K Q x x
    ♡ Q x x
    ◇ x x
    ♣ A J x

41. ♠ A Q 9 x x x   ♡ 10 x x   ◇ x   ♣ K Q 10

You open with 1 Diamond. Partner responds 1 Heart. Opponents pass.

42. ♠ A Q J x
    ♡ K J x
    ◇ A K Q x x
    ♣ x

43. ♠ K x x
    ♡ x x
    ◇ A Q 10 x x
    ♣ K x x

44. ♠ A J x
    ♡ J x
    ◇ A K Q x x
    ♣ K Q J

You open with 1 Spade. Partner raises to 3 Spades. Opponents pass.

45. ♠ K x x x	46. ♠ 10 x x x x	47. ♠ K Q J x
♡ A Q x x	♡ A Q	♡ A K x x x
◊ K x	◊ A K x	◊ Q x
♣ K x x	♣ x x x	♣ x x

You open with 1 Heart. Partner responds with 2 Clubs. Opponents pass.

48. ♠ x x	49. ♠ A x
♡ K J 10 x	♡ K J x x
◊ K Q x x	◊ A 9 x x
♣ A x x	♣ A Q x

You open with 1 Diamond. Partner responds with 1 Spade. Opponents pass.

50. ♠ K x x	51. ♠ x x x x	52. ♠ A K x
♡ x x	♡ K x	♡ x
◊ A K 10 9 x	◊ A Q x x	◊ A 10 9 x x x
♣ x x x	♣ A x x	♣ A Q 10

You open with 1 Spade. Partner responds with 2 No Trump. Opponents pass.

53. ♠ A K Q x	54. ♠ A K 10 x x	55. ♠ A K J 10 x x
♡ K J 10	♡ x x	♡ A x x
◊ A x x x	◊ K x x x	◊ x x x
♣ Q x	♣ x x	♣ x

You are South. The bidding has proceeded as indicated.

56. ♠ K Q 10 x x
♡ A x
◊ x x x
♣ K x x

57. ♠ A K J x x
♡ A x
◊ 10 x x x
♣ x x

South	West	North	East	South	West	North	East
1 ♠	Pass	2 ♣	2 ◊	1 ♠	Pass	2 ♣	2 ♡
?				?			

You open with 1 Diamond. Partner responds with 2 No Trump. Opponents pass.

58. ♠ A x x   ♡ K 10 9 x   ◇ A Q J x x   ♣ x

You open with 1 Spade. Partner responds with 3 No Trump. Opponents pass.

59. ♠ A K x x x   ♡ A x x   ◇ K J x   ♣ x x

You open with 1 Heart. Partner responds with 2 Diamonds. Opponents pass.

60. ♠ x   ♡ A Q J x x   ◇ x x   ♣ K Q 10 x x

You open the bidding with 1 Diamond. Partner responds as indicated.

61. ♠ A Q 10 x   ♡ x x   ◇ A Q J x x   ♣ x x

    (a) 1 No Trump
    (b) 1 Heart
    (c) 2 Clubs
    (d) 2 No Trump
    (e) 2 Hearts

You open the bidding with 1 Spade. Partner responds as indicated.

62. ♠ A K x x x   ♡ Q x x   ◇ x   ♣ K Q 10 x

    (a) 1 No Trump
    (b) 2 Spades
    (c) 2 Diamonds
    (d) 2 Clubs
    (e) 2 Hearts

You are the opener in the following problems. The bidding is indicated.

63. ♠ A K x x x
   ♡ K Q x
   ◇ A Q x
   ♣ J x

64. ♠ A K x x
   ♡ A K x x
   ◇ A Q x
   ♣ K x

OPENER	RESPONDER
1 ♠	4 ♠
?	

OPENER	RESPONDER
1 ♠	4 ♠
?	

65. ♠ Q x x x
    ♡ A x x
    ◇ K J x
    ♣ A 10 x

OPENER	RESPONDER
1 ♣	2 ♣
?	

66. ♠ x x
    ♡ A K x x
    ◇ K x
    ♣ K 10 x x x

OPENER	RESPONDER
1 ♣	1 ♠
?	

67. ♠ A Q J x x
    ♡ J x x
    ◇ x
    ♣ K Q J x

OPENER	RESPONDER
1 ♠	2 ◇
2 ♠	2 N T
?	

68. ♠ K x x
    ♡ A 9
    ◇ x x x
    ♣ A K Q x x

OPENER	RESPONDER
1 ♣	1 ♡
2 ♣	2 ♡
?	

69. ♠ A Q x x
    ♡ A Q x x
    ◇ x x
    ♣ A Q x

SOUTH	WEST	NORTH	EAST
1 ♠	Pass	Pass	2 ◇
?			

70. ♠ A Q x x
    ♡ A Q x x
    ◇ x x
    ♣ A Q x

SOUTH	WEST	NORTH	EAST
1 ♠	2 ◇	Pass	Pass
?			

71. ♠ A K J x x
    ♡ A K x
    ◇ x
    ♣ A Q x x

OPENER	RESPONDER
1 ♠	1 N T
?	

72. ♠ x
    ♡ A K 10 x x
    ◇ A Q x x x
    ♣ J x

OPENER	RESPONDER
1 ♡	1 ♠
2 ◇	2 ♡
?	

73. ♠ J x x   ♡ A 9 x x x x   ◇ x x   ♣ A x

NORTH	EAST	SOUTH	WEST
Pass	Pass	1 ♡	Pass
1 ♠	Pass	?	

REBID QUIZ ANSWERS

1. Pass. You have a balanced hand with only ½ honor trick surplus. (5 winners)

2. 3 Hearts. You have 1½ surplus honor tricks. (6½ winners)

3. 4 Hearts. You can win seven tricks in your own hand.

4. 3 Hearts. You have only 1 honor trick surplus, but good distribution and control (6 winners). A four-card suit may be rebid when it has been supported by partner. A rebid of one of the minor suits might be acceptable but you would not then be confident of your position if partner's next move were to 3 No Trump.

5. 2 No Trump. A balanced hand suitable for No Trump play and containing about 1½ honor tricks surplus.

6. 3 Hearts. You have 6½ winners.

7. Pass. Not quite enough winners for a bid of 3 Hearts. A rebid of 2 No Trump would not be regarded as wrong, however.

8. Pass. Only one trick over a minimum, so game is hopeless.

9. Pass. You have only one trick over your bid and game is hopeless. With a balanced hand you should not rebid the Spades.

10. 3 No Trump. You have two tricks over your bid.

11. 4 Spades. You have 8½ winners. 3 No Trump would also be accepted as correct, a fair gamble that the opposition will not run five Club tricks.

12. 2 No Trump. You have 1½ tricks over your bid. There is a chance for game. You have 19; if partner has more than 6 you have game.

13. Pass. Although you have one trick more than minimum, game is hopeless. You have 15; even if partner has 9 there is no hope for game.

14. 3 No Trump. You have two tricks in excess of an opening bid.

15. Pass. Game is hopeless. You have barely a trick over your bid. Don't rebid Spades. You have only 16 points.

16. 4 Spades. You must go the whole way. Partner may have no more than the King-Queen of Clubs and the game will be a laydown.

17. 2 Clubs. With two short suits you do not choose to play No Trump. 2 Clubs is a much better bid than 2 Spades. Partner may be short in Spades and have length in Clubs and can take his choice.

18. 1 No Trump. Any No Trump bid with a singleton, even a singleton in the suit partner has bid, is undesirable; but it is better when

holding an absolute minimum like this, and a singleton *honor* in partner's suit, to warn partner of weakness with a minimum rebid.

19. 2 Spades. You are satisfied with Spades and have definite additional values. A 2 Heart rebid would be inadequate.

20. 2 Diamonds, not 2 Hearts. You should give partner the choice of
two places.

21. 2 Clubs. This is an awkward hand to rebid. The singleton Spade
argues against a jump to 2 No Trump. The Heart suit itself is not
strong enough for a jump to 3 Hearts. The best procedure is a compromise bid of 2 Clubs, which will probably elicit another bid from partner. 2 Hearts is definitely out, the hand being too strong for it.

22. 2 Diamonds. Cheaper than 2 Hearts and allows an additional
chance for finding a safe landing place. Partner may have:

♠ K x x x x x   ♡ x   ◇ J x x x   ♣ x x

23. 1 No Trump. With this minimum hand you should make the
cheapest rebid available. You must not advertise additional values by
raising to 2 Spades.

24. 3 Diamonds. There are distinct chances for a slam and even a
jump to 4 Spades does not do full justice to this hand.

25. 4 Spades. Partner should make game even if he had a sub-
minimum take-out. He might pass a raise to 3 Spades.

26. 2 Spades. You have definite surplus values, and a raise of partner's major suit is preferable to rebidding your own, which partner may
not like.

27. 2 Diamonds, which affords an additional parking place. Not
2 Hearts.

28. 2 No Trump. You have 1½ honor tricks in excess of your opening bid. Nothing is to be gained by bidding 2 Diamonds.

29. 2 No Trump. You have 1½ honor tricks in excess of the opening.

30. 3 Hearts. You have 7 playing tricks and should strongly invite
partner to bid again.

31. 3 Diamonds (mildly influenced by a slight fit). Had partner's
response been 2 Clubs a rebid of 2 Diamonds would have been sufficient.

32. 2 Hearts. You have more than a minimum but no other rebid is
available.

33. 2 Spades, not 2 No Trump. You are rebidding a questionable
suit. This is necessary because your hand is not strong enough to bid
2 No Trump.

34. 2 No Trump. You have a strong hand and a 2 Spade rebid would not do justice to it.

35. 3 No Trump. If partner's take-out was short of the usual honor tricks and based on an unusually long suit, he can bid 4 Hearts.

36. 2 Spades, not 3 Clubs. Not strong enough to show a new suit at the level of three.

37. 2 Spades. A jump rebid cannot be considered with this trump suit.

38. 4 Spades. A jump to 3 Spades would be improper because partner might pass. A bid of more than 4 Spades would not be safe.

39. 3 Diamonds. A jump shift, announcing interest in a slam. You intend to contract for a Club slam, but there might be seven in the hand and a little investigation is in order.

40. 3 Clubs. You have definite additional values and should make an encouraging rebid. A 2 Spade bid would deny additional values.

41. 2 Spades. A slight underbid. This is better strategy than bidding 3 Clubs, which usually induces partner to bid 3 No Trump, a contract of which you would not be too sure. If partner bids again over 2 Spades you will be in a good position to move forward again.

42. 2 Spades. A force to game. If you rebid only 1 Spade partner might pass, and you should be willing to assume responsibility for a game contract with this hand.

43. 1 No Trump. This is a minimum hand and your rebid should be as cheap as possible.

44. 3 No Trump. You have a reasonable expectancy of winning eight tricks in your own hand. Any lesser bid would risk a pass by partner.

45. 3 No Trump. You are forced to rebid. This rebid best shows the nature of your hand and gives partner a choice between Spades and No Trump.

46. 4 Spades. Even so weak a suit is satisfactory when partner has enough support to give a double raise.

47. 4 Spades. Don't make the mistake of bidding 4 Hearts. That would be considered as a slam try. Partner has guaranteed four cards in Spades, and the Hearts will be useful as a side suit.

48. 2 Diamonds. The cheapest available bid with this mediocre hand. Not 3 Clubs.

49. 3 No Trump. It is pointless to bid Diamonds or raise Clubs. You should have a play for 3 No Trump even with a very weak 2 Club take-out.

50. 2 Diamonds, not 2 Spades. You have normal trump support, but a bare minimum, and you must not give your partner any inducement to proceed.

51. 2 Spades. You have a bare minimum but your hand does possess four trumps and a short suit.

52. 3 Clubs. A jump shift, forcing to game and suggesting slam possibilities.

53. 4 No Trump (not conventional). You have 19 points, partner has at least 13, making a total of 32. If partner has a little more than 13, there should be a slam. If he hasn't, he should pass and you will be safe.

54. 3 Spades. This does not show any additional values; it merely shows a rebiddable Spade suit and tells partner that you have a slight preference for Spades rather than No Trump, because of your two short suits.

55. 4 Spades, indicating a good six-card suit and some additional high card strength.

56. Pass. You have a minimum and are not in a position to make a free rebid. Let partner carry on if he chooses.

57. Pass. Though you have a rebiddable Spade suit you have insufficient surplus values to warrant a free rebid. Leave it to partner.

58. 3 Hearts. You are obliged to go to at least 3 No Trump, so you might as well stop off on the way to try out this suit at no cost whatsoever.

59. 4 No Trump (not conventional). You have 15 and a five-card suit. Partner has at least 16. If he has a maximum 3 No Trump, you may have a slam.

60. 2 Hearts. Your hand is not strong enough to show your second suit at the level of three. Had partner responded with 1 Spade your rebid would have been 2 Clubs.

61. (a) 2 Diamonds, not 2 Spades. Your two short suits militate against No Trump play but you cannot afford a rebid of 2 Spades, as that would make it impossible for partner to return to 2 Diamonds.

(b) 1 Spade. A new suit at the level of one promises no great strength.

(c) 2 Diamonds. You cannot afford to rebid 2 Spades.

(d) 3 Spades. You are forced to bid at least up to 3 No Trump and should try this suit on the way up.

(e) 2 Spades. Since partner is out for a slam there is no danger in your increasing the level.

62. (a) 2 Clubs, not 2 Spades. Give yourself an additional chance to find a safe place.

(b) 3 Spades. You have more than 6 playing tricks.

(c) 2 Spades. Not strong enough to show a new suit at the level of three. A 2 No Trump rebid is out of the question.

(d) 3 Clubs. Do not get excited by the fit. You have not sufficient excess values to warrant a jump.

(e) 3 Hearts. Normal trump support and good distribution justify the raise. It is pointless to complicate matters here by bidding 3 Clubs.

63. Pass. You have a big hand, but a slam is not in sight because partner has a maximum of 1½ honor tricks. The opponents surely have two high-card tricks.

64. 6 Spades. Partner hasn't much in high cards but, what is more important to you, he has plenty of trumps and distributional support.

65. Pass. There is no hope for game. Don't make the mistake of bidding 2 No Trump. That would indicate a strong desire to go to game.

66. 1 No Trump. A rebid of 2 Hearts is improper because it would make it impossible for partner to return to 2 Clubs. The hand is not good enough for that.

67. 3 No Trump, despite the singleton Diamond. The No Trump was partner's idea, not yours. You have already warned that you have a minimum opening. A 3 Club bid would indicate that your hand is unsuitable for No Trump. As a matter of fact, that is not the case.

68. 3 Hearts. You have a good hand and normal trump support for partner's rebid suit. You were previously obliged to underbid.

69. Pass. Partner has announced a bust hand by failing to keep the bidding open. It would be unsafe for you to compete.

70. Double. Partner may have a smattering of strength but insufficient for a free bid, and you are not ready to give up fighting.

71. 3 Clubs. An absolute force to game. Even a slam is not out of the question, despite partner's mild response. A jump to 3 Spades would be highly improper. Partner might pass.

72. 3 Hearts. Partner has not yet indicated any definite values. He has shown a preference but not a raise for Hearts, and the situation should be tested. Partner can decide whether to go on or not.

73. Pass. Be satisfied with a safe part score. Partner's previous pass should convince you that there is no game.

CHAPTER 4

REBIDS BY RESPONDER

THE RESPONDER'S SECOND BID is many times his most important call of the auction. When the opener makes his rebid he tries to describe the nature of his opening, both as to strength and as to type. Similarly, if and when the responder makes his rebid he must clear up any doubt created by his previous response.

Some responses give an accurate description of the hand in one bid and require no further discussion. When the opener bids 1 Spade and partner responds with 2 No Trump, 3 No Trump, 3 Spades or 4 Spades, an exact picture of the hand has been given in one response. But some responses are ambiguous, and must be cleared up on the next round.

For example, the opener bids 1 Club and partner responds with 1 Spade. The responder may have a very powerful hand and may be preparing to engage in considerable bidding pyrotechnics, but again he may have a very weak holding. The next round must make clear which it is.

In a great percentage of hands the responsibility for determining whether or not there is a game in the hand rests squarely on the shoulders of the responder. For those who prefer not to be burdened with memorizing a great variety of figures perhaps the following suggestion will be very helpful to the responder in the all-important process of estimating the probability of game: A game usually results when the combined assets of the partnership amount to two opening bids or the equivalent. *An opening bid faced by an opening bid will generally produce game, provided a convenient contract can be found.*

Let us attempt to clarify this assertion with a few illustrations:

♠ x x   ♡ A K x x x   ◇ J x x   ♣ K J x

You are responder. Your partner opened with 1 Spade. You note that your hand is equivalent to an opening Heart bid. You therefore estimate that there is a probable game in the hand and you start investigating to determine the best contract. You temporarily bid 2 Hearts. Partner makes the discouraging rebid of 2 Spades. Since your estimate is a game on this hand you do not give up. You search for that game by bidding 2 No Trump, even though you do not have complete protection in Diamonds.

♠ J x x   ♡ A K x x x   ◇ x x   ♣ K J x

Your partner has bid 1 Spade. As in the previous case, you estimate there is a game because you have an opening bid yourself. You temporarily bid 2 Hearts. Partner rebids 2 Spades. You know now that he has approximately a minimum hand but that he has a good Spade suit, for which you now have normal trump support. There is no further information to be sought. You know the place, Spades. You know the amount, game. You therefore bid 4 Spades.

♠ J x x   ♡ A K x x x   ◇ x x   ♣ Q x x

Again your partner opens with 1 Spade. You respond with 2 Hearts and partner rebids 2 Spades. This establishes Spades as the proper place. Now for the amount. Are you able to estimate that there is game in the hand? No, because your hand is not quite equal to an opening bid and partner may have a minimum. However, your hand is not far removed from an opening bid and if partner has slight values to spare, you will have, between the two of you, the equal of two opening bids. You therefore raise to 3 Spades. If opener has a minimum he should pass. If he has slight additional values he should proceed to game.

♠ Q x x   ♡ A Q x x   ◇ K x x   ♣ Q 10 x

Your partner opens with 1 Club. You respond with 1 Heart. Partner's rebid is 1 No Trump, which may indicate an absolute minimum. Your hand is the equivalent of an opening bid, for the Queen of Clubs has been promoted by partner's bid in that suit. Since you are facing an opening bid, and the place, No Trump, is settled, it is your duty to contract for game. Bid 3 No Trump.

It would be an error on your part to bid only 2 No Trump, because partner might not be able to carry on.

♠ J x x   ♡ A K x x   ◇ K x x x   ♣ x x

Again your partner opens with 1 Club and you respond with 1 Heart. Partner's rebid is 1 No Trump. While you are satisfied with No Trump as the place, you cannot guarantee a game because your hand is a King short of being an opening bid. It is possible that the opening bidder has a King to spare, in which case there should be game. Your proper procedure is to bid 2 No Trump. If partner has nothing to spare he should pass. If he has approximately the value of a King in excess of his opening bid he should go on to 3 No Trump.

♠ x x x   ♡ A x x x x   ◇ x x   ♣ A x x

Your partner opens with 1 Diamond. You respond with 1 Heart. Partner's rebid is 2 Diamonds. What should you do? Since partner's hand is approximately a minimum there can be no reasonable hope for game and you should pass. When the opening bidder signs off, it is unwise for the responder to continue unless his hand is within half a trick of an opening bid. Notice that the above hand, even with the addition of a half trick, would not be converted into an opening bid. The hand would then contain 2½ honor tricks but not a good suit.

♠ Q x x   ♡ A x x x x   ◇ x x   ♣ A x x

Partner opens with 1 Diamond. You respond with 1 Heart. Partner's rebid is 2 Diamonds. The addition of a King to this hand would convert it to an opening bid. Therefore, if the opening bidder happens to have a King to spare there may be a game. There is still a chance that the partnership assets amount to two opening bids. You should therefore make one move toward game by bidding 2 No Trump.

When your hand is well suited to No Trump you must not waste time telling about your rebiddable suit. For example, you hold:

♠ x x   ♡ A x x   ◇ A K J x x   ♣ J x x

The bidding has proceeded:

North	East	South	West
1 ♣	Pass	1 ♢	Pass
1 N T	Pass	?	

It is proper for you now to go straight to 3 No Trump without worrying about your unprotected Spade suit. Partner will take care of that. You have better than an opening bid and a hand well suited for No Trump play. If you should rebid the Diamonds partner might pass.

RESPONDER CLARIFIES HIS RAISE

When the responding hand has given his partner a single raise in a major suit he has given his partner an approximate idea of his values, but not an exact one. The raise may have been of a very scanty nature, merely to keep the bidding alive, but it may have been a sound raise. The opening bidder rebids to inquire of his partner how good the raise really was. This he does in one of several ways. Let us assume the bidding has proceeded:

Opener	Responder
1 ♠	2 ♠
3 ♠	?

If the responder had a good raise he should bid again. If he had a poor raise naturally he should pass. The question arises, What constitutes a good raise? To those who can count playing tricks a good raise consists of 3½ to 4 playing tricks. Suppose you are the responder with each of the following hands and the bidding has proceeded as shown above.

1. ♠ Q x x x   ♡ x x   ♢ A Q x x   ♣ x x x
2. ♠ K x x   ♡ J x x   ♢ A Q x   ♣ x x x x
3. ♠ Q x x x   ♡ x x   ♢ K x x x   ♣ x x x

With No. 1 you should bid 4 Spades. You have a sound raise which contains 4 playing tricks.

With No. 2 you should bid 3 No Trump. You have a good raise from the standpoint of high cards but since your partner will be unable to ruff anything in the dummy it is more desirable to play for nine tricks than for ten.

With No. 3 you should pass. This is not a good raise but was made only for the purpose of giving partner a chance.

When the opening bidder tests out his partner's raise by a rebid of 2 No Trump, the same general principle applies:

OPENER	RESPONDER
1 ♠	2 ♠
2 N T	?

If your hand is evenly balanced and you have about 2 honor tricks you should raise to 3 No Trump. If you have four trumps and a real raise you should take your partner directly to game. If you have not these requirements you should, as a rule, merely return to three of partner's suit. This bid is not another raise. It is a preference and a sign-off. Its message is, "Partner, I had merely a courtesy raise for you. I prefer your suit to No Trump."

With No. 1 of the preceding examples, responder should leap from 2 No Trump to 4 Spades, announcing a sound raise with four trumps.

With No. 2 he should cheerfully raise to 3 No Trump.

With No. 3 he should merely return to 3 Spades, announcing that he prefers Spades to No Trump, but had a very light raise.

When the responder has given a single raise in a minor suit and the opener rebids to three of the same suit, the responder should try for game at No Trump, even with an unstopped suit, if he has about 1½ honor tricks. For example, you hold:

♠ Q x   ♡ x x x   ◇ A x x x   ♣ K x x x

Partner opens with 1 Diamond, which you raise to two. Partner rebids 3 Diamonds. You should try 3 No Trump.

When a single raise has been given in a major suit and opener names another suit, responder is obligated to speak just once more. For example:

OPENER	RESPONDER
1 ♡	2 ♡
3 ♣	?

The 3 Club bid is a one-round force. It says, in effect, "Partner, I am trying to find out whether you had a good raise or a poor one. Please tell me now. Naturally you must not pass 3 Clubs, because we have agreed on Hearts thus far. If you can bid a game please do so. If not just quietly return to 3 Hearts." Responder will now go directly to 4 Hearts if he has a sound raise:

♠ x x   ♡ K 10 x x   ◊ A x x x   ♣ J x x

But if he held the Queen of Diamonds instead of the Ace, he would have only a courtesy raise and would return to 3 Hearts, inviting opener to pass.

The rebid of 2 No Trump, however, is not forcing. In rare cases—with only three-card trump support and a weak but balanced hand—the responder should pass it. For example, you hold:

♠ 10 x x x   ♡ A J x   ◊ Q x   ♣ x x x x

You have raised partner's 1 Heart to two, and his rebid is 2 No Trump. You should pass. You have too little to raise to game, and the hand should play at least as well at No Trump as at Hearts —better, if partner has only a four-card suit.

REBID BY RESPONDER WHEN OPENER GIVES A SINGLE RAISE

OPENER	RESPONDER
1 ♡	1 ♠
2 ♠	

If the responder has a weak hand he will naturally pass. If his hand is within half a trick of an opening bid he should try for game. If his hand is almost the equivalent of an opening bid he should now bid a game. A raise by the opener shows a little bit more than a minimum, and so the partnership possesses two opening bids. Suppose, in the preceding bidding situation, you are the responder and hold:

1. ♠ A K J x x   ♡ x x x   ◇ x x x   ♣ x x
2. ♠ A K Q x x   ♡ x x x   ◇ Q J x   ♣ x x

With No. 1 you should bid 3 Spades. It is within half a trick of an opening bid. (In fact, with a very conservative partner, a 4 Spade bid might be chanced.) With No. 2, obviously you should bid 4 Spades.

Another case, in which you respond 1 Spade to partner's Heart bid, he raises to 2 Spades, and you hold:

♠ K J 9 x   ♡ x x   ◇ x x x   ♣ A Q 10 x

Your hand, roughly, is within a King of an opening bid, which suggests the possibility of a game because partner's raise shows a little more than an opening bid. You should test out the nature of partner's raise by bidding again. Since partner may have only three Spades you do not choose to insist upon that suit. The proper procedure is to bid 3 Clubs. This may induce partner to contract for game in No Trump if he so chooses, and it may allow him to judge whether or not there is a game in Spades. If he merely returns to 3 Spades you should give up the ghost. However, he may be able to bid 4 Spades when you indicate your additional values.

A similar case:

Opener	Responder
1 ♠	2 ♡
3 ♡	?

If your hand is within a trick of an opening bid you should contract for game. Suppose you hold:

♠ x x x   ♡ A 10 x x x   ◇ K Q x   ♣ x x

With this hand you should bid 4 Hearts. Your hand is about a trick short of an opening bid, but partner's raise from two to three shows a hand that is at least a trick more than an opening bid. Therefore the partnership is in possession of two opening bids.

When a raise is to three in a minor suit the same considerations apply except that the responder must fix his gaze on a No Trump game rather than an eleven-trick game in the minor suit, if his hand is at all suitable for No Trump play. For example:

OPENER	RESPONDER
1 ♠	2 ♣
3 ♣	?

Responder should chance a bid of 3 No Trump on:

♠ 10 x   ♡ A x x   ◇ x x x   ♣ A J 10 x x

REBID BY RESPONDER AFTER HE HAS RESPONDED 1 NO TRUMP

OPENER	RESPONDER
1 ♠	1 N T
2 N T	?

In this sequence of bids opener has shown a very strong hand. In fact, he has 1½ honor tricks in excess of his opening bid. The responder has promised only one trick. If that is all he has, he should permit matters to rest; but if he has about 1½ tricks he is justified in accepting partner's invitation on the basis of the additional half trick in terms of the point count. Responder by his 1 No Trump response has guaranteed that he has 6 points. When partner raises to 2 No Trump, he should go to 3 if he has more than 6. For example, responder holds:

♠ 9 x   ♡ 10 x x   ◇ K Q x x   ♣ K x x x

Responder bids 3 No Trump; he has 8 points.

Occasionally a responder is obliged to bid 1 No Trump with a rather fair hand. If the opener shows signs of life by bidding again the responder may rebid in order to show that he had a maximum 1 No Trump response. For example:

OPENER	RESPONDER
1 ♠	1 N T
2 ♡	?

Responder holds:

♠ J x   ♡ J x x   ◇ A 10 x x   ♣ K 10 x x

Responder had a near maximum No Trump and with supporting cards in both of partner's suits he is justified in speaking again. The recommended rebid is 2 No Trump.

IN A NUTSHELL

If your partner opens the bidding and your hand is equal to an opening bid, there is a good chance for a game. As soon as you find out the correct spot hasten to game. If your hand is almost the equivalent of an opening bid coax your partner to bid a game.

REBID BY RESPONDER WHEN OPENER NAMES ANOTHER SUIT

RESPONDER TAKES HIS CHOICE

A frequently misunderstood obligation of the responder is the one that involves showing a preference between partner's two suits. The responder should not assume the role of captain of the team. His duties are more akin to those of a servant, and he should indicate which of the two suits is preferable according to his holdings.

A preference is sometimes indicated by passing, sometimes by returning to the first suit. In making a choice, length is far more important than high cards in the trump suit. As a rule, it is the duty of the responder to seek the selection of the trump suit in which the partnership has the greatest number.

For example, your partner has bid Spades and Hearts and you have ♠ x x x and ♡ A K. It is your solemn duty to take your partner back to Spades. You should never be heard to say, "But, partner, I have the two top Hearts." Those two top Hearts need not be trumps. They will be winners even with Spades as trumps. Spades will make the better trump suit, because if partner has a losing Heart he can use one of the little Spades to dispose of it.

When the same length is held in each of partner's suits the practice is to prefer the suit he bid first. This has the advantage of giving partner one more chance, if that is your desire, and has the further advantage of returning to the suit in which the partnership will usually have the most trumps. For example:

♠ J x x   ♡ K x x   ◊ A x x x   ♣ x x x

Partner opens with 1 Spade. You respond 1 No Trump. Partner rebids 2 Hearts. You have no actual preference. The fact that you have a King in Hearts and only a Jack in Spades does not make Hearts any better for trumps. The two suits are exactly equal as far as you are concerned, but it would be good practice to return to 2 Spades, because you have a very good 1 No Trump response and would like to give your partner another chance. In fact, should the opener make one more move you will contract for game.

♠ J x   ♡ 10 x x   ◊ x x x x   ♣ A J x x

Your partner opened with 1 Heart. Assume that you elected to respond with 1 No Trump. Partner's rebid is 2 Spades. This is a strong bid and shows that partner has five Hearts and four Spades. You naturally prefer Hearts, and it is your duty to return to that suit even though it increases the contract.

The responder must never refuse to show a preference for the partnership's best trump suit just because he is frightened. Where a preference actually exists he must indicate it. Occasionally there will be no actual preference and the responder may use his own judgment. It is my practice not to show an immediate preference for partner's first suit with a worthless doubleton. In those cases it is my policy to either pass or make some other bid. For example:

♠ A J x x x   ♡ x x   ◊ x x   ♣ 10 x x x

Partner opens with 1 Heart and you respond with 1 Spade. Partner bids 2 Diamonds. Since opener has been unable to make a jump bid you may conclude that there is no possible hope for game. I do not recommend a return to 2 Hearts, although it is partner's first suit; for I am not interested in giving partner any further chance. As far as I am concerned I have no preference between Hearts and Diamonds. Being too weak to make another bid in Spades, I pass. However, holding:

♠ A J x x x   ♡ x x x   ◇ x x x   ♣ x x

I would return to partner's first suit because, holding three trumps, I am at least mildly prepared to play it there.

Some additional cases:

♠ x x x
♡ K 10 9 x
◇ A J x
♣ x x x

Partner opens with 1 Club. You respond with 1 Heart. Partner bids 1 Spade. With more than 1½ tricks you have a perfectly sound one-over-one response and should therefore bid again, since you need not increase the contract. Your proper call is 1 No Trump. With, say, the Queen of Diamonds instead of the Ace, you would pass. Partner's rebid was not forcing.

♠ K x x x
♡ A x x
◇ K x x
♣ 10 x x

Partner opens with 1 Diamond. You respond with 1 Spade. Partner bids 2 Clubs. Regarding the King of Diamonds as a full trick, in view of partner's bid in that suit, your hand is within half a trick of an opening bid and you should make one effort to get to game. This is done by calling 2 No Trump, which is better tactics than a mere Diamond preference.

♠ x x
♡ K x x
◇ K x x x
♣ A 10 x x

Partner opens with 1 Spade. You may have felt this hand was slightly too good for a 1 No Trump response and elected to bid 2 Clubs. Partner rebids 2 Spades, which indicates more or less of a minimum. You should pass. You have already done your noble duty by bidding 2 Clubs, and you should make no effort to get to game merely because all suits are stopped.

♠ K x x x
♡ A K x x x
◇ x x x
♣ x

Partner opens with 1 Spade. You respond with 2 Hearts. Partner bids 3 Clubs. Your proper bid is 4 Spades. You knew all the time there was a game in the hand because you have an opening bid and splendid support for partner. It would be highly improper to bid merely 3 Spades, not that you fear partner will pass but that you will not have given a picture of your strength.

REBIDS THAT FORCE RESPONDER

It is essential for the responder completely to understand the forcing principle. He must know the cases in which he is obliged to bid further, whether he likes it or not, and the cases in which he may pass if he chooses.

The responder is allowed a wider latitude than the opening bidder. In most cases he has made no commitment. His partner is the one with the strong hand and responder may have been bidding just to give the opener another chance. Consequently he is at liberty to drop the bidding at almost any time.

The fact that a responder hears his partner name a new suit does not force him to speak again. That obligation rests only on the shoulders of the opening bidder.

When a responder hears a jump in the same suit, that does not compel him to bid again, although such a jump is forcing on the opening bidder.

When a responder hears his partner jump in No Trump he need not bid again if he does not choose to. Such a jump would be an unconditional obligation to rebid if he had been the opener.

But when a responding hand hears his partner jump in a new suit then he has no right to opinions. He is absolutely bound to speak, and to keep going until game is reached. A jump shift is a force to game whether it is made by opener or responder.

Let us examine a few cases. Suppose your partner has opened with 1 Diamond and you have responded with 1 Heart, holding:

♠ x x x x　♡ K Q 10 x　◇ x x　♣ x x x

If your partner's rebid has been:

(a) 2 Clubs, you should pass. You prefer Clubs to Diamonds and have no interest in making any further bid. As responder you are not forced to speak again just because your partner named a new suit.

(b) 2 No Trump, you should pass. You did your full duty by this hand when you responded with 1 Heart. A jump in No Trump does not force the responder to bid again. If you have as much as your partner needs to go game, he should have gone to 3 No Trump himself.

(c) 3 Diamonds. A jump rebid in the same suit does not force the responder. You should therefore pass.

(d) 3 Clubs. Now you have no choice. The jump in a new suit has forced you to bid again and to keep on going until game is reached. You cannot rebid your own suit. You are unable to support Diamonds. Your hand is not suitable for a Club raise. So there is only one call left for you, namely 3 No Trump. Dutifully make this bid and hold your breath.

Let us observe another case. You hold:

♠ x   ♡ x x x   ◇ Q J x   ♣ A J x x x x

Partner opens with 1 Spade. You respond 2 Clubs. Partner rebids 2 Hearts. What do you do?

You should pass. You are not the opening bidder and the new suit does not force you to speak again. You did everything that could be expected of you when you said 2 Clubs, and since you prefer Hearts to Spades you should seize the opportunity to stop in a reasonably safe parking place. Your partner's hand was:

♠ A J x x x   ♡ A K 9 x   ◇ x x x   ♣ x

You can see what one more word from you would have led to.

IN A NUTSHELL

When a responder hears a new suit mentioned by his partner, he is not forced to bid again (unless there has previously been agreement on a major suit) or where opener jumps in the new suit.

PARTNERSHIP LANGUAGE

As the bidding develops the responder is under the duty first to direct the partnership into the proper contract and secondly to give a portrayal of his strength. Some bids by their nature indicate strong hands. Other bids suggest weakness. It is important to grasp this partnership language.

The constant repetition, at minimum stages, of the same suit indicates great length of suit but not very much strength. However, not every repetition of a responder's suit indicates weakness. When a responder is at perfect liberty to pass and he keeps bidding, even though it happens to be in the same suit he nevertheless shows a willingness to go on. Let us examine a few cases.

OPENER	RESPONDER
1 ♡	2 ♣
2 N T	3 ♣

We are asked to interpret the meaning of the 3 Club bid.

A common sense interpretation is that it cannot be a strong hand. If the responder had a strong hand he would have taken his partner to 3 No Trump. If he had a hand that was not suitable for No Trump but was very strong he could have jumped the bid in Clubs. The plain meaning of his bid is this: "Partner, you will not find my hand helpful for No Trump. You may never be able to use my Clubs." Here is a hand:

♠ x x x   ♡ x x   ◇ x x   ♣ K Q J 10 x x

If partner opens with 1 Heart, you respond 2 Clubs. Partner bids 2 No Trump, which shows a strong hand. If partner has not the Ace of Clubs your hand will be of little value to him. You must therefore give a warning that your hand may not be helpful, and as far as you are concerned must play in Clubs, so you bid 3 Clubs. But if you hold:

♠ x x x   ♡ x x   ◇ x x   ♣ A K Q x x x

It would be highly improper for you to rebid 3 Clubs. You would be painting an improper picture of the hand. Actually you have a good hand for No Trump, for partner will probably win six tricks in Clubs. You should promptly raise to 3 No Trump.

A similar case:

OPENER	RESPONDER
1 ◇	1 ♡
2 ♣	2 ♡
2 N T	3 ♡

What is the meaning of the 3 Heart bid? It is very clear that responder has a weak hand with great length in Hearts, and even the Hearts cannot be very strong; because, if they were, by this time the responder would have been in a position to bid 4 Hearts after opener has shown such strength.

When your partner opens, and later rebids 2 No Trump, if you have a good hand you must not merely repeat your suit. You should either raise the No Trump or jump in your suit.

You are responder, holding:

♠ x x   ♡ A K Q x x x   ◇ x x x   ♣ x x

The bidding has proceeded:

OPENER	RESPONDER
1 ♠	2 ♡
2 N T	?

You should bid either 3 No Trump or 4 Hearts. Definitely not 3 Hearts.

Some more cases:

OPENER	RESPONDER
1 ◇	1 ♠
2 ♣	2 ◇

The question arises, Is the 2 Diamond bid to be construed as encouraging? The answer is No. The responder has shown a mere preference for Diamonds over Clubs. He has never increased the contract and the opener should be very cautious about carrying on.

OPENER	RESPONDER
1 ♠	2 ♠
2 N T	3 ♠

What is the meaning of the 3 Spade bid? It is this: "Partner, I had a very poor raise. I know you are asking me to go game but I am unable to do so. This hand has to play in Spades as far as I am concerned."

OPENER	RESPONDER
1 ♡	1 ♠
2 ♡	2 ♠

What is the meaning of the 2 Spade bid? While it is a repetition of the responder's suit, it is nevertheless an attempt to go forward. Responder was under no obligation to bid. The opener has announced a more or less minimum hand and a willingness to quit. Even if the responder does not like Hearts he should not carry on with a hopeless hand unless he has very great length in Spades. Suppose, in this bidding sequence, responder holds:

1.	♠ K Q J x x	♡ x	◇ x.x x	♣ x x x x
2.	♠ K Q J x x	♡ x x	◇ K J x	♣ x x x

With No. 1 he should give up at 2 Hearts in preference to bidding 2 Spades. Game is hopeless and while the hand might play better at Spades than at Hearts, there is no assurance that partner will quit. But with No. 2, responder should rebid 2 Spades, not because he is dissatisfied with Hearts but because he has within half a trick of an opening bid and there may yet be a chance for game.

To summarize: When the opener invites you to pass (by making a minimum rebid) and you keep bidding, it is a sign of encouragement, even though your rebid is in the same suit.

When the opener names a new suit the responder should make an effort to bid again if he can. With hand No. 2 in the foregoing example, had the bidding proceeded:

OPENER	RESPONDER
1 ♡	1 ♠
2 ♣	

responder would now bid 2 No Trump, rather than 2 Spades. In this sequence of bids:

OPENER	RESPONDER
1 ♠	2 ♣
2 ◇	2 ♠

How do you interpret the 2 Spade bid? On the surface it would appear to be a mere preference and therefore a sign-off. Actually it is not quite so. It is true that the responder has not given a Spade raise, but he previously indicated that he has a fairly good hand by increasing the contract to 2 Clubs. Therefore the 2 Spade bid cannot be treated as being too discouraging. After all, if the responder's hand were not fairly good he could have responded with an immediate raise to 2 Spades instead of taking the trouble to bid 2 Clubs. Responder may hold:

♠ Q J x   ♡ x x x   ◇ x x   ♣ A K x x x

It is apparent that this is the only reasonable bidding sequence for responder to adopt. He surely could not jump to 3 Spades after the 2 Diamond bid. The very fact that he took the trouble to bid 2 Clubs indicates that he has a fairly good hand. If the opener holds:

♠ A K x x x   ♡ x x   ◇ A Q J x   ♣ x x

The bidding would have proceeded in the above manner. After responder's preference for 2 Spades the opener should not give up. He should test his partner out by bidding 3 Spades, which responder will gladly raise to 4 Spades.

Similarly:

Opener	Responder
1 ♡	2 ◇
2 N T	3 ♡

What is the meaning of the 3 Heart bid? Does it show a dislike of No Trump and a mere preference for Hearts, or is it a strong bid? It is a strong bid. The responder is merely saying, "I am not sure whether we should play this hand at 4 Hearts or at 3 No Trump. I wish to give you a choice, partner. You must know I have a good hand because I first took the trouble to bid 2 Diamonds, increasing the contract, and then I again increased the contract to 3 Hearts. If my hand were not that good I would have responded with a mere 2 Heart raise in the first place."

On this sequence of bids the 3 Heart call is forcing. The opener must select a game contract at either No Trump or Hearts. A typical hand justifying such bidding by responder is:

♠ x x   ♡ K x x   ◇ A K J x x   ♣ x x x

RESPONDER'S REBIDS IN SEMI-FORCING SITUATIONS

It has been observed that when the opening bidder makes a jump rebid in the same suit (either his own or partner's) it is only a semi-forcing bid. The responder is strongly invited to bid again, but he need not do so if his hand is below minimum strength. Suppose the responder holds:

1. ♠ K J x x x   ♡ 10 x   ◇ x x x   ♣ x x x
2. ♠ K J x x x   ♡ 10 x x   ◇ x x   ♣ x x x

Opener	Responder
1 ♡	1 ♠
3 ♡	?

With No. 1, responder should pass. His hand is below minimum strength.

With No. 2, responder may chance a raise to 4 Hearts, because he might produce two tricks in the play of the hand. The doubleton Diamond offers one prospect and the Spade holding might produce a trick.

Had the opener's jump rebid been to 3 Spades the same fundamental principle applies. Since his hand is of sub-minimum strength in each case, the responder may pass.

This case is similar:

Opener	Responder
1 ♡	1 N T
3 ♡	?

The responder holds:

1. ♠ 10 x x x   ♡ x x   ◇ K x x   ♣ Q x x x
2. ♠ K x x   ♡ x x   ◇ K x x x   ♣ Q x x x

With No. 1, responder should pass. With No. 2, he should go on to 3 No Trump. He has a sound No Trump response.

A semi-forcing bid need not be responded to, but if the responder does reply, it becomes a force to game:

OPENER	RESPONDER
1 ♡	1 ♠
3 ♡	3 ♠

Responder was not forced to rebid 3 Spades. He could have passed. But since he accepted the semi-force, it now becomes a force to game, and neither partner may pass until game is reached.

RESPONDER'S NEW-SUIT REBIDS ARE FORCING

When the responder names a new suit the opener must bid again, not only on the first round but on subsequent rounds. For example:

♠ A K J x x   ♡ A Q J x   ◇ x   ♣ x x x

Your partner opens with 1 Diamond. You respond with 1 Spade. Partner bids 2 Diamonds. You are quite set on going to game but it is not essential for you to jump the bid in Hearts at this point. You may force another bid from partner by merely naming a new suit. Remember, the opening bidder must bid again every time he hears a new suit. On the next round you will make up your mind just where this hand should play.

This device may be employed by the responder as a temporizing measure when he wishes time to make up his mind where a hand should play. For example you hold:

♠ x x   ♡ x x   ◇ A K J x x x   ♣ A J x

Your partner opens with 1 Spade. You respond with 2 Diamonds. Partner rebids 2 Spades. You know that this hand belongs in game, because you have distinctly more than an opening bid, but you are disinclined to assign this hand to an eleven-trick contract. If partner can stop Hearts you would rather try for 3 No Trump.

You are perfectly safe, therefore, in bidding merely 3 Clubs, a one-round force. This is not Ace-showing. As far as partner is concerned you really have a Club suit. If he does not bid 3 No Trump you will then decide whether to play for 4 Spades or 5 Diamonds.

Here is another interesting use of the new suit force by responder to find the best contract. Responder holds:

♠ K Q J 9 x   ♡ K x x   ◇ x x   ♣ A x x

The bidding has proceeded:

OPENER	RESPONDER
1 ♡	1 ♠
2 ◇	?

The best game contract may be in Spades, Hearts or No Trump, depending upon the texture of opener's hand. If opener has three Spades, that suit should be best. If he has five Hearts that should be the final trump. In the absence of either, 3 No Trump appears to be the most suitable vehicle. How is responder to find out? Merely by bidding 3 Clubs. If opener prefers Spades he will bid 3 Spades and responder's worries are over. If opener rebids Hearts, that's the spot. If opener bids 3 No Trump, responder stops exploring.

When a player takes his partner out of a game contract, to which partner has voluntarily leaped, into a non-game contract, the inference is plain that he is looking for a slam. Otherwise the rescue would be senseless. For example, as responder you hold:

♠ x x   ♡ x x   ◇ K J 10 x x x   ♣ x x x

The bidding has proceeded:

OPENER	RESPONDER
1 ♣	1 ◇
3 N T	?

What should you do? Pass, definitely. Do not make the mistake of bidding 4 Diamonds simply because you do not like No Trump. A player who has jumped to 3 No Trump does not have to be rescued. However, if by single stages the partnership has worked itself into a 3 No Trump contract and one player thinks it is not the proper contract he may go to 4 Clubs or 4 Diamonds if he believes there is no game in the hand.

Again as responder, you hold:

♠ x x x   ♡ A Q x   ◇ x   ♣ K Q 10 x x x

The bidding has proceeded:

OPENER	RESPONDER
1 ♠	2 ♣
3 N T	?

Here you are quite sure that there is slam in the hand and wish to elicit further information from your partner. You may, if you choose, temporize by bidding 4 Clubs, which must be construed not as a rescue bid but as a slam try.

CASES IN WHICH A NEW-SUIT REBID BY RESPONDER IS NOT FORCING

An exception is to be noted to the rule that the naming of a new suit by responder forces opener to speak once more. When the opener's rebid has been a sign-off of 1 No Trump, responder may show a new suit without forcing opener to bid again. For example, you are responder and hold:

♠ K J x x x   ♡ Q x x x x   ◇ x   ♣ x x

The bidding proceeds:

OPENER	RESPONDER
1 ♣	1 ♠
1 N T	2 ♡

The opener may pass; the 2 Heart rebid over 1 No Trump is not forcing. Had the bidding proceeded:

OPENER	RESPONDER
1 ♣	1 ♠
2 ♣	

you would be obliged to pass, because a bid of 2 Hearts would force opener to make another bid, which you do not desire.

The theory is that when opener rebids 1 No Trump he has a balanced hand and consequently has some support for one of your suits, whereas if he bids and rebids his own suit he may not have support for either of yours.

If the responder rebids in a higher-ranking suit, even over 1 No Trump, it is forcing:

OPENER	RESPONDER
1 ♣	1 ◇
1 N T	2 ♠

The 2 Spade bid makes it impossible for opener to return to 2 Diamonds; hence it is a strong bid, made in the expectation of getting to game, and opener must bid again.

A new suit by responder does not force the opener if either of the players has previously passed.

A new suit by responder does not force the opener when it is made directly over an adverse double. Suppose South holds:

♠ J x x   ♡ A Q 10 x x   ◇ A x x   ♣ x x

The bidding:

SOUTH	WEST	NORTH	EAST
1 ♡	Double	1 ♠	Pass

South may pass. Indeed, unless he is very strong he should pass. Since North has not redoubled there can be no game and Spades should be as safe a "spot" as any.

A new suit by responder does not force the opener when it is evident from the preceding bidding that responder is not trying to go places, but is seeking a safe place to land. For example:

OPENER	RESPONDER
1 ♡	1 ♠
2 ♡	2 ♠
2 N T	3 ◇

If responder wished to force opener, he would have bid 3 Diamonds over 2 Hearts.

MEANINGS OF BIDDING SITUATIONS

The significance of the final bid in each sequence is indicated in the following chart:

1.

OPENER	RESPONDER
1 ♠	3 ♠ ?

Game force

2.

OPENER	RESPONDER
1 ♠	2 N T ?

Game force

3.

OPENER	RESPONDER
1 ♠	2 ♣ ?

One-round force

4.

OPENER	RESPONDER
Pass	1 ♠
3 ♠ ?	

Not forcing. Strongly invitational

5.

OPENER	RESPONDER
Pass	1 ♠
2 ♡ ?	

Not forcing

6.

OPENER	RESPONDER
1 ♣	1 ◇
1 ♡ ?	

Not forcing

7.

OPENER	RESPONDER
1 ♡	1 ♠
3 ♠ ?	

Semi-forcing
Strongly invitational

8.

OPENER	RESPONDER
1 ♣	1 N T ?

Weak bid

9.

OPENER	RESPONDER
1 ♡	1 ♠
2 N T ?	

Semi-forcing
Strongly invitational

10.

OPENER	RESPONDER
1 ♠	2 ♠
3 ◊ ?	

One-round force

11.

OPENER	RESPONDER
1 ♡	1 ♠
3 ♡	3 ♠ ?

Game force

12.

OPENER	RESPONDER
1 ♡	1 ♠
2 ♣ ?	

Not forcing

13.

OPENER	RESPONDER
1 ♠	2 ◊
2 ♠	3 ♣ ?

One-round force

14.

OPENER	RESPONDER
1 ♡	1 ♠
1 N T	2 ♣ ?

Not forcing

15.

OPENER	RESPONDER
1 N T	2 ♣ ?

Not forcing

16.

OPENER	RESPONDER
1 N T	2 ♠

Mildly encouraging

17.

OPENER	RESPONDER
1 ♡	2 ◊
3 ♣ ?	

Showing great strength

18.

OPENER	RESPONDER
1 ♠	2 ♠
2 N T	3 ♠

Sign-off

19.

OPENER	RESPONDER
1 ◊	1 ♠
2 ♣	2 ◊ ?

Sign-off

20.

OPENER	RESPONDER
1 ♠	2 ♡
2 ♠ ?	

Not encouraging

21.

OPENER	RESPONDER
1 ♡	1 ♠
1 N T ?	

Not encouraging

22.

OPENER	RESPONDER
1 ♠	2 ♣
2 N T ?	

Strength showing

23.

OPENER	RESPONDER
1 ♠	2 ◊
2 ♠	3 ◊ ?

Mildly encouraging

24.

OPENER	RESPONDER
1 ♠	2 ◊
2 N T	3 ♠ ?

Game force

25.

OPENER	ADVERSARY	RESPONDER
1 ♣	1 ♡	1 N T ?

Strength showing bid

26.

OPENER	RESPONDER
1 ♡	1 N T
2 ♠ ?	

Showing great strength

QUIZ ON REBIDS BY RESPONDER

ANSWERS BEGIN ON PAGE 134

You are responder in each of the following cases. Your holding and the previous bidding are indicated. What is your rebid?

1. ♠ Q 10 x x
   ♡ x x
   ◇ x x x
   ♣ A J 10 x

OPENER	RESPONDER
1 ♠	2 ♠
2 N T	?

2. ♠ A x x
   ♡ J x
   ◇ K x x x
   ♣ Q J x x

OPENER	RESPONDER
1 ♠	2 ♠
2 N T	?

3. ♠ Q x x x
   ♡ K x x x
   ◇ x x x
   ♣ x x

OPENER	RESPONDER
1 ♠	2 ♠
2 N T	?

4. ♠ A 9 x x
   ♡ x x
   ◇ Q x x
   ♣ K x x x

OPENER	RESPONDER
1 ♠	2 ♠
3 ◇	?

5. ♠ x x x
   ♡ 10 x
   ◇ A 10 9 x
   ♣ Q J x x

OPENER	RESPONDER
1 ♡	1 N T
2 ♠	?

6. ♠ J x
   ♡ Q x x
   ◇ Q x x x
   ♣ K J x x

OPENER	RESPONDER
1 ♠	1 N T
3 ♠	3 N T
4 ♡	?

7. ♠ K J
   ♡ J x x x
   ◇ Q 10
   ♣ J 9 x x x

OPENER	RESPONDER
1 ♠	1 N T
2 ◇	2 ♠
3 ♠	?

8. ♠ K x x
   ♡ x x x
   ◇ K J x
   ♣ x x x x

OPENER	RESPONDER
1 ♡	1 N T
2 ♠	?

9.
♠ J x
♡ 9 x x
◊ Q x x x
♣ A x x x

Opener	Responder
1 ♡	1 N T
2 ♠	?

10.
♠ x x x x
♡ 10 x x
◊ J x
♣ A 9 x x

Opener	Responder
1 ♡	1 N T
3 ♣	?

11.
♠ A Q J x x x
♡ x x x
◊ x x x
♣ x

Opener	Responder
1 ♡	1 ♠
2 ♠	?

12.
♠ x x
♡ A x x x x
◊ x x x
♣ K Q x

Opener	Responder
1 ♠	2 ♡
2 ♠	?

13.
♠ x x
♡ Q J x
◊ K x
♣ A Q J 9 x x

Opener	Responder
1 ♠	2 ♣
2 ♠	?

14.
♠ x x
♡ x x x
◊ K x x
♣ A K J x x

Opener	Responder
1 ♠	2 ♣
2 ♠	?

15.
♠ A 10
♡ 10 x x
◊ J x x
♣ A K x x x

Opener	Responder
1 ♠	2 ♣
2 ♠	?

16.
♠ x x
♡ x x x
◊ x x x
♣ A K x x x

Opener	Responder
1 ♠	2 ♣
2 ◊	?

17.
♠ x x x x
♡ x x x
◊ A x x x x
♣ J

Opener	Responder
1 ♣	1 ◊
1 ♠	2 ♠
3 N T	?

18.
♠ x x
♡ Q 10 x
◊ x x x
♣ A K x x x

Opener	Responder
1 ♡	2 ♣
2 ◊	?

19. ♠ x
    ♡ 10 x x
    ◇ A x x
    ♣ A K x x x x

Opener	Responder
1 ♡	2 ♣
2 ♡	?

20. ♠ J x x
    ♡ A K x x x
    ◇ A x x
    ♣ 10 x

Opener	Responder
1 ♠	2 ♡
2 ♠	?

21. ♠ Q x x x
    ♡ A 9 x x x
    ◇ x
    ♣ K x x

Opener	Responder
1 ♠	2 ♡
3 ♠	?

22. ♠ x x x
    ♡ x
    ◇ K Q J x x x
    ♣ x x x

Opener	Responder
1 ♡	2 ◇
3 ♡	?

23. ♠ K 10 x x x
    ♡ x x x
    ◇ Q x x
    ♣ x x

Opener	Responder
1 ♣	1 ♠
2 N T	?

24. ♠ x x
    ♡ A x x
    ◇ J x x
    ♣ K Q 10 x x

Opener	Responder
1 ♡	2 ♣
2 N T	?

25. ♠ A J x x
    ♡ Q x x
    ◇ K Q x x x
    ♣ x

Opener	Responder
1 ♡	2 ◇
2 N T	?

26. ♠ Q x x
    ♡ A J x x
    ◇ K Q x x x
    ♣ x

Opener	Responder
1 ♠	2 ◇
2 N T	?

27. ♠ A J x x x
    ♡ x
    ◇ J 10 x x
    ♣ K x x

Opener	Responder
1 ◇	1 ♠
2 ♡	?

28. ♠ Q x x
    ♡ A x x x
    ◇ x x x
    ♣ A x x

Opener	Responder
1 ♠	2 ♠
3 ♠	?

29.
♠ x x x
♡ K 10 x
◇ A K J x x
♣ J x

OPENER	RESPONDER
1 ♡	2 ◇
3 ♣	?

30.
♠ x
♡ K J x x x
◇ x x
♣ K 10 x x x

OPENER	RESPONDER
1 ♠	2 ♡
2 ♠	?

31.
♠ A K x x
♡ x x
◇ Q J x
♣ K Q J x

OPENER	RESPONDER
1 ♠	2 ♣
2 ♡	?

32.
♠ Q J 9 x
♡ J x x
◇ Q J
♣ A 9 x x

OPENER	RESPONDER
1 ◇	1 ♠
1 N T	?

33.
♠ K x x
♡ x x
◇ K Q 9 x x x
♣ J x

NORTH	EAST	SOUTH	WEST
1 ♣	Pass	1 ◇	1 ♡
1 N T	Pass	?	

From the information furnished in the following bidding diagrams answer these questions:

Is the last bid forcing?

Does it show great strength, or mild strength, or is it discouraging?

Can you tell the approximate distribution of the player making the last bid?

34.
OPENER	RESPONDER
1 ♠	1 N T
2 ♠	2 N T
3 ♡	?

35.
OPENER	RESPONDER
1 ◇	2 ♣
2 ♠ ?	

36.	OPENER	RESPONDER		37.	OPENER	RESPONDER
	1 ♡	2 ◇			1 ♠	2 ♣
	3 ♣?				2 ♠	2 N T
					3 ♠?	

38.	OPENER	RESPONDER		39.	OPENER	RESPONDER
	1 ◇	1 ♠			1 ♠	2 ♡
	2 ♡	2 N T			2 N T	3 ♠?
	3 ♡?					

40.	OPENER	RESPONDER		41.	OPENER	RESPONDER
	1 ♠	2 ♣			1 ♡	2 ◇
	2 ♠	3 ◇			2 ♡	2 ♠
	3 N T	4 ♠?			3 ◇	3 ♡?

42.	OPENER	RESPONDER		43.	OPENER	RESPONDER
	1 ♡	2 ◇			1 ♠	2 ♠
	2 ♡	3 ◇?			3 ♣?	

44.	OPENER	RESPONDER		45.	OPENER	RESPONDER
	1 ♠	3 ♣			1 ♠	2 ◇
	3 N T?				2 N T?	

46.	OPENER	RESPONDER	47.	OPENER	ADVERSARY	RESPONDER
	1 ◇	1 ♠		1 ♠	Double	2 ♡?
	1 N T	2 ♣?				

QUIZ ANSWERS—REBIDS
BY RESPONDER

1. 4 Spades. You have 4 playing tricks. This is a good raise. If you had returned to only 3 Spades partner would think you had a poor raise.

2. 3 No Trump. You have a good raise that consists of high cards.

3. 3 Spades. You have only 3 playing tricks and therefore not a good raise. If partner had 7 playing tricks he would have bid 4 Spades himself.

4. 4 Spades. Your original raise was a very sound one and partner's 3 Diamond call is a "fishing" bid, made in an effort to find out what

kind of a raise you have made. To reply, "A bad one"—you bid 3 Spades. To reply, "A good one"—you bid 4 Spades.

5. 2 No Trump. You have a mediocre hand but partner has shown a very strong one and you should "honor his reverse" since you have slightly over a minimum No Trump response.

6. 4 Spades. Partner has shown a six-card Spade suit and four Hearts. This gives the partnership eight Spades as against only seven Hearts.

7. 4 Spades. You haven't much but it's just in the right spots. Your Spades and Diamonds should just about solidify both of partner's suits and he is obviously short in the others.

8. 3 Hearts. It is your duty to return to the suit in which the partnership has numerical superiority, even though it involves an increase in the level. That's your partner's business. Besides, you have a sound response.

9. 3 Hearts. When partner has shown a 5-4 you should not insist on No Trump, having sketchy stoppers in partner's short suits.

10. 3 Hearts. This is preferable to raising the Clubs, because partner is marked with a five-card Heart suit. If he had four Hearts and four Clubs he would probably have opened with 1 Club. Furthermore, with such a hand he would no doubt have jumped to game in No Trump.

11. 4 Spades. You have 5½ winners and partner's bidding indicates he should take at least 4½ tricks.

12. Pass. Partner has indicated a minimum and you would need within half a trick of an opening bid to try again. You do not have this.

13. 2 No Trump. This hand is about the equal of an opening bid and therefore holds forth promise of game. An eleven-trick game is not desirable and you do not care for Spades, so 2 No Trump is the only bid open to you. A mere rebid of 3 Clubs would be a move forward but would indicate a hand whose value was almost exclusively Clubs.

14. 2 No Trump. You have the equivalent of an opening bid opposite a partner who has opened the bidding, which makes game prospects very bright. Since the only reasonable chance for game is No Trump you should try it despite the lack of a Heart stopper. (Responder may chance a suit in the hope that opener has it.)

15. 3 Spades. You have the equal of an opening bid and partner has opened the bidding. There should be game if you can find the right contract. With two unguarded suits you do not wish to try No Trump so the only thing left is to raise the rebid Spade suit.

16. Pass. You have no good bid to make. You prefer Diamonds to Spades. Since partner did not bid 2 No Trump over 2 Clubs it is difficult to see how anything could be gained by bidding 3 Clubs.

17. 4 Spades. It is your first duty to see that the hand is played in the right contract. The bid of 4 Spades does not show additional values. It merely announces that this hand will be a good dummy for Spades but not for No Trump.

18. 2 Hearts. This may sound like a mere preference but partner will know you have a fairly good hand since in your first response you elected to increase the contract in a new suit.

19. 4 Hearts. Partner's minimum rebid dampens the slam prospects, but since you have somewhat more than an opening bid you should be certain of game and must bid it in partner's suit, for which you have normal support, once partner has rebid it.

20. 4 Spades. You have a good substantial opening and partner has opened. This spells game and you have normal trump support for the rebid suit. You must bid game yourself.

21. 5 Spades. This hand has enormous playing strength in support of Spades. A mere "pressure" raise to 4 Spades would be inadequate and would sound as though you might be stretching a point. If you translate the singleton Diamond into an Ace you have the equivalent of an opening bid.

22. Pass. You did all that could be expected of you when you bid 2 Diamonds. The jump rebid in the same suit does not force responder.

23. Pass. You performed your full duty when you responded with 1 Spade. The jump in No Trump does not force you, for you are not the opener. If your hand has all partner needs to make game he should have jumped to 3 No Trump himself.

24. 3 Hearts. This gives partner the choice of going on in Hearts or No Trump. Partner might have a five-card Heart suit which he has not yet had time to describe.

25. 3 Hearts. It is essential to show support for partner's major suit. This gives him various choices. If he has some weak four-card Spade suit he may try it out at this point or he can go on in Hearts or No Trump.

26. 3 Hearts. This serves a dual purpose: First, finding a possible spot; second, permitting partner to rebid to 3 Spades if he has a five-card suit, in which case you will support his suit.

27. 4 Diamonds. Partner has shown a very strong hand. His 2 Heart rebid makes it impossible for you to return to 2 Diamonds. A mere bid of 3 Diamonds would simply be a return to your partner's first suit. You must indicate a fine raise by jumping to 4 Diamonds.

28. 3 No Trump. While you have no ruffing values you have more in high cards than could be expected from your single raise. You should accept partner's invitation to go game, but you should try for nine tricks rather than ten. Partner can then take his choice.

29. 4 Hearts. Partner has shown a very fine hand by rebidding at the level of three. The hand has great possibilities and a mere return to 3 Hearts would not be sufficient. There is no fear that partner has a four-card Heart suit. With four Hearts and four Clubs he would have opened with 1 Club.

30. Pass. You are treading on thin ice and might fall in any minute. It is true that one of your suits will probably play better than Spades, but unfortunately you cannot afford to find out. Resign yourself to a small loss in cases of this type.

31. 4 Spades. This is a stronger bid than 3 Spades, inasmuch as you have previously shown another suit. The objection to bidding 3 Spades is that if partner automatically goes to four you will feel that you have not done justice to the hand and will be tempted to act above the game level. This would not be safe.

32. 2 No Trump. Your Diamond holding should be looked upon as a full trick for playing purposes, which makes your hand not far removed from an opening bid in strength. If partner has slight surplus values there is a chance for game.

33. 2 No Trump. Your hand will produce a number of tricks for partner. A rebid of Diamonds would be improper for it would suggest that your hand would be of doubtful value at No Trump.

34. The 3 Heart bid is not especially encouraging. If opener had a good hand he would have shown the Hearts immediately. It is apparent that opener did not like the No Trump and is trying to find a better spot. Opener probably has five Spades and four Hearts, or possibly six Spades and four Hearts, but not very much honor strength, just a minimum opening bid.

35. The 2 Spade bid is not forcing but it is a reverse and shows a strong hand, because the bid makes it impossible for responder to return to 2 Diamonds. Opener probably has five Diamonds and four Spades and at least 4 honor tricks.

36. The 3 Club bid is not forcing but it shows a very strong hand, since it increases the level so sharply. The opener is marked with a five-card Heart suit and either four or five Clubs. The Hearts cannot be a four-card suit because with four Hearts and four Clubs the correct opening bid would have been 1 Club.

37. The 3 Spade bid is a discouraging bid. Responder has shown a good hand but opener has nothing to say except that he has six Spades and just about 2½ honor tricks.

38. The 3 Heart bid is forcing. The opener shows a very strong hand including six Diamonds and five Hearts. The rebid of the Hearts shows a five-card suit and the fact that the Diamonds were bid first indicates that they are longer. Both partners have shown strength.

39. The 3 Spade bid is forcing. Responder has shown a very good hand. If it were not of game caliber responder would not have bid 2 Hearts but should have responded with a mere raise to 2 Spades. Responder may merely be giving opener a choice between 4 Spades and 3 No Trump. He probably has five Hearts and three Spades.

40. Not forcing, but responder has a very good hand, apparently including five Clubs, four Diamonds, three Spades and a singleton Heart.

41. Forcing; responder has shown a very fine hand including five Diamonds, four Spades and three Hearts.

42. Not forcing; but the 3 Diamond bid, although it is repeating the same suit, is nevertheless encouraging. If responder did not have any hopes he would resign at 2 Hearts even though he had a long Diamond suit. Except for his length in Diamonds, he has not shown any particular distribution.

43. The 3 Club bid is a one-round force. It is true that ordinarily a new suit does not force the responder to speak, but when a major suit has already been agreed upon the showing of any other suit is a one-round force. Opener may be testing out the nature of the Spade raise or may be attempting to reach a game at No Trump, so his distribution is not yet revealed.

44. The 3 No Trump bid, in response to a jump shift, indicates a balanced hand with no surplus values. It is not forcing.

45. The 2 No Trump bid is not forcing, but shows a strong hand of balanced distribution. Remember, it makes it impossible for responder to return to 2 Spades.

46. The 2 Club bid is not forcing. This is one of the exceptions to the rule. When opener signs off with 1 No Trump the naming of a new, lower-ranking suit is not forcing, so that if responder had a game-going hand it would be necessary for him to jump to 3 Clubs. Responder probably has five Spades and four or five Clubs.

47. The 2 Heart bid is not forcing and does not show a very strong hand. This is logical because if the responder had a strong hand he would have redoubled.

CHAPTER 5

SLAM BIDDING

THROUGH THE YEARS we have formed the habit of treating slam bidding as a distinct topic apart from bidding tactics in general. Despite the fact that I share this guilt with other writers, I think it is a bad idea and has led to a great deal of unsound thinking on the subject of slams.

True enough, there are certain bids which by their very nature carry direct slam inferences—a jump in a new suit, for example, or a cue-bid in a suit adversely bid. But the development of the bidding that reaches a slam should not differ widely from the style employed in getting to game. If we have a method for determining that a hand will take ten tricks with Hearts as trumps, why is that method not equally suitable for determining that we have eleven tricks with Diamonds as trumps, or twelve tricks at a Spade contract? The big thing in slam bidding is to determine whether or not the partnership resources amount to twelve tricks. A simple thought, indeed, but as hard to sell to the public as was, long ago, the proposition that the earth is round.

What about Aces, you ask? You may find that your side can win twelve tricks but unfortunately the enemy can cash two tricks first. Naturally this is a condition to be avoided. After it is determined that the partnership has the necessary winning tricks then comes the check-up. Various conventions have from time to time been devised for the purpose of making this check-up, but bear it in mind that the purpose of these conventions is not to find out if you have a slam. Regular bidding methods are employed for that purpose. The conventions are calculated to find out if the opponents can win two tricks in a hurry. In other words, conventions like the Blackwood are not for the purpose of getting to a slam. They are for the purpose of staying out of one that cannot be made.

Among the teams that it is my pleasure to coach, I do not encourage the members in the use of the standard artificial slam conventions, but occasionally some player will come to me for special permission to use her favorite 4 No Trump bid.

"It's perfectly all right with me," I usually reply, "provided you first make sure you have a slam." And I'm not jesting.

The query so frequently heard, "Do you like Blackwood?" is not unlike asking a golfer if he likes a No. 9 iron. It wouldn't be the club to use from the driving tee; it has its special uses. And so has Blackwood. To employ that convention on every slam is very much like using the same golf club for every stroke.

One of the principal objections to the use of Blackwood by the average player is the lack of restraint which its employment seems to induce. Some of my students, who know my preference for common sense methods of bidding slams, but who cannot resist the glamor that artificial slam conventions seem to provide, will come to me upon occasion and announce with a triumphant air, "Professor, we used Blackwood and got to a slam."

"I'm not surprised," is my wonted reply, "it's one of the surest ways of getting there. Inertia takes care of that. If you really want to brag, come to me some day and tell me that you used Blackwood and stayed out of a slam, at which point I shall doff my hat." (My fedora is as good as new.)

SLAM VALUATION

In slam bidding, the big thing is the diagnosis, that is, determination that the partnership has twelve or thirteen trick-winners. We have observed that when the partnership possesses the sum total of two opening bids game will usually result. In other words, if both partners are satisfied with Spades as trump and each one has the equivalent of an opening bid the hand should produce ten tricks. If the partnership has a surplus of about an Ace and a King the total is increased to about $11\frac{1}{2}$, making a slam highly probable. If, in addition to the two opening bids, the partnership has a surplus of about two full tricks, a slam is a moral certainty.

The question arises, How can we determine that the partnership has 1½ or 2 tricks in excess of two opening bids? This may be done in several ways. Let us examine a simple case. You hold:

♠ K x x x x　♡ A x x　◇ x x　♣ A 9 x

Your partner opens with 1 Diamond. You respond with 1 Spade. Your partner raises to 3 Spades. What is your diagnosis? You should diagnose a slam. You have approximately the equivalent of an opening bid. Your partner opened the bidding, and then jumped. We have observed that a jump rebid by the opener must be based upon a total of 1½ honor tricks in excess of the opening bid. It now needs simple arithmetic. Partner has an opening bid plus 1½ tricks and you have an opening bid. This gives the partnership two opening bids plus 1½ tricks and makes a slam very probable.

What should you bid? Our suggestion is just 6 Spades. You say, What if there is a grand slam in the hand? The answer is, if your partner has bid correctly it simply does not add up. Here is partner's hand:

♠ A x x x　♡ x　◇ A K x x x　♣ K Q x

Let us take another example:

♠ 10 x x　♡ A 9 x　◇ A K J x　♣ Q J x

Your partner opens with 1 Club. You respond with 1 Diamond. Partner's rebid is 2 No Trump. What should you do? Let us make a diagnosis. You have a good, substantial opening bid yourself. Partner has an opening bid plus 1½ tricks (else his jump to 2 No Trump was unsound). The partnership possesses two opening bids plus about 2 tricks. There can be no doubt as to a slam. This isn't a question of Aces, it is a question of tricks. Since you have no five-card suit you are not deeply interested in a grand slam. Partner's hand:

♠ A J x　♡ K Q x x　◇ Q x　♣ A K x x

This leads us to the following conclusion: If you hold a responding hand which is as good as an opening bid and your partner opens the bidding and jumps, there should be a slam.

In other words, *an opening bid faced by an opening bid and followed by a jump equals a slam.* All of this, of course, assumes that there is a suitable contract and that the hand is not a misfit. We assume for the purpose of this rule that your partner's jump is in a declaration that you like.

Estimating slams on direct No Trump bidding is nothing more complicated than simple addition of assets. If partner opens with 1 No Trump you know that he has in the vicinity of 4 honor tricks. If partner opens with 2 No Trump you know that he has about 5½ tricks; with 3 No Trump, about 6½ tricks. So by adding partner's tricks to your own you can tell at a glance within ½ trick of what the partnership strength is. Remember that the deck contains about 8 honor tricks. If the partnership possesses a little over 7 honor tricks and a five-card suit, your chances for a slam are splendid. Without a five-card suit it will usually require almost all the high cards in the pack to produce a slam. With 37 or 38 you should be willing to chance a grand slam; with 33 or 34, a small slam. This assumes a balanced hand. With a good five-card suit you may get by with a point less. And with a six-card suit, with 2 or 3 points less.

If partner opens with a bid of 2 Spades you may assume that he can take nine tricks in his own hand. By simply adding these to the total of tricks you are confident your hand will produce you will usually arrive, with a fair degree of accuracy, at the full trick-taking capacity of the combined holding. Due allowance, of course, must be made for questions of controls and duplication. Check-up methods will be illustrated in the ensuing pages.

SLAM DIAGNOSIS BY OPENER, WHEN RESPONDER JUMPS

You open and partner jumps: 1 Spade—3 Spades. If you have no excess values you merely contract for game. Partner's response is based on a hand that is equivalent to an opening bid. You have an opening bid. This spells game. Where you have excess values it follows that your hand will produce tricks in excess of game.

If you have 1 honor trick in excess you probably will be able to produce eleven tricks and might in a mild way suggest the possibility of a slam. Try once, and if partner does not react favorably quit at game, allowing for a possible bad break which would reduce your number from eleven to ten.

If you have 1½ honor tricks in excess of your opening bid, the total will come to 11½ tricks, which should induce you to exercise your sporting blood. On hands of this type you might make two tries for a slam. You should surely be safe for five-odd, even if partner subsequently appears unenthusiastic.

If you have 2 honor tricks in excess of your bid let no evil power keep you out of a slam. It is in this class of hands that you should give serious thoughts to a grand slam.

Your judgment should also be influenced by the distribution of your hand—the more even it is the more pessimistic you should be. With a 4–3–3–3 distribution you will usually need about a trick more than you might think. A two-suiter that fits with partner responds very favorably to slam treatment. A singleton is a desirable feature in declarer's hand when a slam is contemplated. It guarantees against a loss of two tricks in that suit and gives you time to develop the hand.

Let us examine a few cases. In each you open with 1 Spade and partner jumps to 3 Spades. Your hand:

♠ A K x x x   ♡ x x   ◇ A x x   ♣ K x x

With this hand you have one trick in excess of an opening bid. You should therefore be mildly suspicious of a slam. The distribution of the hand is unfavorable and therefore you must step lightly. When you are only mildly suspicious of a slam you must not jeopardize game by experimenting above the level of your game contract. Therefore on hands of this type any such bid as 4 No Trump or 5 Spades is barred because there is no absolute assurance that a contract of five would be safe. However, a mild slam try can be made by a bid of 4 Diamonds. This will denote possession of the Ace and permit responder to carry on if he so desires. You will take no further aggressive action.

♠ A K x x x   ♡ x   ◇ A x x x   ♣ K x x

Here you have one trick in excess of your opening bid, with the additional advantage of a singleton, which is very vital for slam purposes, and you may be slightly more aggressive than in the preceding example. A contract of five-odd will probably be safe.

♠ A K x x x ♡ x x ◇ A x x ♣ K Q x

You have 1½ tricks in excess of your opening bid, making this a pretty sure slam. Hands of this type should be absolutely safe for eleven tricks, so if you employ any of the 4 No Trump conventions you can do so with no danger on this hand, although it is doubtful that it will be of great assistance; the low-card losers in Hearts and Diamonds will still be doubtful in your mind.

♠ A K x x x ♡ x x ◇ A Q x ♣ K Q x

You have 2 honor tricks in excess of the opening bid, so that a slam is a certainty. Here any 4 No Trump convention may be employed if you choose and a contract of six must be reached. It is almost inconceivable that partner can jump from 1 Spade to 3 Spades opposite this hand without the Ace of Hearts or the Ace of Clubs.

In the following example you have opened with 1 Spade and partner responds with 2 No Trump. You have slightly more than two tricks in excess of the opening bid. This makes a slam a certainty and your correct rebid is 6 No Trump:

♠ A K J x ♡ K x x ◇ A K x ♣ Q J x

You have 21 points; partner has 13 to 15. This adds to a sure small slam with no reasonable chance for a grand slam.

BIDS CARRYING SLAM IMPLICATIONS

I. A JUMP IN A NEW SUIT

A jump shift by the responder is the most frequent method of announcing an early interest in a slam. Since the mere naming of a new suit by responder forces the opener to speak again it is unnecessary to jump in a new suit when game is your only objective. The jump shift should therefore be reserved exclusively for those hands in which you have slam aspirations.

2. A JUMP FROM ONE OF A SUIT TO 3 NO TRUMP

This bid must suggest slam possibilities if the opener has a good hand, because the responder has a minimum of 3½ honor tricks. The bid enables the opener to count the partnership assets at once, but at the same time it warns him that the responder's distribution is probably 4–3–3–3.

It is to be borne in mind that a response of 3 No Trump after an opening bid of one in a suit shows a hand equivalent to a 1 No Trump bid (16 to 18 points).

3. CUE-BIDS

Another bid carrying a definite slam inference is the cue-bid, that is, a bid in the opponent's suit. This shows ability to win the first trick in that suit (either a void or the Ace).

A cue-bid is made with the idea of reaching slam. Occasionally it may be used for the purpose of getting to 3 No Trump, when it is apparent from the bidding, which has not been vigorous, that the partnership cannot aspire to a slam. Normally, however, the cue-bid is not used merely for the purpose of getting to game. Direct methods are more effective for such purposes. There are many slams, however, which cannot be reached unless partner is shown control of the adverse suit.

Before a cue-bid is in order there must be an agreement on the trump suit, either expressed or implied. Let us take an illustration.

♠ ——   ♡ K 10 x x x   ◇ A K x x   ♣ Q J x x

Your partner opens with 1 Heart and the opponent overcalls with 1 Spade. There is no question as to game in Hearts, and if your partner happens to have strength in Clubs, you will make either six or seven. At this point a cue-bid of 2 Spades is in order. It says, "Partner, I can take care of your Spade losers. I have plenty of trump support. I absolutely guarantee a game and I am looking for a slam. Tell me more about your hand." If your partner rebids the Hearts you should now call 4 Diamonds. If your partner follows this with a 5 Club bid you may safely contract for 6 Hearts. You are not in a position to bid seven because you may lose to the King of Clubs. If your partner's hand is as follows:

♠ x x x   ♡ A Q x x x x   ◇ x   ♣ A K x

he can contract for a grand slam.

A cue-bid has an additional advantage. If partner's strength happens to be in the suit which you have cued he will realize its lack of value. In the last case, assuming that your partner held:

♠ A K x   ♡ A Q x x x x   ◇ x   ♣ x x x

He would realize that his 2 honor tricks in Spades were absolutely useless and a slam should be avoided.

It is important to bear in mind the fact that a cue-bid is not justified merely because of the void in the adverse suit. Such a bid must be supported by at least 3 honor tricks to promise a slam.

CHOICE BETWEEN A CUE-BID AND A SUIT BID

When you can either show your own suit or make an immediate cue-bid, the former should be preferred. While it is very difficult to describe a good suit late in the bidding, it is never too late to show that you have control of the adverse suit.

For example, your partner opens with 1 Spade. The opponents bid 2 Clubs. You hold:

♠ K Q x x   ♡ A J x x x   ◇ x   ♣ A Q x

This hand certainly has a slam air about it and is strong enough to justify an immediate cue-bid in Clubs, but that would not be the best strategy. The recommended bid is merely 2 Hearts. The hand is strong enough for a jump shift to 3 Hearts but a simple one-round force is recommended in order to conserve bidding space, since there are so many features about your hand that you wish to describe. When on the next round you make a cue-bid in Clubs your partner will realize that you are headed for a slam. He will know also that you have a Heart suit. You will tell him later that you have very fine Spade support.

THE SINGLETON IN SLAM BIDDING

Aces and Kings alone do not make a slam. Quite as many slams are dependent upon the possession of a singleton.

Let us take an example. You are South and hold:

♠ A K Q x x   ♡ x x x   ◇ K x x   ♣ J x

The bidding has proceeded:

SOUTH	WEST	NORTH	EAST
1 ♠	Pass	2 ◇	Pass
2 ♠	Pass	3 ♣	Pass
3 ◇	Pass	4 ♠	Pass
?			

What should South do?

The unimaginative player would pass, of course, because he would feel that he had already shown the full strength of his hand. The player with vision would stop to picture his partner's holding, and would realize that there was only one Heart loser because partner must have a singleton or a void in that suit. The King of Diamonds would solidify that suit and at worst there would be a Club finesse for the slam. North holds:

♠ J 9 x   ♡ x   ◇ A Q x x x   ♣ A Q x x

The recognition of the singleton in Hearts is the interesting feature of the hand. It may be stated as a principle of bidding that when a player names three suits and incorporates a jump in his sequence of bids he shows a singleton or void in the fourth suit.

If North held a doubleton Heart he might bid three suits, but then he would not be justified in jumping to 4 Spades. Over the 3 Diamond bid it would be sufficient to bid only 3 Spades, or North might show only one of his suits and jump to 4 Spades.

Had South held precisely the same hand in high cards:

♠ A K Q x x   ♡ K x x   ◇ x x x   ♣ J x

he would have passed 4 Spades quickly because he would have realized that his King of Hearts opposite his partner's singleton or void was practically a useless card.

In the next case you are South and hold:

♠ J x   ♡ J x x x   ◇ K x   ♣ A K J x x

The bidding has proceeded:

SOUTH	NORTH
1 ♣	1 ◇
2 ♣	3 ♠
3 N 'T	5 ♣
?	

What do you do?

Despite the minimum you should bid 6 Clubs, because you have the right King. Had it been the King of Hearts you would not do so. Your partner is marked with, at most, a singleton Heart. He has shown five Diamonds, four Spades, and at least three Clubs. This is his hand:

♠ A Q x x   ♡ x   ◇ A Q J x x   ♣ Q 10 x

This is just one of those hands in which the important consideration is not the number of Aces and Kings, but the extent of the fit, the possession of a singleton, or of the holding of specific cards. One King might serve the purpose while another King might not. Or the possession of one Ace rather than another may decide.

FINDING THE SINGLETON

A sudden leap beyond game, when nothing has previously been said about a suit the opponents have bid, should be taken as a request to partner to bid a slam if he has no more than one loser in the adverse suit. An illustration from a tournament:

NORTH

♠ K Q x x x
♡ 10 x
◇ x
♣ K Q 10 x x

SOUTH

♠ A J 10 9 x
♡ A K J x x
◇ x x
♣ A

The bidding is:

SOUTH	WEST	NORTH	EAST
1 ♠	2 ♢	3 ♣	Pass
3 ♡	Pass	4 ♠	Pass
5 ♣	Pass	6 ♠	

The bidding follows routine lines up to South's 5 Club bid. This must not be construed as any desire to play Clubs, since Spades have been so vigorously supported. The bid therefore denotes possession of the Ace of Clubs and implies a desire for partner to bid a slam if he can take care of the adverse Diamonds. Had North's hand contained one Heart and two Diamonds he would have been obliged to return to 5 Spades; no slam could be made. The key to the slam was the singleton Diamond.

At one table where this hand was played North responded with 4 Spades over West's 2 Diamond bid, a call, incidentally, which I cannot endorse. South in turn made a very good bid. He bid 5 Spades. An overcall of game under these circumstances he felt would be understood by partner to ask what his holding was in Diamonds, the adverse suit. North so read it and, holding a singleton Diamond, elected to bid 6 Spades. The bidding had become too crowded for South to show his Aces. If he had elected to bid 5 Hearts over 4 Spades North could have done no better than to bid 5 Spades and the question of the singleton Diamond could never have been answered.

Another illustration of this principle:

NORTH

♠ x x x
♡ Q J x
♢ A K x x
♣ A K x

SOUTH

♠ x
♡ A K 10 9 x
♢ x x
♣ Q 10 x x x

The bidding:

	North		South
1	◇	1	♡
2	♡	3	♣
4	♣	4	♡
5	♡	6	♡

North's raise to 2 Hearts was a slight underbid but no satisfactory call was available at that point. South realized that if his partner had high Clubs there might be a chance for a slam so he tested for one round by bidding 3 Clubs. North, having previously underbid, was delighted at the opportunity to show the high Clubs, which he was quite sure partner was fishing for, and South, of course, could do no more than return to 4 Hearts. At this point it was clear to North that Hearts, Diamonds and Clubs were in good shape. The only question was Spades. North therefore bid 5 Hearts, overbidding a game, and saying, in effect: "Partner, we have talked about everything but Spades. What is your condition in that respect? If you have only one loser in that suit I believe we can make a slam. If you have two losers you will naturally quit at five." South, holding a singleton Spade, properly bid 6 Hearts. Had South held two Spades he would have passed.

It is equally important to know when there is no singleton in the crucial spot:

Opener	Responder
♠ A K J 10 x x	♠ Q x
♡ Q x	♡ J x
◇ A Q x x	◇ K 10 x x x x
♣ x	♣ A Q 10

The bidding:

	Opener		Responder
1	♠	2	◇
3	♠	4	♣
4	◇	4	♠
5	♠	Pass	

When the opener jumped to 3 Spades, his partner had good reason to be slam minded—his own hand was about equal to an opening bid, opposite an opening bid and a jump. The Spade suit is now accepted as trump by inference, and the responder's bid of 4 Clubs must be construed as an Ace-showing bid. This, incidentally, is the proper procedure even if you are playing any of the 4 No Trump conventions. There should be no hurry about the 4 No Trump asking bid. Opener's showing of the Diamond support at this point is natural and responder can do no better than show his Spade support in response. It is the opener's bid of 5 Spades that is the subject of our attention. What is its meaning?

Logically, it means this: "Partner, we have talked about everything else and the only thing that worries me is the Heart situation. How are you fixed in that department? If you have only one Heart loser I think we can make a slam." Responder must stop despite the strong bidding of his partner. With a singleton in Hearts he would, of course, have proceeded to a slam. Similarly, with a singleton Heart opener would have bid six himself.

THE RIGHT SINGLETON—THE RIGHT ACE

NORTH

♠ x x
♡ Q
◇ A Q x x
♣ A K J 10 x x

SOUTH

♠ A x x
♡ x x x
◇ K J 10 x x
♣ Q x

The bidding:

NORTH	EAST	SOUTH	WEST
1 ♣	Pass	1 ◇	1 ♠
3 ◇	Pass	3 ♠	Pass
6 ◇	Pass	Pass	Pass

South's cue-bid may appear to be a little on the aggressive side, but I think fully justified. When one regards the Queen of Clubs as an almost certain winner, in view of partner's bidding, the hand closely approximates an opening bid in strength. With a splendid fit already established a slam is by no means a fanciful notion. Furthermore, if North manifests no interest in a slam, the knowledge that South has the Ace of Spades may induce him to bid game at No Trump and that may be the best contract.

When North learns of South's possession of the Ace of Spades, he is able to bid a slam in Diamonds, trusting that the Club suit can be established for discards. Note that South had the right Ace. Had it been the Ace of Hearts, the partnership would have been subject to the immediate loss of two Spade tricks. Note also that North had the right singleton. A short Spade holding would not have served the purpose. You see, a comptometer cannot do all those things.

SLAM TRY BELOW GAME

It would appear to be good hard business reasoning that it. is better, when convenient, to try for a slam below the game level. You will have explored slam possibilities and are in a position to quit if necessary without jeopardizing the game itself.

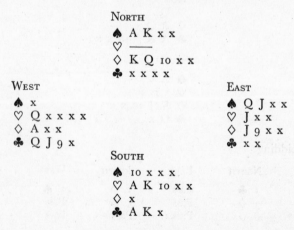

NORTH
♠ A K x x
♡ —
♢ K Q 10 x x
♣ x x x x

WEST
♠ x
♡ Q x x x x
♢ A x x
♣ Q J 9 x

EAST
♠ Q J x x
♡ J x x
♢ J 9 x x
♣ x x

SOUTH
♠ 10 x x x
♡ A K 10 x x
♢ x
♣ A K x

The bidding is given as it actually took place:

NORTH	EAST	SOUTH	WEST
1 ◇	Pass	1 ♡	Pass
1 ♠	Pass	3 ♠	Pass
4 ♠	Pass	5 ♣	Pass
5 ♠	Pass	Pass	Pass

Down one!

There is nothing in all of bridge that makes one feel more like a "sucker" than to be set a trick at an unnecessary bid of five in a major suit. Here the risk was incurred with no reward for the added hazard. South should have planned his bidding tactics so that he could try for a slam below the game level. South's second bid of 3 Spades is indefensible. Such a bid announces a willingness to contract for game but does not suggest a slam. Once the Spade bid is heard South should visualize a slam and should at this point make a definite slam signal, that is, *a jump in a new suit*. His call should be 3 Clubs. North, a little nervous about his partner's Heart response, and having already described the values of his hand, may be reluctant to raise the Clubs and may step lightly by bidding 3 Diamonds. South is now at liberty to jump to 4 Spades, if he chooses, for his second slam try. By this time North will know very well that South has an enormous hand and is interested in big things, but North is still able to check out at a safe level by passing.

BLASTING

In many circles there is a lasting stigma attached to bidding a slam and being set one. This induces a tendency towards over-cautiousness which deprives these players not only of the increased revenue that is the reward of the daring, but, what is probably more important, the thrill of bringing in a big one. The bridge player, unlike the fisherman, derives no pleasure in telling about the one that got away.

The science of slam bidding is very fascinating. There are many ways in which ingenuity can be exercised in the effort to learn this, that and the other thing about your partner's hand. There are other features that can be ascertained in a purely mechanical manner, such as by the showing of Aces (either wholesale or retail).

Occasionally a hand comes up in which no amount of science can help you to determine definitely that a slam can be made. Success may depend upon your partner's holding a doubleton of some suit or an odd Jack. In those cases blasting, or taking the bull by the horns, may be the best bet.

Occasionally unscientific treatment of the hand is apt to produce the best results. This is particularly true when everything depends on the luck of the opening lead. If the opposition is not given too many suggestions during the auction there is at least an even chance that the opening lead will be favorable, as witness the following hand:

NORTH

♠ —
♡ A Q J x x x
◇ K J x x x
♣ 10 x

WEST

♠ J x x
♡ x x
◇ Q x x x
♣ A x x x

EAST

♠ K 10 9 x
♡ x
◇ 10 9 x
♣ K J x x x

SOUTH

♠ A Q x x x x
♡ K 10 x x
◇ A
♣ Q x

The bidding:

NORTH	EAST	SOUTH	WEST
1 ♡	Pass	1 ♠	Pass
2 ♡	Pass	6 ♡	

South knew that it might depend on the opening lead, which would be either Diamonds or Clubs. Of course, partner might

have the Ace of Clubs, in which case South would certainly wish
to be in a small slam, although not necessarily in a grand slam.
North might have the King of Clubs, which would make the
chance of fulfillment very bright. Finally, East might not lead a
Club. In the actual case East elected to lead the ten of Diamonds
and the contract was brought home without any difficulty. A
Club lead, of course, would have defeated the contract, but there
are many players who would not have led a Club with East's
hand.

Another illustration of the same principle:

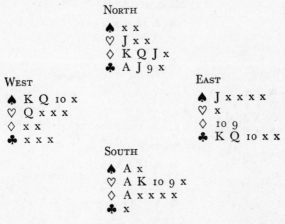

NORTH
♠ x x
♡ J x x
◇ K Q J x
♣ A J 9 x

WEST
♠ K Q 10 x
♡ Q x x x
◇ x x
♣ x x x

EAST
♠ J x x x x
♡ x
◇ 10 9
♣ K Q 10 x x

SOUTH
♠ A x
♡ A K 10 9 x
◇ A x x x x
♣ x

The bidding:

SOUTH	WEST	NORTH	EAST
1 ♡	Pass	2 ◇	Pass
6 ◇			

I will quote the player who sent this hand to me: "I wasn't
sure we could make six, and I wasn't sure that we couldn't make
seven, but I was quite sure that I was not going to help the
defense and was willing to take my chances on a slam, so I bid
6 Diamonds.

"East opened the King of Clubs and the contract was fulfilled
by drawing trumps and establishing Hearts for the Spade discard.

I had decided against a fake jump in Spades for two reasons. First, partner might not catch on in time and get me overboard. Secondly, it would afford West an opportunity to double the Spade bid if from his holding he could suspect horse thievery, and this would suggest the lead of that suit to his partner."

POSITIONAL SLAMS

A slam can frequently be made when played from one side of the table but not when played from the other. Let us examine a case or two.

NORTH
♠ A 10 9 x x
♡ A 10 x x
◇ x x
♣ J x

WEST
♠ J x
♡ J x x x
◇ A Q x x
♣ x x x

EAST
♠ x x
♡ K x x x
◇ J 10 9 x x
♣ x x

SOUTH
♠ K Q x x
♡ Q
◇ K x
♣ A K Q 10 x x

South opened with 1 Club and when North responded with 1 Spade he leaped to four, lest North might not be able to carry on. North, having two Aces, and knowing that his partner could not be relying on more than one trick, properly tried for a slam by bidding 5 Hearts. South now elected to bid 6 Clubs, which North should have passed. North actually went to 6 Spades which was defeated with a Diamond opening.

South had used good judgment. When it was merely a question of game in his mind he went to 4 Spades, but when it turned into a slam hand he realized that it was important for him to be declarer, so that the King of Diamonds could not be attacked on the opening lead. If North happened to have five Spades he could obtain a discard of a Diamond. North should have realized that South had a definite purpose in bidding 6 Clubs rather than 6 Spades, and North's own weakness in Diamonds should have told him what the purpose was. South might have bid (and made) 6 No Trump, but he trusted his partner's choice of a contract.

When a player holds K x of a suit he should try to be declarer himself. When he holds two worthless cards of any unmentioned suit he should try to permit partner to play the hand in case his partner happens to have the King or a tenace position. For example:

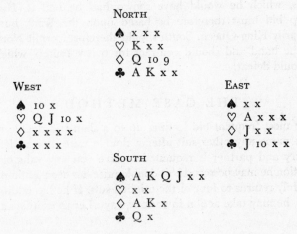

NORTH
♠ x x x
♡ K x x
◇ Q 10 9
♣ A K x x

WEST
♠ 10 x
♡ Q J 10 x
◇ x x x x
♣ x x x

EAST
♠ x x
♡ A x x x
◇ J x x
♣ J 10 x x

SOUTH
♠ A K Q J x x
♡ x x
◇ A K x
♣ Q x

When I saw this hand played the bidding was:

SOUTH	NORTH
1 ♠	2 ♣
4 N T (Blackwood)	5 ◇
5 ♠	Pass

The contract was fulfilled where the bidding stopped at five. In some cases South went on to six, which was defeated by a Heart opening. South's use of Blackwood indicated bad judgment. Even if North had held two Aces South would have had no way of telling whether or not the slam could be made.

The bidding of this hand should follow natural lines. South opens with 1 Spade. Let us assume that North responds with 2 Clubs. South should jump to 4 Spades, having the ability to take more than eight tricks in his own hand.

North will reason: I have virtually the equal of an opening bid. My partner has opened the bidding and jumped. There is a very probable slam. In view of my possession of the King of Hearts, in which suit partner may have nothing of value, I should try to be declarer. I will do so by making a natural bid of 4 No Trump.

South should now realize that his partner lacks the Ace of Hearts, which he would have shown had he had it. His No Trump bid must therefore be based upon the King, but not necessarily King-Queen. South should therefore permit North to play the hand and should contract for 6 No Trump, which no lead could defeat.

THE CASE METHOD

The most frequent bid leading up to a slam is a double raise. If you name any other suit after a double raise, it is a definite slam try and partner is requested to give you any valuable information he may possess. If his double raise has been a minimum, he merely returns to four of the original suit. If he has additional values, he may take action in various ways. Let us examine a few cases.

1.   ♠ A K x x x   ♡ x   ◇ K x x x   ♣ A x x

You open with 1 Spade. Partner raises to three. You have one trick in excess of your opening bid and satisfactory distribution, including a singleton. There should be a mild suspicion of a slam. The proper procedure is to bid 4 Clubs. This is forcing for one round, since Spades have been agreed upon. If partner merely returns to 4 Spades you relax in the knowledge that you have done your duty. If he shows one of the other Aces you can still do no more than return to 4 Spades, but you will be in a position to accept a further invitation should it be extended by partner.

2. ♠ A K x x x ♡ A x x ◇ x x ♣ A x x

You open with 1 Spade. Partner raises to three. You have 1½ honor tricks in excess of your opening bid, which makes a slam very probable despite the fact that your distribution is not attractive. The proper procedure is to bid 4 Clubs. This affords partner the opportunity to bid 4 Diamonds, which in turn will allow you to bid 4 Hearts, showing both your Aces below the game level. It is for this reason that it would be poor tactics over the 3 Spade bid for you to show the Ace of Hearts first. Partner could not then show the Diamond Ace without going above game, which he might fear to do.

3. ♠ K Q 10 x ♡ K x x x ◇ A x ♣ x x x

Your partner opens with 1 Diamond. You respond with 1 Spade. Opener now jumps to 3 Spades. What is your diagnosis? You should suspect a slam. Your hand is almost equal to an opening bid. Your partner has opened the bidding and jumped. You should make one mild try by bidding 4 Diamonds. This merely indicates possession of the Ace, not a desire to play at Diamonds (since Spades have been agreed upon). You should leave the rest to your partner. If he does not go on toward a slam, at least you have done your duty.

4. ♠ A Q J x x ♡ A x x ◇ x x x ♣ x x

Partner opens with 1 Club. You respond with 1 Spade, which he raises to three. What is your diagnosis? Since you have the ingredients of an opening bid and partner has opened the bidding and jumped, there is a good chance for a slam even though your distribution is not very attractive. You should suggest a slam by bidding 4 Hearts. Since Spades have been definitely agreed upon the 4 Heart bid designates the Ace and an interest in a slam, and cannot be construed as showing a suit.

5. ♠ 10 x x ♡ A K x x x ◇ K Q x ♣ x x

Partner opens with 1 Spade. You respond with 2 Hearts and partner jumps to 3 Spades. You should diagnose a probable slam.

You have the equivalent of a substantial opening Heart bid. Your partner has opened the bidding and jumped. You are satisfied with his trump suit. Since you have no Ace to show you should tell your partner that you are interested in a slam, in the only way available to you, and that is by overbidding a game in Spades. The proper procedure is to bid 5 Spades. Do not make the mistake of bidding only 4 Spades, which you would have done in this sequence without the King and Queen of Diamonds.

6.　♠ x x　　♡ A K x x x　　◇ K Q x　　♣ x x x

Your partner opens with 1 Spade. You bid 2 Hearts. Partner raises to 4 Hearts. Here again you should suspect a slam. You have an opening bid while partner has opened the bidding and jumped. You have no Ace to show and should indicate your desire for a slam in the only way open to you, by bidding 5 Hearts.

7.　♠ A K J x x　　♡ J x　　◇ x x x　　♣ K Q x

Your partner opens with 1 Heart. You respond with 1 Spade. Partner jumps to 2 No Trump. You have a good substantial opening bid. Partner has opened the bidding and jumped. You should have a splendid play for a slam and ought to bid 6 No Trump yourself. There is no advantage in playing this hand in Spades. Your Spades will take tricks at No Trump.

8.　♠ x x　　♡ A K x x x　　◇ A J 10　　♣ x x x

Your partner opens with 1 Spade. You respond with 2 Hearts. Partner raises to 3 Hearts. There is some chance for a slam. You have slightly better than an opening bid. Your partner has an opening bid plus one trick (as shown by the fact that he raised you to three). The partnership therefore possesses two opening bids and more than one trick. You should suggest slam possibilities by bidding 4 Diamonds.

9.　♠ x　　♡ K Q x x x　　◇ K x x x　　♣ K x x

Partner opens with 1 Club. You respond with 1 Heart, which partner jumps to three. Should you suspect a slam? Yes. You may regard the King of Clubs as a sure winner, in view of partner's opening in that suit, so you have the equal of an opening bid, while your partner has opened the bidding and jumped. You have no Ace with which to suggest a slam but you may do so by bidding 4 Clubs. Partner probably has the Ace of his suit, so in this case he will realize that you are showing the King. If his next bid is 4 Diamonds you should gamble it out for a slam because of the singleton Spade. As far as your partner is concerned you might have had two small Spades. His complete hand was:

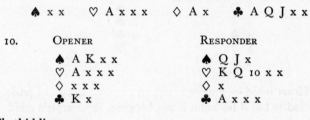

♠ x x　♡ A x x x　◇ A x　♣ A Q J x x

10.

OPENER	RESPONDER
♠ A K x x	♠ Q J x
♡ A x x x	♡ K Q 10 x x
◇ x x x	◇ x
♣ K x	♣ A x x x

The bidding:

OPENER	RESPONDER
1 ♠	2 ♡
3 ♡	4 ♣
5 ♡ or 5 ♣	6 ♡

When opener raises to 3 Hearts responder should realize there are slam possibilities because he has the equivalent of an opening bid himself. Partner, for his raise to three, should have an opening bid plus one trick. Responder can investigate below the game level by bidding 4 Clubs, showing the Ace of that suit. The opener has a choice. He may bid 5 Clubs to show the King directly, or he may jump to 5 Hearts, as if to say, "Partner, we have talked about everything else but Diamonds. What is your situation there?" In view of the Diamond singleton the responder can comfortably bid 6 Hearts. The responder may have had an even stronger hand, containing the Queen of Clubs, but with two small Diamonds in his hand the slam would not have been successful. By the same token, the opener might have had a better hand including the King and Queen of Diamonds but not the King of Clubs and the slam would not have been successful.

11. | OPENER | RESPONDER |
|--------|-----------|
| ♠ K Q x | ♠ A 10 9 x x x |
| ♡ A Q J x x x | ♡ K x |
| ◇ A x | ◇ x x x |
| ♣ x x | ♣ A x |

The bidding:

OPENER	RESPONDER
1 ♡	1 ♠
3 ♡	3 ♠
4 ♠	5 ♣
5 ◇	5 ♡
7 N T	

The 3 Heart rebid by opener is not an absolute force but partner is expected to bid if his hand is not hopeless. Responder's rebid of 3 Spades is just marking time. West raises to 4 Spades, showing that his previous jump was influenced by Spade support. Responder now shows the Ace of Clubs, whereupon opener shows the Ace of Diamonds. At this point responder, by his bid of 5 Hearts, is attempting to indicate the King of that suit, Spades having already been agreed upon. The opener is now able to count thirteen tricks, relying on six Hearts, five Spades (as far as he knows) and the two Aces.

12. | OPENER | RESPONDER |
|--------|-----------|
| ♠ x | ♠ A x x |
| ♡ A x x x | ♡ K Q x x x |
| ◇ K Q J x x | ◇ x x |
| ♣ K x x | ♣ A x x |

The bidding:

OPENER	RESPONDER
1 ◇	1 ♡
2 ♡	2 ♠
3 ♡	4 ♣
5 ♣	6 ♡

When opener raises responder's Heart bid to two, responder
realizes there is a good chance for a slam because he has more
than an opening bid and partner has an opening bid and a raise.
He therefore starts investigating by bidding 2 Spades. This is a
one-round force, Hearts having so far been agreed upon. Opener
should now have jumped to 4 Hearts; his return to 3 Hearts,
which is a sign-off, was an underbid. Responder nevertheless
makes a further slam try by showing the Ace of Clubs, still below
the game level. At this point the opener, realizing the importance
of the singleton Spade and the King of Clubs, both of which
provide second-round control of the black suits, redeems himself
by showing this feature. His bid of 5 Clubs accepts the slam try,
whereupon the responder contracts for slam.

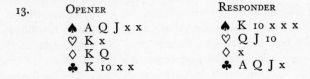

13.

	OPENER	RESPONDER
♠	A Q J x x	K 10 x x x
♡	K x	Q J 10
◇	K Q	x
♣	K 10 x x	A Q J x

The bidding:

OPENER	RESPONDER
1 ♠	3 ♠
5 ♠	?

In actual play responder accepted the invitation and contracted
for a slam in Spades because he had a very good 3 Spade bid.
Naturally, two Aces were lost and the slam defeated. The question arose as to the place of the guilt. In this hand the Blackwood
Convention, to be sure, would have kept the partnership from
error, but still the pitfall should have been avoided. Responder
contended that opener should have been satisfied merely to contract for game and should not have invited the slam. The opener
argued that he had a full trick over and above his bid and was
justified in issuing one invitation. With this I concur. Responder
should have realized that the opponents had both the red Aces,

else South would have bid 4 Diamonds or 4 Hearts as a slam try. South's 5 Spade bid was very clear. It said, "Partner, I have a fine hand but I have no Aces to show you, other than in trumps."

The moral: If partner has a reasonable opportunity to show an Ace and fails to do so, you are to assume that he does not have it.

THE BLACKWOOD CONVENTION

This is perhaps the most widely used of all the slam conventions, and, I venture to say, the most subject to abuse. On the surface it appears to be a very simple device. In actual practice, however, the exercise of very fine judgment is required to attain the ultimate in results by its use.

This convention should not be employed as a substitute for thinking. The conduct of certain bridge players gives one the impression that they have a desire to insert a nickel in the Blackwood Juke Box and expect a slam to come bursting forth.

The original sin is in the assumption that the Blackwood Convention may be employed in all slams. Nothing can be farther from the truth. Permit me to quote from the writings of the author himself, Easley Blackwood:

"We do not pretend that the Blackwood Convention will solve all your slam problems because there are certain types of hands that cannot be covered by Blackwood."

"In some deals both the Blackwood Convention and cue-bidding are impossible because an exchange of information between the partnership is either unnecessary or unobtainable. When that happens a player must use his own initiative and jump directly into a slam."

"The Blackwood Convention is so easy and simple that it can be learned in less than five minutes and for that reason it is subject to abuse, and players are warned against trying it too often."

"During the preliminary rounds a player must make certain that Blackwood will produce better results than either cue-bidding or a direct try for slam."

When the preliminary rounds of bidding have indicated that a slam is probable, and a suit has been agreed upon, either player may institute the convention by calling 4 No Trump. No special holding is required, but the player making the 4 No Trump bid must be quite convinced that the hand will play safely for eleven tricks.

The responses are as follows:

> With no Aces bid 5 Clubs
> With one Ace bid 5 Diamonds
> With two Aces bid 5 Hearts
> With three Aces bid 5 Spades
> With four Aces bid 5 No Trump

After Aces have been shown the 4 No Trump bidder may ask for Kings by bidding 5 No Trump. However, there is the very distinct proviso that the 5 No Trump bid must never be made unless it has been previously determined that the partnership is in possession of all four Aces.

In other words, the opener late in the bidding calls 4 No Trump. Responder bids 5 Diamonds, showing one Ace. The opener now bids 5 No Trump, asking for Kings. Responder knows that the opener has three Aces. Otherwise he could not tell that the partnership has all four Aces and would not be privileged to call for Kings.

The responder to the 5 No Trump bid shows the number of his Kings exactly as he shows the number of his Aces in response to 4 No Trump.

Not every 4 No Trump bid is part of the convention. A suit must have been mentioned on the way up. If an opening No Trump bid is raised to 4 No Trump, that is simply an assist and is not part of the convention.

The player who makes the conventional 4 No Trump bid must be careful to plan so that any response by partner will not embarrass him. Such might be the case when the agreed suit, for example, is Clubs. The 4 No Trump bidder must in that case have at least 2 Aces, because otherwise the partnership will be in a slam after a 5 Diamond response, and the opposition will hold two Aces.

It is essential to determine whether or not information as to how many Aces partner has will solve your problem. After all, many a hand with all the Aces has no chance to produce a slam. A singleton or even a doubleton in partner's hand may be the decisive factor.

Another important consideration is which of the two players should start the convention. As a general rule the stronger of the two hands should be given the opportunity to do so, because he can better judge what the hands will produce. For example:

NORTH

♠ A x x
♡ K x x
◇ A x x x
♣ A J x

SOUTH

♠ K Q J x x
♡ A Q x
◇ K Q J
♣ K x

After Spades have been agreed upon, which of these two players should start the 4 No Trump bid? If North does it, he will find out that the partnership has all the Aces and Kings but he will be worried about a losing Diamond and possibly a losing Heart. If, however, South is the one who starts the convention he will be able to bid 7 No Trump immediately he learns that partner has three Aces and one King.

When it may be desirable for partner to start the 4 No Trump bid the bidding may be steered in that direction by making temporary bids of various types to afford him the opportunity, when the four level is reached, to ask for Aces.

Assuming that the bidding has proceeded in a very aggressive manner and that a slam becomes probable, is it desirable for you or your partner to initiate the 4 No Trump bid with these hands?

1.   ♠ A x x x   ♡ x x x   ◇ A 10 x   ♣ A K x

With this hand you should permit partner to bid the 4 No Trump, because you can give specific information about your hand which will help partner decide. If you bid the 4 No Trump and find out that your partner has one Ace and three Kings, you will still be worried about small card losers.

2. ♠ A Q J x x   ♡ A Q x x   ◇ x x   ♣ A x

With this hand you may properly initiate the Blackwood Convention, because specific information about Aces and Kings will permit you to judge the possibilities of the hand.

3. ♠ Q J x x   ♡ A 9 x x x   ◇ x x x   ♣ A

With this hand it is much better for your partner to start the convention, because information about Aces and Kings will not solve your problem.

It is an integral part of the Blackwood Convention that the 4 No Trump bidder is the captain of the team. When he hears the response he, and he alone, decides on the final contract, and the responder must abide by his decision.

There is one exception: When the bidding has shown that the partnership has all four Aces, the responder may exercise his own judgment as to the final contract. Occasionally the responder, instead of telling how many Aces he has, may bid a slam directly when his hand contains a void. This might be done in a case where, let us say, Diamonds are the agreed suit, and partner has asked for Aces. The Blackwood response would be 5 Diamonds, showing one Ace, but the responder has a void in an unmentioned suit and fears that the Blackwood bidder will be discouraged and pass the 5 Diamond bid. He may exercise his discretion by bidding a slam directly over the 4 No Trump bid. For example:

♠ A K x x x   ♡ Q x x   ◇ Q J 10 x x   ♣ ——

Your partner has opened with 1 Heart, has vigorously supported your Diamonds, and then bids 4 No Trump (Blackwood). Your conventional response would be 5 Diamonds, showing one Ace. This may discourage partner from bidding a slam, so you may take control of the situation and bid 6 Diamonds instead of telling about your Ace.

There is an important amendment to the Blackwood Convention. When cue-bids have been made on preliminary rounds to show Aces or voids, and subsequently the Blackwood 4 No Trump is called, any Ace that has previously been cue-bid or any Ace in a suit that partner has cued must not be shown. For example, you hold:

♠ K Q J   ♡ 10 9 x x x   ◇ A x x x   ♣ x

Your partner has opened with 1 Heart, which you have jumped to three. Your partner now bids 4 Clubs, an obvious cue-bid. You bid 4 Diamonds, showing the Ace. Partner now bursts forth into Blackwood. Your normal response would be 5 Diamonds, showing one Ace, but since you have previously made a cue-bid indicating this Ace it does not count and you are obliged to respond with 5 Clubs, showing no Ace other than Diamonds. If instead of the King of Spades you held the Ace, your proper response would be 5 Diamonds, showing one Ace other than the one which you cued.

BLACKWOOD RESPONSE AFTER INTERFERENCE BID

Occasionally, after a 4 No Trump bid, an adversary will insert an overcall in order to interfere with the normal response. If you do not choose to double for a penalty the Aces are indicated as follows:

The responder starts to count Aces from the suit in which the overcall has been made. For example: After the Blackwood 4 No Trump bid an opponent bids 5 Diamonds. You have two Aces which you wish to show, so you start counting at 5 Diamonds; a pass would show no Aces, 5 Hearts would show one Ace, 5 Spades would show two Aces, 5 No Trump would show three Aces and 6 Clubs would show all four.

There is one other exception which permits the responder to set the final contract. When the 4 No Trump bidder mentions an unbid suit at the five level after partner's response, the responder is forced to call 5 No Trump, which becomes the contract. This is done in cases where it is learned that the adversaries have two Aces but that No Trump will be the best contract.

SLAM QUIZ

(ANSWERS BEGIN ON PAGE 172)

In each of the following cases the previous bidding is indicated. You are South. What is your present bid?

1. ♠ A J 10 9 x x
   ♡ J 10 x
   ◊ J x
   ♣ A x

NORTH	EAST	SOUTH	WEST
1 ◊	Pass	1 ♠	Pass
2 N T	Pass	?	

2. ♠ A J x x x
   ♡ A K J x
   ◊ Q x
   ♣ J x

NORTH	EAST	SOUTH	WEST
1 N T	Pass	3 ♠	Pass
3 N T	Pass	?	

3. ♠ x
   ♡ K Q J x x x
   ◊ K J x
   ♣ A Q x

SOUTH	WEST	NORTH	EAST
1 ♡	Pass	3 ♡	Pass
?			

4. ♠ x
   ♡ A K x x x x
   ◊ K x
   ♣ A J x x

SOUTH	WEST	NORTH	EAST
1 ♡	Pass	3 ♡	Pass
4 ♣	Pass	4 ◊	Pass
?			

5. ♠ A K J x x
   ♡ A K Q x x
   ◊ —
   ♣ K Q J

SOUTH	WEST	NORTH	EAST
2 ♠	Pass	3 ♠	Pass
?			

6. ♠ A 10 9 x
   ♡ K 10 9
   ◊ Q J x x
   ♣ K x

NORTH	EAST	SOUTH	WEST
1 ♡	Pass	1 ♠	Pass
3 ♡	Pass	?	

7. ♠ 10 9 x x x
   ♡ J
   ◊ A x x
   ♣ A K 10 x

NORTH	EAST	SOUTH	WEST
1 ◊	Pass	1 ♠	Pass
3 ♠	Pass	?	

8. ♠ K 9 x x x
   ♡ A x x
   ◊ J x
   ♣ A x x

NORTH	EAST	SOUTH	WEST
1 ◊	Pass	1 ♠	Pass
3 ♠	Pass	?	

9. ♠ x x x
   ♡ A J x x
   ◇ J 10
   ♣ A Q 10 x

NORTH	EAST	SOUTH	WEST
1 ◇	Pass	1 ♡	Pass
3 N T	Pass	?	

10. ♠ x x
    ♡ K x x x x
    ◇ A x
    ♣ Q 10 x x

NORTH	EAST	SOUTH	WEST
2 N T	Pass	?	

11. ♠ A Q x x x
    ♡ K
    ◇ K Q x x x
    ♣ Q x

SOUTH	WEST	NORTH	EAST
1 ♠	Pass	3 ♡	Pass
4 ◇	Pass	4 ♡	Pass
?			

12. ♠ x x
    ♡ K Q x x x
    ◇ A J 10 9 x
    ♣ J

SOUTH	WEST	NORTH	EAST
1 ♡	Pass	3 ♡	Pass
?			

13. ♠ K 9
    ♡ A K Q x x
    ◇ J 9 x x
    ♣ x x

NORTH	EAST	SOUTH	WEST
2 ♠	Pass	3 ♡	Pass
3 ♠	Pass	?	

14. ♠ K x
    ♡ 9 x x x x
    ◇ Q x
    ♣ x x x x

NORTH	EAST	SOUTH	WEST
2 ◇	Pass	2 N T	Pass
3 ♡	Pass	?	

15. ♠ x x
    ♡ A J x x
    ◇ K Q x x x
    ♣ Q x

NORTH	EAST	SOUTH	WEST
2 ♠	Pass	3 ◇	Pass
3 ♠	Pass	4 ♡	Pass
4 ♠	Pass	?	

16. ♠ x x x
    ♡ K J x
    ◇ Q J
    ♣ x x x x x

EAST	SOUTH	WEST	NORTH
Pass	Pass	1 ♠	2 ♠
Pass	3 ♣	Pass	5 ♣
Pass	?		

17. ♠ A x
    ♡ x x
    ◇ K Q 10 x x x
    ♣ x x x

NORTH	EAST	SOUTH	WEST
1 ♠	Pass	2 ◇	Pass
2 ♡	Pass	3 ◇	Pass
5 ◇	Pass	?	

18. ♠ x x x
    ♡ A J 10
    ◇ Q x
    ♣ A 9 x x x

NORTH	EAST	SOUTH	WEST
1 ◇	Pass	2 ♣	Pass
5 ♣	Pass	?	

19. ♠ A Q J x x
    ♡ K
    ◇ K x x x
    ♣ K x x

NORTH	EAST	SOUTH	WEST
1 ♡	Pass	1 ♠	Pass
4 ♡	Pass	?	

20. ♠ A Q 9
    ♡ A K x x
    ◇ A K x x
    ♣ K x

SOUTH	WEST	NORTH	EAST
1 ♡	Pass	4 ♡	Pass
?			

21. ♠ A x x x x
    ♡ A 10 x
    ◇ K x x
    ♣ J x

NORTH	EAST	SOUTH	WEST
4 ♠	Pass	?	

22. ♠ A 9 x x
    ♡ K 10
    ◇ A K J x
    ♣ A K x

SOUTH	WEST	NORTH	EAST
1 ◇	Pass	1 ♠	Pass
?			

23. ♠ A x x
    ♡ A K 9 x
    ◇ K x
    ♣ A 10 x x

SOUTH	WEST	NORTH	EAST
1 ♣	Pass	1 ◇	Pass
1 ♡	Pass	4 ♡	Pass
4 ♠	Pass	5 ♣	Pass
?			

24. ♠ J
    ♡ K Q x x
    ◇ x x x
    ♣ A Q x x x

NORTH	EAST	SOUTH	WEST
1 ♡	Pass	2 ♣	Pass
3 ◇	Pass	?	

25.	♠ A K Q J x x x			26.	♠ A x
	♡ —				♡ A K Q J x
	◊ A Q 10 x				◊ A x x
	♣ x x				♣ K Q J

NORTH	EAST	SOUTH	WEST	SOUTH	WEST	NORTH	EAST
1 ♡	Pass	?		2 ♡	Pass	3 ♡	Pass
				?			

SLAM QUIZ—ANSWERS

1. 5 Spades, or with a conservative partner 6 Spades. You have the equivalent of an opening bid and partner has opened the bidding and jumped. Your hand has the further desirable feature of containing two controls.

2. 6 No Trump. An addition of partnership assets will indicate that you hold about 8 honor tricks, which, with a five-card suit, should produce a slam. Since partner's rebid was a minimum you should not be inclined to try for seven. A bid of 4 Hearts at this point is not recommended because of the possibility that partner might pass. Fur-.nermore, since partner has an evenly balanced hand there probably would be no advantage to playing this hand at a suit. You have a point count of 16 plus a 5-card suit so that the partnership is guaranteed a minimum of 32 points in addition to your length of suit.

3. 4 Clubs. You should, of course, be very much interested in a slam. You have a full trick more than your opening bid in honor strength, and additional trumps and splendid distribution. If partner cooperates by showing the Ace of Diamonds or Spades you should be willing to contract for a slam.

4. 5 Diamonds. You have definitely determined to bid at least 6 Hearts, but there is a chance for a grand slam and this bid will indicate the King of Diamonds, inasmuch as partner has already shown the Ace. When you subsequently bid 6 Hearts partner may be able to go the whole way if he holds the Ace of Spades, and either a singleton Club or the King and one other. The Blackwood Convention at this point would not necessarily enable you to bid a grand slam with safety because even if you learn that partner has both Aces and the King of Clubs there is still the concern about a possible loser in Clubs. Should partner have three Clubs you should not choose to bid the grand slam in the hope of capturing the Queen.

5. 4 Hearts. You make a waiting bid at this point to afford partner an opportunity to show the Ace of Clubs, should he have it. If partner

shows the Ace of Diamonds you must be satisfied with six. If it is the Ace of Clubs you will naturally bid a grand slam. Incidentally, a bid of 4 Hearts at this point is absolutely forcing, since Spades have been agreed as the final contract.

6. 5 Hearts. You have approximately an opening bid and partner has opened and jumped. You should suggest slam possibilities to partner.

7. 6 Spades. You have an opening bid and partner has opened and jumped. Don't be frightened by the anaemic complexion of your trump suit. If you are off a trump trick partner will have everything else.

8. 6 Spades. You have approximately an opening bid. Partner has opened and jumped. That's all you have to know. With this type of hand you are not particularly interested in a grand slam, so I do not suggest taking time out to show your Aces.

9. There is a very strong likelihood of a slam. You have nearly an opening bid and partner has opened and made a powerful jump. You should bid 4 or 5 No Trump, depending upon the habits of your partner.

10. 3 Hearts. A temporary bid, made with the intention of inviting a slam on the next round. Partner has at least 5½ honor tricks and you have about two. Possession of 7½ honor tricks and a five-card suit makes a slam very probable. If partner rebids 3 No Trump you should raise to 4 No Trump. You have a point count of 9, which guarantees that the partnership has a minimum of 31 points.

11. 5 Hearts. It is not true that you have already shown all your values. The King of Hearts is a full trick added to your hand. Partner is slamming without that card, which he must be counting as a loser.

12. 4 Hearts. It would be completely pointless to show the Diamonds. Furthermore, a 4 Diamond bid in this sequence indicates a desire to search for slam. Any such wild impulse should be restrained.

13. 6 Spades. On simple arithmetic partner can take at least nine tricks. You can take at least three. Partner cannot have two losers in a minor suit, else he would not have a two-bid. Figure it out.

14. 5 Hearts. You have a very good hand under the circumstances. If you bid only 4 Hearts it would merely show a preference for Hearts as trumps.

15. 5 Spades. This is an almost certain slam. Partner has guaranteed to take at least nine tricks in his own hand. You will take at least two. You are therefore safe for eleven tricks.

16. 6 Clubs. Partner has been willing to gamble it out for eleven tricks though you might have nothing at all but four Clubs. Your red cards must fit with partner's values and your hand will produce two or three unexpected tricks.

17. 6 Diamonds. Partner has bid three suits, including a jump, which promises a singleton in the fourth suit. It is inconceivable that partner has less than two Aces on this bidding. Just try to figure out a hand on which he would bid that strongly with only one Ace!

18. 6 Clubs. You have considerably more than you might have had for your 2 Club bid. The Queen of Diamonds is a very probable winner and the fact that your hand contains two Aces renders it very suitable for a slam play.

19. 6 Hearts. You have an opening bid and partner has made an opening bid and a super-jump. The King is ample support for that type of suit. If you are a Blackwood player this is an acceptable spot for its use. You may gamble that the Hearts are solid. If you learn that partner has three Aces and the missing King you may chance a grand slam.

20. 6 Hearts. Partner has just what you need, plenty of trumps and distribution.

21. Pass. Partner cannot have more than 2½ honor tricks, so slam is out of the question.

22. 3 Clubs, absolutely forcing to game and suggesting slam possibilities. The alternative bid is 4 Spades. A jump to three would be improper, since partner might pass. The Blackwood 4 No Trump bid would be wrong because the hand is by no means safe for five. You could readily lose two Hearts and a Spade. With this hand it is not so much a question of Aces and Kings as it is of solidity.

23. 5 Diamonds. Hearts have been agreed upon and a small slam appears to be a cinch. If you show partner the King of Diamonds he may be able to go hunting for bigger game.

24. 6 Hearts. You have virtually an opening bid. Partner has opened and made a "super" jump. If there is seven in the hand he will be able to bid it.

25. 2 Spades. Despite the complete misfit in Hearts this hand possesses slam possibilities and your suit can stand on its own feet.

26. 4 Hearts. You have told your full story. You can win exactly nine tricks, of which you have already spoken. If partner can win three he will surely act over your 4 Heart bid.

CHAPTER 6

OVERCALLS

THE PROPER USE of the overcall may spell the difference between a winning and a losing player. Losses incurred by indiscriminate overcalling may at times be so staggering that a somewhat lengthy dissertation on this topic is in order.

An overcall is a competitive bid made when an opponent has opened the bidding. It must not be confused with a response made when partner opens the bidding and an opposing call is inserted, for example:

NORTH	EAST	SOUTH	WEST
1 ♠	2 ♣	2 ◇	

South's 2 Diamond bid is not regarded as an overcall. It is simply a free response and is discussed in the chapter on Responses. But in this sequence:

EAST	SOUTH	WEST	NORTH
1 ♠	2 ◇		

The 2 Diamond bid is an overcall.

Naturally, with a partner who has opened the bidding you are in a position to take a certain amount of liberty, but when an opponent opens the bidding and you may be all alone in the world, the exercise of greater care is indicated. The idea developed some years ago that if the bidding is opened adversely and you hold 1½ honor tricks and a biddable suit, you should make your presence felt by overcalling. That was in the days before people learned how to double.

Every overcall should serve some specific purpose. There are several considerations that might induce you to enter the bidding. One of the most important is to suggest a lead to your partner.

For example, you hold:

♠ K Q J x x   ♡ K x x   ◇ x x x   ♣ x x

Your right-hand opponent opens with 1 Club. The potentialities of the hand are as yet unknown, but it is not looking too far ahead to visualize a possible adverse 3 No Trump contract, or possibly a game contract in Hearts. As far as you are concerned the lead most ardently desired is a Spade, a suit which your partner could hardly be expected to select for his opening shot should it become his duty to lead. An overcall of 1 Spade is therefore in order, even though you have no real expectation of playing the hand or desire to go places. This suggests a danger in overcalling with Jack- or ten-high suits.

On some hands you may be able to outbid the opponents for a part score. You may hold a fairly good hand on which, for some reason or other, you do not choose to make a take-out double. For example:

♠ x   ♡ A K 10 9 x   ◇ A J 9 x x   ♣ J x

Your opponent bids 1 Spade. It is usually not good policy to double with two-suiters, because the bidding might become too involved before you have a chance to show both suits. Your best bet is to overcall with 2 Hearts. The next time it will probably be convenient to show the Diamonds and partner can exercise his choice without increasing the contract. With hands that are stronger or more flexible, strength-showing bids other than overcalls are made. They will be discussed some pages hence.

You have heard much about nuisance or bother bids. Many times the person most bothered by your bid is your patient partner. Remember this: Unless you are playing against someone who has been attacked by Dracula, you must not expect him to fold up and collapse into his shelter just because you overcall his 1 Club bid with 1 Diamond.

Overcalls can have a certain nuisance value. This is when they deprive the opponents of some bidding space. Suppose, for example, the bidding is opened with 1 Diamond and you overcall with 2 Clubs. You have deprived the opponent of the opportunity to respond at the level of one in either Hearts or Spades. This may prove embarrassing to him. If, however, the opening bid is 1 Spade and you overcall with 2 Clubs you have deprived the responder of nothing, because he would have had to bid at that level anyhow. In such cases a 2 Club overcall gives the enemy all the best of the bargain. They can either double you (even on suspicion, because a fulfilled 2 Club contract will not yield a game) or they can go on.

There is the further disadvantage of providing the declarer with clues that will be of assistance to him in the play of the hand. An overcall, far from being a nuisance to the opponents, will many times be of actual assistance in the bidding. Let us suppose that you are South and hold the following hand:

♠ Q J x   ♥ Q 10 x   ♦ x x   ♣ A Q x x x

The bidding has proceeded:

NORTH	EAST	SOUTH	WEST
1 ♠	2 ♦	?	

What should you do? Well, the first thing you should do if you have the slightest regard for the social amenities is to turn to East and say politely, "Thanks for the overcall," and follow it up with a bid of 2 Spades. In the absence of the overcall you would have been in some quandary about your response. The giving of a mere single raise would have been inadequate and yet a bid of 2 Clubs, followed by a subsequent Spade raise, would have been somewhat on the aggressive side. The overcall by East clarified your response because it made it clear that you had a hand on which you were willing to make a free raise.

If you have come to the conclusion that you have a sound purpose in overcalling you should then inquire into the risk. You must expect to be doubled every time you overcall and you must be prepared to find a very anaemic dummy. Figure out what the damages are going to be. If they come to more than 500 points you cannot afford the luxury of overcalling. This little guide takes care of such questions as vulnerability and the level of your bid.

In overcalling, the number of high cards held is of minor importance. When you go down 700 do not ever be heard to sing the song of the sucker, "But partner, I had 3½ honor tricks." The important consideration is the type of trump suit you have. I have said many times before, and I have had no reason to change my mind, that in order to overcall you should have a good trump suit or plenty of credit with the local bank. A good rule of thumb is *not to overcall at the level of two unless you can promise that you will not lose more than two trump tricks.*

Suits like these are treacherous:

> A Q 9 4 2
> K J 7 3 2

Such suits may produce very few tricks against an unfortunate trump break, whereas the following combinations, no richer in honor count, give you the comfort of logs on the fire:

> K Q J 9 7
> Q J 10 9 8

With trump suits like these there can be no feeling of impending disaster.

REOPENING THE BIDDING

When an opponent opens the bidding and his partner fails to keep it alive, you may take great liberties in competing for the part score. You have the distinct comfort of knowing that one of your opponents is "broke," and the other was not able to open with a demand bid. It follows, therefore, that your partner probably has a smattering of strength. In this position you may compete on a prayer. For example, you are South with this hand:

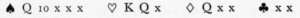

♠ Q 10 x x x   ♡ K Q x   ◊ Q x x   ♣ x x

The bidding has proceeded:

WEST	NORTH	EAST	SOUTH
1 ♣	Pass	Pass	?

You should contest the auction by bidding 1 Spade. Partner must not expect too much of you in this situation.

THE JUMP OVERCALLS

In a certain number of cases when the opponents open the bidding you will have a feeling that you probably have a better hand than they have, a hand that you believe can produce game for your side with only a smattering of strength from partner. In some of these cases you will make a take-out double, which will be discussed later. In other cases, when you have a very good trump suit and therefore a rather definite idea of where the hand is going to play, you may paint this picture by making a jump overcall, that is, by bidding exactly one more than is actually necessary. For example:

East	South	West	North
1 ◇	2 ♡		

or

East	South	West	North
1 ♣	2 ♠		

South's bid in each case denotes that he can probably make in his own hand what he bids, and partner is asked to support with 1 honor trick or abnormal distribution. For example, you hold:

♠ A K Q x x x   ♡ x   ◇ A Q J   ♣ x x x

Your opponent opens the bidding with 1 Heart. Your best bid is 2 Spades, a jump overcall, one more than is necessary. You have a little over eight winning tricks, including 3½ honor tricks. This is not a forcing bid. It is a strong invitation to partner to respond with very little strength, but partner is at liberty to pass if he has nothing. With 1 honor trick partner should make a response. In this case he need not have more than Q x or three small in trumps, because he knows you have a very fine trump suit. If he has a short suit and some trump support he may raise with as little as ½ honor trick. Another case:

♠ A Q 10 x x   ♡ A K J x x   ◇ x x   ♣ x

Your opponent bids 1 Diamond. A jump overcall of 2 Spades is recommended, with the intention of showing Hearts on the next round. Game can be made with very little help from partner provided he has a preference for one of your suits. However, holding:

♠ A Q 10 x x   ♡ x   ◇ x x   ♣ A K J x x

If the opponent opens with 1 Diamond a jump overcall of 2 Spades is not recommended because the bidding may get too high before you can show your second suit, as would be the case, for example, if partner elected to bid 3 Hearts. A simple Spade overcall is recommended, to increase the chance that Clubs can be shown at a reasonable level. Another hand:

♠ A x x   ♡ x x   ◇ A K Q J x x   ♣ x x

If your opponent opens the bidding with either a Club or a Heart bid, a jump overcall in Diamonds is recommended. This suggests to partner that he gamble the hand out at No Trump if he can stop the adverse suit and develop two winners in the play of the hand.

DOUBLE JUMP OVERCALLS

The strength-showing jump overcall is a bid of exactly one more than necessary; as 2 Spades over 1 Diamond. A jump of two or more tricks does not show strength. It is a preëmptive bid, made on the same type hand as an opening preëmptive bid. For example, the opening bid on your right is 1 Heart and you hold:

♠ Q J 10 x x x x   ♡ x   ◇ Q J 9 x   ♣ x

You may overcall with a jump to 3 Spades on this hand, if you are sure your partner will not misunderstand and interpret it as a strong bid. The 3 Spade bid may keep the opponents out of a 4 Heart contract. Such a bid is dangerous when vulnerable, however. If the opponents have all the cards, you give them a choice between doubling you and going on to their own best contract, whichever they think is more profitable.

♠ x   ♡ x x   ◇ x x   ♣ A Q J 10 x x x x

A jump to 4 Clubs, not vulnerable, is justified on this hand.

THE 1 NO TRUMP OVERCALL

This is a strong bid and is not very complicated. It is just about the same as any opening 1 No Trump bid, with the proviso that the adversaries' suit must be safely stopped. It is a bid to use when you are prepared to play at 1 No Trump if partner is weak, and are willing to go on to game if partner raises. The hand will, as a rule, meet with the technical requirements for a take-out double, but the double has the disadvantage of compelling you to bid No Trump on the next round, when a higher level will have been reached. Suppose you hold:

♠ K Q x   ♡ A K x   ◇ A Q J x   ♣ 10 x x

Your opponent opens the bidding with 1 Spade. If you double and partner responds with 2 Clubs or 2 Diamonds you will feel obliged to try 2 No Trump, which may not be safe if partner is weak. The best strategy is to overcall the Spade bid with 1 No Trump. If partner is weak you are prepared to play it there. If partner raises you are willing to try for game.

USE OF THE 1 NO TRUMP BID TO REOPEN

When an adverse opening bid of one in a suit has not been kept alive and you are in fourth position, it has been pointed out that you can take great liberty in competing for the part score. You may do so in some cases by calling 1 No Trump. Partner must not construe this as a normal 1 No Trump call, but merely as a refusal to sell out so cheaply. For example, you are South and hold:

♠ A Q   ♡ Q x x   ◇ K 9 x x   ♣ J x x x

The bidding:

West	North	East	South
1 ♠	Pass	Pass	?

You may bid 1 No Trump. If partner has values he may speak. If he hasn't much you may as well play it at 1 No Trump. Partner must realize that you cannot have a really good hand, else you would have doubled first and then bid No Trump later. He must not raise the No Trump unless he passed with a very good hand.

ACTION BY PARTNER
OF OVERCALLER

Partner of overcaller is many times in a strategic position to judge the entire possibilities of the hand. He knows approximately how much partner has; knows that he has a good trump suit and that he can come within two or three tricks of making his bid. The partner is therefore in a position to add his own assets to those shown by the overcaller, and thus to form a conclusion as to game possibilities.

There is seldom any point in raising an overcall unless there is a chance for game. If the partner believes there is a chance for game he may raise, assuming, of course, that he is satisfied with the trump named in the overcall.

Normal trump support for an overcall is less than that required to support an opening bid, because, while an opening bid may be based on a four-card suit, an overcall usually is not. The overcaller's partner may presume that the overcaller has a good five-card suit, so three small trumps are sufficient support, or even Q x, particularly if the overcaller's side is vulnerable. For example, you are South and hold:

♠ x x x   ♡ Q 10   ◇ K J 9 x x   ♣ K Q x

With both sides vulnerable the bidding has proceeded as follows:

SOUTH	WEST	NORTH	EAST
Pass	1 ♠	2 ♡	Pass
?			

What should you do? Your partner's vulnerable overcall has shown the ability to take at least six tricks, and is based upon a good Heart suit. Your hand should develop at least three tricks for partner, which means that you have some reasonable prospects of going game. What do you bid? Surely not 3 Diamonds. In the first place, partner might pass. He is not the opener. Secondly, if he is placed in a position where he is obliged to rebid Hearts you will not know whether he had any additional values, or whether he just couldn't stand 3 Diamonds, and you will be called upon to bid 4 Hearts blindly, if at all. Your proper procedure is to raise to 3 Hearts. If partner wishes to leave it he may do so. If partner wishes to go on you have given him an inducement to do so.

Similarly, you are South and hold:

♠ x x x   ♡ 10 x x   ◇ K Q x   ♣ A K x x

With North and South vulnerable the bidding has proceeded:

WEST	NORTH	EAST	SOUTH
1 ♠	2 ♡	Pass	?

What should you do? You have normal trump support for a vulnerable overcall at the level of two and your hand has a reasonable chance to develop 4 playing tricks. Since partner has promised to take six, the total reaches ten, and you should bid 4 Hearts. A bid of 3 Clubs would be little short of an atrocity. Partner might pass. He did not open the bidding, and is not obligated to make any further bids.

Another illustration. You are South and hold:

♠ A K x   ♡ x x x x   ◇ x x x x   ♣ K x

North and South are vulnerable. The bidding has proceeded:

WEST	NORTH	EAST	SOUTH
1 ♡	1 ♠	Pass	?

What should you do? Your partner has guaranteed to take five tricks. You can take three. The hand should be safe for eight tricks. You therefore raise to 2 Spades.

Again, as South you hold:

♠ K 9 x x   ♡ x   ◊ A 10 x x   ♣ Q 10 x x

North and South are vulnerable. The bidding has proceeded:

West	North	East	South
1 ◊	1 ♠	Pass	?

What should you do? Partner has promised to take five tricks. You can produce at least four. You should therefore jump to 3 Spades. This is not forcing, since partner was not the opener. He may drop it if he had a questionable overcall, but he should be given a strong inducement to go on to game if he chooses.

If you are satisfied with your partner's overcall but have a suit of your own you should think twice before showing it. Remember that he has not invited you to bid, that he has not shown a hand of general strength, all his values may be massed in his own suit, and he may not have the slightest interest in yours. It is usually not good policy to show your own suit unless you have such a hand that you would have overcalled independently of your partner.

Where you have a choice between showing your own suit and supporting your partner's overcall, if your partner has bid a major suit by all means support him. If your partner has bid a minor suit you may try the major if your hand is sufficiently strong. To illustrate, as South you hold:

♠ K x x   ♡ x x   ◊ A Q J x x   ♣ x x x

The bidding has proceeded:

West	North	East	South
1 ♡	1 ♠	2 ♡	?

Here your problem is whether to compete by bidding 3 Diamonds or by raising to 2 Spades. The bid of 2 Spades is recommended. But if you held:

♠ A Q J x x   ♡ x x   ◊ K x x   ♣ x x x

and the bidding proceeded

WEST	NORTH	EAST	SOUTH
1 ♡	2 ◇	2 ♡	?

you should try 2 Spades. If partner doesn't like it and is obliged to bid 3 Diamonds you are prepared to support him.

DO NOT RESCUE AN OVERCALL WHEN IT IS NOT DOUBLED

As South you hold:

♠ x x   ♡ x   ◇ 10 x x   ♣ K 10 9 x x x x

The bidding has proceeded:

WEST	NORTH	EAST	SOUTH
1 ♠	2 ♡	Pass	?

What should you do? This is no hand with which to seek involvements. Offer up a prayer of thanksgiving that you have not been doubled and don't do anything that might put such ideas in the enemy's mind. Pass quickly. If you permit matters to rest you will probably learn that West, the opener, who rather likes his hand, will rescue your partner and save you the trouble. But if partner is doubled at 2 Hearts you might give serious consideration to bidding 3 Clubs.

Moral: *Do not rescue a partner who has not been doubled.*

RESCUING

What if partner's overcall has been doubled for penalties? Should you rescue? That involves the use of good, sound judgment. "Never rescue" would be just as bad advice as "Always rescue."

Suppose you are South and hold:

♠ x   ♡ x x x   ◇ A K 10 9 x   ♣ J x x x

The bidding has proceeded:

WEST	NORTH	EAST	SOUTH
1 ♡	1 ♠	Double	?

Should you rescue to 2 Diamonds? By all means NO. In the first place you have no means of knowing that 2 Diamonds will be a better contract than 1 Spade. Secondly, a rescue would increase the commitment to eight tricks. And finally, your hand as dummy will produce two tricks for your partner, which is as many as he had the right to expect. Again, as South you hold:

♠ x x   ♡ x x x   ◇ Q J 10 9 x x   ♣ x x

The bidding has proceeded:

WEST	NORTH	EAST	SOUTH
1 ♠	2 ♣	Double	?

Should you rescue to 2 Diamonds? As a dummy your hand is completely useless. If you rescue to 2 Diamonds you are sure of winning four tricks in your own hand plus whatever high cards partner might contribute. Since you will be developing four tricks which would not otherwise exist, a rescue to 2 Diamonds is recommended.

SHOWING ADVERSE STOPPERS WHEN PARTNER HAS OVERCALLED

Bidding No Trump for the sole purpose of showing stoppers in the suit adversely bid is not good policy. Remember, when partner has merely overcalled you should take no action unless you think there is some chance for game. Do not keep the overcaller's bid open as though he were the opener. For example, as South you hold:

♠ x x x x   ♡ x x   ◇ A Q x   ♣ Q x x x

The bidding has proceeded:

WEST	NORTH	EAST	SOUTH
1 ◇	1 ♡	Pass	?

What should you do? Nothing. Do not bid 1 No Trump to show that you have Diamonds stopped. That would indicate a desire to go on, a desire which you do not have. At least, you shouldn't,

IN A NUTSHELL

Don't overcall at the level of two, unless you can promise to lose no more than two trump tricks.

Don't overcall with No Trump unless your hand is as good as an original No Trump bid.

When your partner has merely overcalled, don't try to keep the bidding alive unless you hope to go game.

Don't rescue a partner who has not been doubled.

DEFENSIVE BID QUIZ

ANSWERS BEGIN ON PAGE 191

What action do you take with each of the following hands, in the situation indicated?

The opponent has opened with 1 Club. You are next to speak and hold:

1.	2.	3.
♠ A K Q 9	♠ A x x	♠ x
♡ x x	♡ x x x	♡ A K 10 x x x
◇ A x x x	◇ A Q 10 x x	◇ A Q J x x
♣ x x x	♣ x x	♣ x

The opponent has opened with 1 Spade. You are next to speak and hold:

4.	5.	6.
♠ 10 x	♠ x x x	♠ K Q 10 x
♡ A J x x x	♡ x x	♡ x
◇ K x x	◇ A K x x x	◇ A J x x x
♣ K x x	♣ K x x	♣ K x x

The opponent has opened with 3 Spades. You are next to speak and hold:

7.   ♠ Q 10 x x x   ♡ x x   ◇ x x   ♣ A K x x

The opponent has opened with 4 Spades. You are next to speak and hold:

8.   ♠ A x   ♡ K Q x   ◇ K Q J x   ♣ A 10 x x

You are South; the bidding has proceeded:

WEST	NORTH	EAST	SOUTH
1 ◇	2 ♡	Pass	?

9. ♠ Q x x x x x
    ♡ x
    ◇ x x x
    ♣ x x x

10. ♠ K Q x x
    ♡ 10 x x
    ◇ x x
    ♣ Q x x x

11. ♠ x x x x
    ♡ x x
    ◇ A x x x
    ♣ K x x

12. ♠ K x x x
    ♡ x x x
    ◇ x x x
    ♣ J x x

13. ♠ x x x
    ♡ 10 x
    ◇ x x x
    ♣ Q J 9 x x

14. ♠ A x
    ♡ J x x
    ◇ J x x x x
    ♣ K Q x

You are South; the bidding has proceeded:

WEST	NORTH	EAST	SOUTH
1 ◇	1 ♡	Pass	?

15. ♠ K 10 x x
    ♡ Q x x x
    ◇ x x
    ♣ A x x

16. ♠ A Q 10 x x
    ♡ J 10 x
    ◇ x x
    ♣ K x x

17. ♠ A Q x
    ♡ x x x
    ◇ K J x
    ♣ Q J x x

18. ♠ x x x x   ♡ x x   ◇ A Q x   ♣ Q x x x

In the following problems you are South. The bidding has proceeded as indicated:

19. ♠ Q x x
    ♡ A x x x
    ◇ A 10 x
    ♣ Q 10 x

20. ♠ A K Q J x x
    ♡ x
    ◇ A Q 10 x
    ♣ x x

SOUTH	WEST	NORTH	EAST	EAST	SOUTH	WEST	NORTH
Pass	1 ♡	2 ♠	Pass	3 ♡	?		
?							

21. ♠ A Q x x
    ♡ K 10 x
    ◇ A 10 x
    ♣ A 9 x

You are vulnerable. Opponents
are not.

EAST	SOUTH	WEST	NORTH
1 ♠	?		

22. ♠ K Q x
    ♡ A K x
    ◇ A Q J x
    ♣ 10 x x

You are vulnerable. Opponents
are not.

EAST	SOUTH	WEST	NORTH
1 ♠	?		

23. ♠ Q J x
    ♡ A J
    ◇ A K Q x x
    ♣ 10 x x

You are vulnerable. Opponents
are not.

EAST	SOUTH	WEST	NORTH
1 ♠	?		

24. ♠ J 9 x x
    ♡ x x
    ◇ J x
    ♣ A K Q x x

You are vulnerable.

WEST	NORTH	EAST	SOUTH
1 ◇	1 ♠	2 ♡	?

25. ♠ A K 10 x x
    ♡ K x
    ◇ x x x
    ♣ K J 10

You are vulnerable.

WEST	NORTH	EAST	SOUTH
1 ◇	1 ♡	Pass	?

26. ♠ Q 10 x
    ♡ J x x x x x
    ◇ A x
    ♣ x x

WEST	NORTH	EAST	SOUTH
1 ♠	2 ♣	Pass	?

27. ♠ Q 9 x
    ♡ x x
    ◇ A K 10 x
    ♣ K J 9 x

You are vulnerable.

WEST	NORTH	EAST	SOUTH
1 ♡	1 ♠	Pass	?

28. ♠ Q x x
    ♡ x x
    ◇ A K x
    ♣ K J 10 9 x

You are vulnerable.

WEST	NORTH	EAST	SOUTH
1 ♡	1 ♠	Pass	?

29. ♠ x x x
     ♡ A x
     ◇ A 9 x x
     ♣ K J x x

You are vulnerable.

WEST	NORTH	EAST	SOUTH
1 ♠	2 ♡	Pass	?

30. ♠ K J 9 x
     ♡ x x
     ◇ Q x x x
     ♣ 10 x x

WEST	NORTH	EAST	SOUTH
1 ♠	2 ♡	Pass	?

31. ♠ Q 10 x
     ♡ x
     ◇ J 10 x
     ♣ K J 10 x x x

Both vulnerable.

WEST	NORTH	EAST	SOUTH
1 ♠	2 ♡	Pass	?

32. ♠ x
     ♡ x x x
     ◇ Q J 10 9 8 6
     ♣ Q x x

WEST	NORTH	EAST	SOUTH
1 ♡	1 ♠	Double	?

33. ♠ Q J 10 9 8 6
     ♡ x
     ◇ J x x
     ♣ J x x

You are vulnerable.

WEST	NORTH	EAST	SOUTH
1 ♠	2 ♡	Double	?

34. ♠ x x x
     ♡ K Q x
     ◇ J 10 x x x x
     ♣ J

EAST	SOUTH	WEST	NORTH
1 ♡	Pass	2 ♡	2 N T
Double	?		

35. ♠ K 10 x
     ♡ Q x x
     ◇ x
     ♣ A K Q J x x

Both vulnerable.

WEST	NORTH	EAST	SOUTH
1 ♠	2 ◇	Double	?

36. ♠ A x x
     ♡ Q 10
     ◇ K J 10 x x x
     ♣ K x

You are vulnerable.

WEST	NORTH	EAST	SOUTH
Pass	Pass	1 ♣	1 ◇
2 ♣	2 ♡	Pass	?

37. ♠ x x
♡ Q J x x x x
♢ J x x
♣ J x

38. ♠ x x
♡ 10 x x
♢ A K J x
♣ A 9 x x

You are vulnerable.

EAST	SOUTH	WEST	NORTH	WEST	NORTH	EAST	SOUTH
1 ♠	Pass	2 ♠	3 N T	1 ♠	2 ♡	Pass	?
Double	?						

DEFENSIVE BID QUIZ ANSWERS

1. 1 Spade. This is a rare case in which you may overcall with a four-card suit. You have 5 playing tricks.

2. 1 Diamond, if not vulnerable; a doubtful overcall when vulnerable.

3. 2 Hearts. A jump overcall, strongly invitational but not forcing.

4. Pass. Too dangerous to overcall. You could easily lose more than two trump tricks. You have good defensive strength.

5. Pass, for the same reason as in the preceding case.

6. Pass. Your brightest prospect is to set a trap for the opponents. One step in the wrong direction and the enemy is yours.

7. Pass. It is very tempting to double for penalties but there is an objection to such action. Such a double is more or less "optional" and partner may exercise his option by bidding Hearts if he has length in that suit. Pass and accept a sure profit.

8. Double. You have no assurance you can make five of anything. If partner happens to have a very long suit he is at perfect liberty to take the double out. He must know you are doubling, not particularly on Spade strength, but on outside values.

9. Pass. You cannot support Hearts and partner is unlikely to have Spade support.

10. 3 Hearts. You have normal trump support for the jump overcall and more than 1 honor trick.

11. 2 No Trump, showing a stopper in the adversaries' suit and some definite values.

12. Pass. Your partner's bid is only a strong invitation, which you are unable to accept with less than 1 trick.

13. Pass. You have no values and must decline partner's strong invitation.

14. 4 Hearts. You have normal trump support and 2 honor tricks. A single raise would therefore be inadequate. There is no point in bidding No Trump to show the remote Diamond stopper.

15. You have 4 playing tricks. Bid 2 Hearts if not vulnerable (partner has promised to take four tricks). Bid 3 Hearts if vulnerable (partner has promised to take five tricks).

16. 1 Spade. There is a chance to get somewhere. A bid of 2 Hearts would also be acceptable.

17. 1 No Trump. This is a strong bid and invites partner to continue. Had partner opened the bidding you would have responded with 2 No Trump.

18. Pass. Do not bid 1 No Trump, to show the Diamond stopper. It is not necessary to keep an overcall open nor is it necessary to deny partner's suit.

19. 3 Hearts. This hand has enormous possibilities. Partner has promised to take eight tricks and you can take at least three. Slam possibilities should be suggested by cue-bidding the adverse suit. Spade support will be confirmed subsequently.

20. 4 Spades. You require ever so little from partner to produce game and should gamble it out yourself by bidding 4 Spades. If you bid only 3 Spades partner will gain the impression that you are merely putting up some kind of fight.

21. 1 No Trump. This gives an exact picture of your hand. If you double partner will be obliged to respond with two of a suit and you will then have to try 2 No Trump, which will be somewhat more risky.

22. 1 No Trump, for the reasons outlined in the preceding problem. If partner has not a voluntary raise you will not go game, in which case 1 No Trump will be the best contract. If he does raise you may test your luck.

23. 1 No Trump. Even though, or rather because, you have a good five-card suit. If there is any future in this hand it is at No Trump and nowhere else.

24. 4 Spades. You have tremendous playing strength for partner and his vulnerable overcall indicates that he has a good suit. It would be pointless to jump in Clubs, and a bid of only 3 Clubs would be outlandish. Partner might pass. Remember, he is not the opener.

25. 2 Spades. There can be no possible question of a game and you must make a bid which absolutely forces partner. A bid of only 1 Spade would not, since he is not the opener.

26. Pass. There is no point in showing your emaciated six-card Heart suit. You are not going places and you might drive partner to 3 Clubs, which you would not like.

27. 4 Spades. Your hand will develop about five tricks in the play and partner should be able to take that many. A 4 Spade bid is therefore in order, or with an aggressive partner possibly 3 Spades would be sufficient. Don't give any thought to bidding one of the minors.

28. 4 Spades, for the reasons given in the preceding problem. If you choose you might bid 3 Clubs, but since no slam is visualized there is not much to be gained by such action.

29. 3 Hearts. This is a fine hand opposite a vulnerable overcall, and you have normal trump support for the type of suit your partner should have, if he has not been badly brought up.

30. Pass, quickly. It would not make sense to show the stoppers in the adverse suit.

31. Pass, promptly. Thank your stars you have not been doubled yet. Don't do anything that might induce the enemy to start firing.

32. 2 Diamonds. This is the type of hand on which a rescue bid is indicated. For Spades you have an absolutely worthless dummy. If you play the hand yourself you can take four tricks in Diamonds, plus whatever your partner can contribute in high cards.

33. 2 Spades. For the same reason outlined in the previous answer. You have four sure Spade tricks despite the adverse bid. Only with a thoughtful partner should you take this step. Any other kind will not permit you to play it in Spades and will keep on bidding. That won't be good.

34. Pass. You can't tell what partner may be up to but you should not rescue to 3 Diamonds. In the first place, as far as you know he can make his bid, and secondly, he may wish to escape to Clubs. Don't get in his way.

35. 3 No Trump. Partner has apparently run into a bad break in Diamonds, but he should have a couple of high cards in his hand. A 3 Club bid would get you nowhere.

36. 3 Hearts. It is true partner is not rich in high cards but he surely has a good Heart suit, which is all you need to give you some sort of chance for game. Remember, he bid voluntarily.

37. Pass. Partner has not invited your cooperation. Permit him to work out his own destiny. His bid is no doubt based on a long minor suit. He is not interested in Hearts.

38. 4 Hearts. This is simple arithmetic. Partner can take six tricks and you should take four.

CHAPTER 7

TAKE-OUT DOUBLES

THE TAKE-OUT DOUBLE is perhaps the most abused and at the same time the most neglected bid in contract. It is strange that it should be so, for it is one of the most valuable tools in the bridge artisan's kit. The take-out double is the most common method of showing strength when partner has not yet spoken and only the enemy's voice has yet been heard.

At this point it may be appropriate to identify a take-out double, that is, to distinguish it from the penalty double.

The following facts should be borne in mind:

The double of 2 No Trump is always for penalties.

The double of 1 No Trump is intended primarily for penalties, but partner may use his own judgment and refuse to leave it in if his hand has no defense and contains a long suit.

The double of an opening three-bid has caused a great deal of confusion. As a general rule it should be treated the same as a double of one of a suit. In other words, partner's suggestion is that you bid, but at that level you may exercise a certain amount of discretion and pass if you think it better to play for penalties.

A double, in order to be for a take-out, must be made at the doubler's first opportunity to double that suit. For example:

SOUTH	WEST	NORTH	EAST
1 ♠	Pass	1 N T	Pass
2 ♠	Double		

This is a double for penalties. If West wished to hear from his partner he would have doubled 1 Spade.

After partner has made any bid all doubles are for penalties. For example:

SOUTH	WEST	NORTH	EAST
1 ♣	1 ♦	Double	

This is a penalty double, since North's partner has already bid
1 Club.

REQUIREMENTS FOR THE TAKE-OUT DOUBLE

The standard high-card requirement for the take-out double
is 3 honor tricks. One may go a little below this, but not much,
with a hand that is very well suited for the purpose. Then again,
even with more than 3 honor tricks a take-out double may be in-
advisable.

The high-card holding is only one consideration. There are
other factors of equal, if not greater, importance. The doubler
must never forget that he is forcing his partner to bid.

It is a good idea to make up your mind in advance what suit
partner will probably bid. (It's usually your worst suit. That's
bridge life.) If that response is going to embarrass you, something
is wrong with your double. In other words, don't force your partner into a position which you yourself are going to find awkward.
For example:

♠ A Q x x   ♡ x   ♦ A J x x   ♣ A x x x

Both sides are vulnerable. Your right-hand opponent opens with
1 Spade. What should you do? The casual player would double
without trying to visualize partner's probable response. Let's be
realistic. It's sure fire partner will reply with 2 Hearts. What
then? You would have a problem for Mr. Anthony. Do you intend to try 2 No Trump over 2 Hearts? I don't like your case.
Partner may have nothing. You should have thought of all this
before you doubled. You would then have refused to double and
decided instead on "snake in the grass" tactics, that is, just waiting for the enemy to bid themselves into trouble.

In a word, the doubler, in addition to promising certain high
cards, guarantees safety. He says, in effect, "My hand will be a
good dummy for you," or "I have a very convenient suit in which
I myself can play the hand."

If your hand will be a very good dummy for partner regardless of the suit he may bid, you may double with as little as 2½ honor tricks. For example:

♠ K 10 x x   ♡ K J x x   ◇ A Q x x   ♣ x

The opponent bids 1 Club. You have about 2½ honor tricks, but this is a sound double, because your hand will be a fine dummy for any suit partner may bid.

Possession of a good five-card suit is no bar to the use of the double. For example:

♠ A K J 10 x   ♡ K x x x   ◇ x x   ♣ A x

An opponent opens the bidding with one of a minor suit. To make a mere overcall in Spades would not describe the strength of your hand and would risk partner's passing with a smattering of strength sufficient to produce game. The best procedure is to double first and to bid Spades thereafter. This will give your partner an accurate picture of the strength of your hand. There is the further consideration that partner might be very short in Spades and have some length in Hearts, in which case game might be available in that suit.

The take-out double is a technical bid announcing, "I have a good hand, partner. I will tell you more about it later. Meanwhile, just answer my questionnaire."

A DOUBLE TO REOPEN THE BIDDING

There is one instance in which a take-out double may be made with as little as 2 honor tricks. That is to prevent the bidding from dying out, when the adversaries have quit at a low level. For example, as South you hold:

♠ A J x x   ♡ K x x x   ◇ K x x   ♣ x x

The bidding has proceeded:

WEST	NORTH	EAST	SOUTH
1 ♣	Pass	Pass	?

What should you do? In this situation one is frequently heard to say, "Oh, well, they did not bid a game. One Club won't hurt us. Let them have it." This is the wrong attitude to adopt. The proper attitude is, "Why should they be permitted to play a hand so cheaply when we can probably make a part score?" South, in this sequence, may deduce that partner has a certain amount of strength. East is woefully weak, since he was unable even to keep open a Club bid. He quite definitely has less than one trick. North's hand may have been just as short of the requirements for a take-out double or an overcall. You should give your partner a chance to compete by making a take-out double. North must make allowances in situations of this kind and should not presume that you have a normal type of double. You should be very careful not to proceed further after doubling, because in that case partner will assume that your double was of the standard three-trick variety.

IN A NUTSHELL

Double for a take-out only when you are prepared for partner's probable response and can guarantee safety.

RESPONSES BY PARTNER OF DOUBLER

When partner makes a take-out double it is your absolute duty to respond irrespective of the weakness of the hand. *The only excuse for passing is the ability to defeat the opponents in the bid which your partner has doubled.* Do not be afraid to bid with a "bust" hand. Your partner has promised full responsibility. If you suffer a loss blame it on him.

If your response can be made at the level of one, a four-card major should be shown in preference to a five-card minor, provided the four-card major is headed by a high honor. For example:

♠ x x x   ♡ Q x x x   ◇ x   ♣ K x x x x

Your partner has doubled 1 Diamond. You should respond with 1 Heart, rather than 2 Clubs.

Considerations of safety may dictate a departure from this rule. Suppose that as South you hold:

♠ J x x x　　♡ x x　　◇ J x x x x　　♣ x x

The bidding has proceeded:

WEST	NORTH	EAST	SOUTH
1 ♣	Double	Pass	?

With a hand this weak it is better policy to respond with 1 Diamond rather than 1 Spade.

Some players make an exception to the above rule when they have a fairly good hand and hope to get a chance to show both suits in response. For example:

♠ K 10 x x　　♡ x x　　◇ x x　　♣ A x x x x

Partner doubled an opening bid of 1 Heart. The above rule calls for a response of 1 Spade. Some players, however, prefer to respond with 2 Clubs, hoping to get another chance, at which time they will bid 2 Spades. This will give partner an accurate description of the hand; he will know responder held five Clubs, four Spades and a fairly good hand.

There is one objection to this type of strategy. When you respond in a minor suit partner may become discouraged and not carry on the bidding; whereas if you respond with a major suit you are almost certain to get another chance.

When the responder holds two suits and a good hand, the practice is to show the higher-ranking suit first, with the intention of showing the other suit on the next round. For example:

♠ x x x　　♡ x x　　◇ A 10 x x　　♣ K Q x x

Partner has doubled a bid of 1 Heart. You should respond with 2 Diamonds. This hand is strong enough to warrant two bids from you and Clubs should be shown on the next round if desirable. Again:

♠ K 10 x x   ♡ A Q x x   ◇ x x x   ♣ x x

Partner has doubled a bid of 1 Diamond. Respond with 1 Spade, fully intending to bid Hearts on the next round unless Spades are vigorously supported.

Occasionally you will find that the only four-card suit in your hand has been bid by the opponents. This presents an embarrassing problem. Do not respond with No Trump unless you can very safely stop the adverse suit. Rather than bid No Trump you may be obliged to respond in a three-card suit. In that case you should select the cheapest possible bid you can make. For example:

♠ 10 x x   ♡ J x x   ◇ Q x x x   ♣ x x x

Your partner has doubled a bid of 1 Diamond. Do not respond with 1 No Trump. Your Diamond stopper is too sketchy. Respond with your cheapest three-card suit. In this case you are obliged to bid 1 Heart.

If your hand contains four cards in a major and also a safe stopper in the opponent's suit a choice of responses is presented. As a rule it is better policy to name a major than to respond in No Trump. For example:

♠ J 10 x x   ♡ K J x   ◇ Q J x   ♣ x x x

Partner has doubled a bid of 1 Heart. Respond with 1 Spade rather than 1 No Trump. If partner shows any enthusiasm you may bid No Trump later.

But when you have the adversaries' suit well stopped and your hand contains more than 1 honor trick you may respond in No Trump in preference to showing a four-card minor suit. For example:

♠ K 10 9 x   ♡ x x   ◇ Q x x   ♣ K 10 x x

Partner has doubled 1 Spade. This is a fairly good hand under the circumstances. You have definitely more than 1 honor trick, and the adversaries' suit is safely stopped. You could respond with 2 Clubs but that will probably lead nowhere, and a better response is 1 No Trump. It will be noted that the No Trump response to partner's double denotes a fairly good hand. In some quarters the unsound practice exists of using the No Trump response to partner's double to indicate a bad hand. This should be avoided.

To summarize: Where the doubler's partner has a choice between No Trump and a suit, he should prefer No Trump if his suit is a minor, but if he holds a major that suit should be given preference to the No Trump.

If you have a very hopeless hand it is good policy to keep the bidding at the lowest possible level. For example, if you have two four-card suits and a "bust" it is preferable to bid the lower-ranking, rather than the better of the two. To illustrate:

♠ x x   ♡ x x x   ◇ J x x x   ♣ x x x x

Partner has doubled a bid of 1 Spade. With this hopeless hand it is better to respond with 2 Clubs than with 2 Diamonds. If you respond in Diamonds and partner wishes to bid Clubs he will be driven to three.

IN A NUTSHELL

You must respond to partner's take-out double, even with a "bust."

RESPONDING WITH STRONG HANDS

Among the shortcomings of the average bridge player, few are more outstanding than his inability to judge the value of his hand when partner has made a take-out double. Most players are inclined to underestimate the value of their hands in this position.

The following table should be of assistance, in a general sort of way, in judging the value of the responding hand.

If you have 1 honor trick you have a fair hand.

If you have 1½ honor tricks you have a good hand.

If you have 2 honor tricks you have a probable game.

When you have more than 2 honor tricks game becomes a moral certainty, provided you reach the proper contract.

It is important to know that any distributional situations in your favor will promote a fair hand to a good hand, and a good hand to a probable game. A six-card suit, with 1 honor trick, for example, becomes a good hand, and a six-card suit with 1½ honor tricks is more than just a good hand. It represents a probable game.

When you hold a hand in which you have a probable game it is generally good strategy to so advise your partner at once. This is done by bidding one more than is necessary in response. You may bid one more than necessary even though your suit is not very robust. For example:

♠ Q J x x   ♡ A J x   ◇ x x x   ♣ K J x

Partner has doubled a bid of 1 Diamond. You have more than 2 honor tricks, which means that you very probably have a game. The proper response is 2 Spades, one more than necessary. This does not necessarily indicate a good Spade suit.

When your best suit is a minor and you hold over 2 honor tricks, the same principle should be followed. That is, your strength should be shown by bidding one more than necessary. But if this would require a jump to three you ought to have a fairly good minor suit. Holding minor-suit strength as well as protection in the suit adversely bid, a jump should be made in No Trump, thus:

♠ Q J 10   ♡ J x x   ◇ K J x   ♣ K Q x x

Partner has doubled 1 Diamond. You have more than two tricks and a jump is indicated. The recommended response is 2 No Trump, rather than a jump in the minor suit. But:

♠ x x   ♡ Q J 10   ◇ A 10 x   ♣ K Q J x x

Partner has doubled a bid of 1 Spade. The proper response is 3 Clubs.

THE BUSINESS PASS OF PARTNER'S TAKE-OUT DOUBLE

It has been pointed out above that doubler's partner is under an absolute duty to respond, however weak his hand may be.

The double should be passed only when you are quite sure you can defeat the contract.

This does not refer to doubles of 1 No Trump, which are essentially for penalties and should almost always be left in. Reference is being made to take-out doubles of suit contracts.

The double of one in a suit should never be left in with less than three sure trump tricks. Bear in mind that if you pass the double of one in a suit, an energetic partner will select a trump for his opening lead. Are you prepared for it? If you are not, then definitely your business pass is improper.

Inexperienced players sometime pass a take-out double with the assertion, "Partner, I just did not have anything to bid." It is an ironclad principle of bidding that one never passes his partner's take-out double because he is frightened. On the contrary he does so because he is ambitious. You need strength to pass.

PROCEDURE BY DOUBLER'S PARTNER AFTER AN INTERVENING BID

When your partner has doubled the opening bid and opener's partner, who speaks before you, takes action, you are no longer under the duty to respond. You have been relieved of that obligation by the enemy. A bid by you at this point is therefore voluntarily made and denotes some measure of strength. It is not, however, regarded as a free bid in the general meaning of that term. The requirements are not nearly so stringent as they would be if partner had opened the bidding and second hand had overcalled. By doubling, partner is trying to get a message from you, and the opponents are trying to obstruct your communications. You will sometimes find it necessary to stretch a point to get through the message to your partner.

Bear in mind that if you have 1½ honor tricks you should regard your hand as a good one and you should make a free bid. Even with less high-card strength you may take action if you have a long suit or an unbalanced hand. For example:

♠ A Q x x   ♡ x x   ◇ x x x x   ♣ x x x

Your partner has doubled a bid of 1 Heart. Opener's partner bids 2 Hearts. You may make a free bid of 2 Spades.

♠ x x x   ♡ K x x   ◇ A Q x x   ♣ x x x

Partner has doubled a bid of 1 Spade. Opener's partner bids 2 Clubs. You should make a free bid of 2 Diamonds.

♠ x x   ♡ x x x   ◇ Q J x   ♣ A x x x x

Partner has doubled a bid of 1 Heart. Opener's partner bids 1 Spade. You should make a free bid of 2 Clubs. Had the opener's partner bid 2 Hearts it would have required a bid of three to show your suit, which in this case would have been somewhat doubtful wisdom, but still a close question.

You are South and hold:

♠ K x x x x x   ♡ x x   ◇ x x x   ♣ x x

The bidding has proceeded:

West	North	East	South
1 ♣	Double	1 ♡	?

A free bid of 1 Spade is recommended because of the length of the suit and the cheapness at which it can be shown. But:

♠ x x   ♡ K x x x x x   ◇ x x x   ♣ x x

The bidding has proceeded:

West	North	East	South
1 ◇	Double	2 ♣	?

A free bid of 2 Hearts, while it cannot be condemned, is open to mild question, because of the increased level at which the suit must be shown. If partner's suit is Spades he will have to show it at the level of two, which may leave you in a somewhat awkward position.

PROCEDURE BY DOUBLER'S PARTNER WHEN AN OPPONENT REDOUBLES

If your partner makes a take-out double and the opener's partner redoubles you are relieved of the obligation to bid, because the auction reverts to your partner and permits him to take himself out. A pass by you indicates, in most cases, that you have nothing to say at the present time and you would prefer to have your partner take himself out of the redouble. It implies that you are more or less willing to have him select any of the suits, that you have no special choice. However, a bid at this point does not promise strength and should not be regarded as a free bid. Partner has asked you for your best suit. If you can afford to show it the chances are you should. If you have a five-card suit it is generally good practice to show it regardless of its texture. Even a four-card suit may be shown if it does not consume any bidding space.

For example:

♠ x x x　　♡ K J x x　　♢ x x x　　♣ x x x

Partner has doubled a bid of 1 Diamond. The next hand redoubles. It is proper for you to bid 1 Heart. This does not consume any bidding space. If partner wishes to bid 1 Spade or 2 Clubs he can do so at the same level as if you had passed. Had the opening bid been 1 Club, doubled by your partner and redoubled, it is doubtful that you should bid the Heart with a hand this weak, inasmuch as partner's suit might be Diamonds. A Heart bid would force him to the level of two to name his suit, whereas had you passed he could have rescued himself from the redouble by a bid of 1 Diamond.

ACTION BY DOUBLER AFTER PARTNER RESPONDS

A great many players are able to visualize partner's possible strength. Few, however, learn to visualize partner's probable weakness. Generally speaking, a doubler who has already advertised his strength should underbid on subsequent rounds, and the responder, who has made no promises, should adopt an aggressive attitude. In actual play, however, the opposite is true. The doubler keeps rebidding his values while his partner, who never did care for his hand, cannot seem to work up any enthusiasm.

Let us take an illustration. As South you hold:

♠ A K 10   ♡ x x   ◇ K 10 x   ♣ A K J 10 x

The bidding has proceeded:

West	North	East	South
1 ♡	Pass	Pass	Double
Pass	2 ♣	Pass	?

What do you do?

Most players could not resist the impulse to make a jump raise in Clubs. They do not stop to realize that opposite an opening bid and a partner who may be extremely weak, an eleven-trick contract would not have a very good prospect of success. However, if partner can manage to stop the Heart suit a game contract at No Trump might be worth risking. The proper procedure, therefore, is to bid only 3 Clubs. A jump to 4 Clubs would be improper on another ground, the simple one that you have no assurance that your partner will not lose four tricks. Let us examine the complete hand:

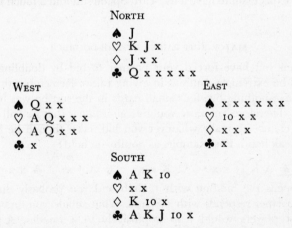

NORTH
♠ J
♡ K J x
◇ J x x
♣ Q x x x x x

WEST
♠ Q x x
♡ A Q x x x
◇ A Q x x
♣ x

EAST
♠ x x x x x x
♡ 10 x x
◇ x x x
♣ x

SOUTH
♠ A K 10
♡ x x
◇ K 10 x
♣ A K J 10 x

It will be observed that a contract of 3 No Trump can be fulfilled, the bid which North should hazard after partner raises to 3 Clubs. The singleton Spade should not act as a bar to such action, inasmuch as partner's strong bidding clearly indicates that he has some strength in that suit.

Sometimes the doubler can tell by partner's response that chances for game are very remote and that the bidding should therefore not be continued. For example, as South you hold:

♠ A Q x x   ♡ x x   ◇ A 10 x   ♣ K J x x

The bidding has proceeded:

EAST	SOUTH	WEST	NORTH
1 ♡	Double	Pass	2 ◇
Pass	?		

What should you do?

You have a minimum double and partner was unable to jump the bid, so he cannot have a very strong hand. You have no choice but to pass. Since partner did not respond with 1 Spade it is highly unlikely that he will be found with four of that suit so that it would be risky, if not pointless, for you to bid 2 Spades. Partner would expect you to have a five-card Spade suit and a much better hand.

MAJOR SUIT RAISES BY THE DOUBLER

When you have forced your partner to bid by doubling you should be extremely cautious in giving raises. Remember that he may have nothing but four small cards in the suit he was forced to bid. Therefore any raise you give guarantees that he will have a fair chance to make whatever you bid, even though he has a very weak hand. For example, as South you hold:

♠ A K Q x x   ♡ K x x   ◇ A J x   ♣ x x

East opens the bidding with 1 Club and you properly double. Your partner responds with 1 Spade. What should you do?

Most players would leap impulsively to 4 Spades. A little analysis will show such action to be unsound. Partner was forced to speak and may be trickless. In that case even a contract of 3 Spades will not be safe. Let us examine the complete hand:

NORTH

♠ J 10 x x
♡ Q x x
◇ x x x
♣ Q x x

WEST

♠ x x
♡ J 9 x x
◇ K 10 x x
♣ J 10 x

EAST

♠ x x
♡ A 10 x
◇ Q 9 x
♣ A K x x x

SOUTH

♠ A K Q x x
♡ K x x
◇ A J x
♣ x x

It will be noted that declarer, against proper defense, will be obliged to lose two tricks in each of the side suits and could barely fulfill a contract of one-odd.

No sounder advice can be given the doubler than this: *When partner's response has been forced, never jump to any contract that you cannot reasonably expect to fulfill in your own hand.*

When a doubler follows up his original double with a free raise (after his right-hand opponent has bid again) he confirms a very fine double and a hand that possesses game-going possibilities. For example, as South you hold:

♠ x   ♡ A 9 x x x   ◇ A Q x   ♣ K Q x x

The bidding has proceeded:

EAST	SOUTH	WEST	NORTH
1 ♠	Double	Pass	2 ◇
2 ♠	?		

What should you do? Nothing. No action would be safe. A raise to 3 Diamonds, when partner may have nothing, may prove disastrous, as may likewise a bid of 3 Hearts. You have done justice to your holding by making an immediate double. You can afford to pass the bid around to partner, who, if he has anything at all, will remember the double and will not permit the opponents to run off with the contract.

ACTION BY DOUBLER'S PARTNER WHEN DOUBLER RAISES

With an indifferent hand the doubler's partner will have no problem when the doubler raises his response, but if he holds a good hand it will be his duty to take further action.

It will be borne in mind that with $1\frac{1}{2}$ honor tricks or more the responder must consider that he holds a good hand. For example:

♠ J x x x　　♡ A x x　　♢ x x x　　♣ K x x

Your partner has doubled an opening bid of 1 Diamond. You have responded with 1 Spade, which partner raises to two. Holding over $1\frac{1}{2}$ honor tricks, you have a good hand. A player holding a good hand should make one more bid if the doubler gives him a raise. Your proper procedure is to bid 3 Spades. Remember that partner has offered to fulfill an eight-trick contract, though he knows you may have little or nothing, and you should surely be safe for nine tricks. Another case:

♠ J x x x　　♡ A x x　　♢ x x　　♣ A x x x

The bidding has proceeded as in the previous example. You hold 2-plus honor tricks, which, after partner's double, indicate a probable game. A probable game becomes a biddable game when your partner raises. You should bid 4 Spades. Do not be concerned about the complexion of your trump suit. As far as your partner is concerned you have nothing more than four small Spades and he should not raise your forced response unless he has four trumps.

ACTION BY OPENER'S PARTNER

THE REDOUBLE

When your partner's opening bid has been doubled by your right-hand opponent, your proper procedure is not always clearly indicated. What you do at this point may determine the success or failure of the hand.

A superstition that seems to have gained popularity is the one to the effect that "a bid over a double shows weakness." This is an unsound doctrine, but it is easy to see how the confusion has arisen. It has for many years been a definitely accepted convention that when partner opens the bidding and the next hand doubles, a redouble by the third player denotes a good hand. It may or may not denote support for partner, but the paramount consideration is the desire to get across this information, "Partner, do not be intimidated by the double. I think we have the best hands. I'll tell you more about mine later."

If, therefore, the partner of the opening bidder fails to redouble, the inference is very plain that he does not have a very strong hand. This does not necessarily mean that he has a weak hand. He may have just enough to feel that he should show his partner some values and yet cannot afford to wait for fear the bidding will get too high before his next bid. Briefly, if partner's opening bid has been doubled:

With a good hand you redouble.

With a bad hand you pass. To bid for the sole purpose of announcing you are broke is really silly. It proceeds from the argument that it is wise to spend money to let the world know you are poor. The only time a bid with a bad hand should be countenanced is when responder is able to give partner a raise.

With an in-between hand you usually bid immediately. (Sometimes with a hand that is not quite good enough to redouble you may decide to await developments and enter the auction later, but make sure you can afford to bid later.)

Let us take a few practical examples:

♠ x   ♡ K Q 10 x   ◇ A Q x x   ♣ A 10 x x

Your partner's opening bid of 1 Spade has been doubled by your right-hand opponent. Although you do not like Spades you have a very good hand. The proper procedure is to redouble to announce your strong holding. If you contend, "What if this hand should be played at 1 Spade redoubled?" the answer is, that with all your high cards your partner will surely be able to take seven tricks and the redouble of 1 Spade will produce a game. If, however, as is more probable, the opponents elect to bid, they will fall into your trap and you can make a devastating penalty double of any suit that they choose to play.

Here it is essential to point out a very important convention that applies to this case: A player who redoubles becomes the temporary captain of the team. The opening bidder is requested to pass the next bid around to the redoubler, who promises to double or bid.

♠ 10 x x   ♡ A K J x x   ◇ K x x   ♣ x x

Again your partner's opening bid of 1 Spade has been doubled. You have a good hand and your proper procedure is clearly defined. You should redouble. There will be plenty of time to show the Hearts later, if expediency so dictates.

The question arises, what strength is required to justify a redouble? Roughly speaking, a hand that has game-going possibilities. Not merely a hand on which you believe that partner can make his contract. You do not expect the hand to be played there.

♠ J x x x   ♡ x   ◇ x x x   ♣ Q x x x x

Again your partner's opening bid of 1 Spade has been doubled. With this hand you should bid 2 Spades, not particularly to show weakness but with the intention of taking this cheap opportunity to show some Spade support. This may make it possible for partner to sacrifice at 4 Spades, if he believes such procedure will be profitable, should the opponents arrive at a contract of 4 Hearts. The bid has the further advantage of making it somewhat more difficult for the doubler's partner to respond. He must now bid three of some suit and may fear to do so. If in the same bidding situation you hold:

♠ Q J x x x   ♡ x   ◇ x x x   ♣ J x x x

With this hand you might be justified in bidding 3 Spades. You will note that while this is a jump it cannot be interpreted as showing strength, because over a double the accepted way to indicate strength is by a redouble. Since you fail to redouble, your partner must realize that you do not have a good hand. The 3

Spade bid is made merely as a barricade. In the majority of cases it will make it more embarrassing for the partner of the doubler to enter the auction, and you are not anxious to hear from the opposition.

♠ x x ♡ x x x ◇ x x x ♣ A K J x x

Your partner's opening bid of 1 Spade has been doubled by your right-hand opponent. Your hand is neither good nor bad. It might be called an in-between hand. If you do not bid now you will find no convenient opportunity to show your values at a later stage. The proper procedure, therefore, is to bid 2 Clubs. Similarly:

♠ A K x x ♡ x x x ◇ x x x ♣ A K x

As South you open the bidding with 1 Spade. West doubles. Your partner bids 3 Spades and East passes. What should you do?

Definitely pass. Despite your 4 honor tricks you do not have a very strong hand; it contains an unusually large number of losers. It is inconceivable that your partner can take care of enough of them to produce a game, for in that case he would have had a good enough hand to redouble. Partner's jump to 3 Spades is a barricade bid, intended to embarrass East.

The complete hand:

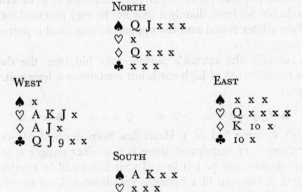

NORTH
♠ Q J x x x
♡ x
◇ Q x x x
♣ x x x

WEST
♠ x
♡ A K J x
◇ A J x
♣ Q J 9 x x

EAST
♠ x x x
♡ Q x x x x
◇ K 10 x
♣ 10 x

SOUTH
♠ A K x x
♡ x x x
◇ x x x
♣ A K x

It will be seen that even a 3 Spade contract is down one. But the opponents can make 4 Hearts if they are permitted to get together in the bidding.

As previously stated, with a poor hand the opener's partner should pass the take-out double. For example:

♠ x x   ♡ x x x   ◇ Q x x   ♣ K x x x x

Your partner opened with 1 Spade. The next hand doubles. It is poor strategy for you to bid 2 Clubs. Nothing is to be gained by taking action. You should pass.

Occasionally when partner's opening bid is doubled you will have just a smattering of strength and your course of action will not be clear. For example:

♠ x x   ♡ A x x   ◇ K x x x   ♣ x x x x

Your partner's opening bid of 1 Spade has been doubled by the next hand. What should you do? Your high card holding, in conjunction with your partner's bid, is such that you are quite persuaded that you can prevent the opponents from going game. In other words, this hand may develop into a dog fight for a part score. If you advise partner that you have a little something he may be able to carry on the fight for a round or two. This bit of information you may convey by an immediate bid of 1 No Trump. If you do not act immediately it may not be very practical for you to bid on a later round and the opponents may steal a part score from you.

Occasionally the opener's partner may bid over the double with a hand devoid of high cards but containing a long suit. For example:

♠ Q J x x x x   ♡ x   ◇ x x x   ♣ x x x

Partner's opening bid of 1 Heart has been doubled by second hand. From your standpoint there is a distinct danger that the 1 Heart double may be left in and your hand will be completely worthless. A take-out of 1 Spade is recommended, on the theory that you will probably find greater safety in that contract. Without a six-card suit such a bid would be extremely doubtful, inasmuch as you would be in a less favorable position to promise safety in that suit.

There is one other case in which opener's partner may take out with a very weak hand. That is when the opener's 1 No Trump bid has been doubled. For example:

$$\spadesuit \text{ x} \qquad \heartsuit \text{ x x} \qquad \diamondsuit \text{ J x x x} \qquad \clubsuit \text{ Q 10 x x x x}$$

Partner opened with 1 No Trump. Next hand doubles. There is a very distinct danger that the double will be left in and may prove costly. In this case a rescue to 2 Clubs is recommended.

USE OF THE TAKE–OUT DOUBLE BY OPENING BIDDER

The take-out double may also be used by the opening bidder to force a partner who has previously declined the opportunity to make a bid. For example, as South you hold:

$$\spadesuit \text{ K J x x} \qquad \heartsuit \text{ A K 9 x} \qquad \diamondsuit \text{ x} \qquad \clubsuit \text{ K Q x x}$$

The bidding has proceeded:

SOUTH	WEST	NORTH	EAST
1 ♣	1 ◇	Pass	Pass
?			

What should you do?

Naturally you are going to carry on the fight and it would be pointless for you to guess whether to rebid in Spades or in Hearts. There is no necessity for you to do so. Partner has not yet spoken. Therefore a double by you is still for a take-out. There is a tendency in some quarters to confuse this with a business double because the *doubler* has previously bid. That is not the test. The test is whether the partner of the doubler has previously bid. If he has, the double is for penalties; if he has not, it is to be construed as a take-out double. In this case, since North has not bid South's double insists that he do so. Here the double will provide for every contingency. If partner has either Hearts or Spades he will name the suit. If he has neither he may return to 2 Clubs, or, if he has great length in Diamonds, he may elect to pass and play the hand at 1 Diamond doubled. Such practice entirely eliminates guess work.

A FEW SPECIALIZED SITUATIONS

EXPOSING THE PSYCHIC BID

As South you hold:

♠ x x x   ♡ J 10 9 x x   ◇ A x x x   ♣ x

The bidding has proceeded:

West	North	East	South
1 ♣	Double	1 ♡	?

What should you do?

Had East not bid, your response would have been 1 Heart, a response, incidentally, of which you would not have been ashamed, for you have slightly better than a fair hand under the circumstances. If partner has a sound double East will be unable to fulfill the contract of 1 Heart. You should therefore double for penalties. It is very probable that East is playing horse and is trying to rob you of your bid. When you double it is obviously for penalties, partner having already bid (the double being construed as a bid). North will therefore realize that you would have had a sound Heart response and will act accordingly.

To put it in another way: Whenever your partner has shown strength by either an opening bid or a double, and your right-hand opponent steals your bid, double for business.

CUE-BIDDING AS A RESPONSE

As South you hold:

♠ A   ♡ 10 9 x x   ◇ K 10 9 x   ♣ K J x x

What should you do if the bidding has proceeded:

WEST	NORTH	EAST	SOUTH
1 ♠	Double	2 ♠	?

You have more than 2 honor tricks and splendid distribution. There can be no possible question but that you have a game in one of your three suits. On the surface a bid of 3 Hearts is in order, but there are certain objections to this. The weakness of the Heart suit makes the bid at this level a bit uncomfortable. Partner may expect a better suit. Also, a free bid at this level, while it denotes a really good hand, does not necessarily promise a game. The best procedure is to force partner to select the suit. This should be done by a cue-bid in the adverse suit. The recommended call is 3 Spades, announcing the ability to win the first Spade trick, and asking partner to select the suit in which the game contract will be played.

THE IMMEDIATE CUE–BID

This is the strongest of all defensive bids. It is absolutely forcing to game and announces practically the equivalent of an opening two-bid. It promises the ability to win the first trick in the suit adversely bid, either with the Ace or by ruffing.

For example, an opponent opens with 1 Diamond. You hold:

♠ A K Q x   ♡ K J 10 x x   ◇ ——   ♣ K Q J x

You are unwilling to play for less than game, and conceivably a slam, in one of your three suits. You prefer not to make a take-out double; first, because of the slight risk that partner might have sufficient strength in Diamonds to make a penalty pass, and you have no special desire to play against 1 Diamond doubled; secondly, because if you double and partner responds with a weak hand, he may lose his nerve somewhere along the line and drop the bidding short of game. The proper procedure therefore is an immediate cue-bid of 2 Diamonds. This forces partner to keep bidding till game is reached and you may then proceed to display your wares in leisurely fashion, without the necessity for resorting to jump bids on the way up.

Partner is expected to respond to the cue-bid exactly as he would to a take-out double.

THE 4 NO TRUMP OVERCALL

The overcall of an adverse opening bid of four in a suit with 4 No Trump is really a glorified take-out double and tells partner that you are prepared to play the hand at five of his best suit. It is unconditionally forcing, and partner must under no circumstances pass. Nervousness is no excuse. You are not asking for strength, you are merely looking for numbers (of trumps).

For example, an opponent, not vulnerable, opens with 4 Spades. You are vulnerable and hold:

♠ x   ♡ A K J x   ◊ K Q 10 x   ♣ A Q J x

While there is little doubt of your ability to defeat the adverse contract, there is a grave question in your mind as to whether the penalty will prove worth while. You prefer to play for game in one of your suits. The proper procedure is to bid 4 No Trump. Partner is then in duty bound to name his best suit other than Spades.

THE 3 NO TRUMP OVERCALL

This overcall is used in its natural sense and indicates a desire to play at that contract. It is by no means a request to partner to show any suit, and he should resist the impulse to show even a six-card suit unless he has a most extraordinary hand from the standpoint of distribution.

Against an opening 3 Spade bid, you might chance a 3 No Trump overcall with:

♠ K x   ♡ J x   ◊ A 10 x   ♣ A K Q x x x

With a Spade lead you have a fair prospect of taking eight immediate tricks, and are willing to muddle along for the ninth. You are naturally not eager to have your partner enter the auction with some broken-down six-card Heart suit.

TAKE-OUT DOUBLE QUIZ

ANSWERS BEGIN ON PAGE 222

In all these problems you are South; the bidding situation is indicated, and you are next to speak. What do you do?

Both vulnerable. East opens with 1 Club:

　1.　♠ Q x x　　♡ K J 10 x x x　　◇ A K x　　♣ x

Both vulnerable. East opens with 1 Spade in each of the following:

2. ♠ A Q x x	3. ♠ x	4. ♠ x x x
♡ x	♡ Q x x	♡ A Q x
◇ A 10 x x	◇ K J 10 x x x	◇ A K x
♣ A J x x	♣ A K x	♣ x x x x

　　5.　♠ x　　♡ A K 10 9 x　　◇ A J 9 x x　　♣ J x

East opens with 1 Club:

　6.　♠ A Q x x　　♡ x　　◇ A Q x x　　♣ A J x x

East opens with 1 Diamond:

　7.　♠ A J　　♡ K J x x　　◇ x　　♣ A K Q J x x

East opens with 1 Heart:

　8.　♠ A Q 10 9 x x　　♡ x　　◇ A K x x　　♣ K x

East opens with 1 Diamond:

　9.　♠ A Q 9 x x　　♡ A J 10 x x　　◇ x x　　♣ x

The bidding is indicated in the following cases:

10. ♠ A K J x	11. ♠ A Q 9 x x
♡ A K 10 x	♡ A J 10 x x
◇ x	◇ x x
♣ J 10 9 x	♣ x

SOUTH	WEST	NORTH	EAST	WEST	NORTH	EAST	SOUTH
1 ♠	2 ◇	Pass	Pass	1 ◇	Pass	2 ♣	?
?							

12. ♠ Q
    ♡ A 9 x x x
    ◇ A K Q J 10 x
    ♣ x

WEST	NORTH	EAST	SOUTH
1 ♣	Pass	1 ♠	?

13. ♠ A 10 x
    ♡ K 9 x x
    ◇ K Q 9 x
    ♣ x x

EAST	SOUTH	WEST	NORTH
1 ♣	Double	Pass	1 ♡
2 ♣	?		

14. ♠ A J 9 x
    ♡ A Q 10 x
    ◇ Q J x x
    ♣ x

EAST	SOUTH	WEST	NORTH
1 ♣	Double	Pass	1 ♡
2 ♣	?		

15. ♠ A Q J x
    ♡ A 10 x x
    ◇ x x
    ♣ K x x

EAST	SOUTH	WEST	NORTH
1 ◇	Double	Pass	2 ♣
Pass	?		

16. ♠ K Q 10 x x
    ♡ A Q 10 x
    ◇ K Q x
    ♣ x

EAST	SOUTH	WEST	NORTH
1 ♣	Double	Pass	1 ♠
Pass	?		

17. ♠ A x x
    ♡ K Q 9 x x x
    ◇ A K
    ♣ K x

WEST	NORTH	EAST	SOUTH
1 ♣	Pass	1 ♠	Double
Pass	2 ◇	Pass	?

East bids 1 Diamond:

18. ♠ K 9 x x   ♡ A K J x x x   ◇ x x   ♣ x

East bids 1 Heart:

19. ♠ K 9 x x   ♡ x   ◇ x x   ♣ A K J x x x

In each of the following cases partner has doubled and the next player has passed. What is your response?

Partner has doubled a bid of 1 Heart:

20. ♠ x x x
    ♡ A J x
    ◇ J x x
    ♣ A Q x x

21. ♠ Q x x
    ♡ x x
    ◇ A K x x x
    ♣ Q J x

22. ♠ x x
    ♡ K Q J 9 x
    ◇ K x x x
    ♣ x x

23. ♠ J x x
    ♡ Q x x x
    ◇ x x x
    ♣ x x x

24. ♠ Q x x x
    ♡ K Q x
    ◇ x x x
    ♣ x x x

25. ♠ x x
    ♡ K J x x
    ◇ Q x x
    ♣ Q J x x

26. ♠ Q 10 x x   ♡ x   ◇ A x x x   ♣ A x x x

Partner has doubled a bid of 1 No Trump:

27. ♠ x x x
    ♡ K x x
    ◇ J x
    ♣ K Q 10 x x

28. ♠ A K Q x
    ♡ x x x
    ◇ x x x x
    ♣ x x

29. ♠ Q 9 x x
    ♡ A x
    ◇ 10 x
    ♣ 9 8 x x x

30. ♠ x
    ♡ K 10 x x x x
    ◇ J x x
    ♣ x x x

Partner has doubled a bid of 1 Club:

31. ♠ x x x   ♡ x x x x   ◇ x x x   ♣ x x x

The bidding is indicated in the following hands:

32. ♠ x x
    ♡ Q J x x x
    ◇ x x x
    ♣ K J x

33. ♠ A 9 x x
    ♡ x x
    ◇ 10 x
    ♣ Q J 10 x x

WEST	NORTH	EAST	SOUTH	WEST	NORTH	EAST	SOUTH
1 ♠	Double	2 ◇	?	1 ♡	Double	4 ♡	?

34. ♠ K 10 9 x x
    ♡ J 10 x
    ◇ x x x x
    ♣ K

35. ♠ 9 x x x x
    ♡ x x x
    ◇ x x x
    ♣ J x

WEST	NORTH	EAST	SOUTH	WEST	NORTH	EAST	SOUTH
1 ◇	Double	Pass	1 ♠	1 ♡	Double	Redbl.	?
Pass	2 ♠	Pass	?				

36. ♠ x x x
    ♡ 10 9 x x x
    ◇ x
    ♣ K Q J x

WEST	NORTH	EAST	SOUTH
1 ♠	Double	3 ♠	?

37. ♠ Q J x
    ♡ A 10 x
    ◇ x x
    ♣ 9 x x x x

WEST	NORTH	EAST	SOUTH
1 ♠	Double	Pass	2 ♣
2 ◇	2 N T	Pass	?

38. ♠ J x x x x
    ♡ J 9 x x x
    ◇ x
    ♣ x

WEST	NORTH	EAST	SOUTH
1 ♠	Double	Pass	?

39. ♠ Q x x
    ♡ 9 x x
    ◇ A K x x x
    ♣ x x

SOUTH	WEST	NORTH	EAST
Pass	1 ♣	Double	Pass
2 ◇	Pass	2 ♡	Pass
?			

40. ♠ x x x x
    ♡ x
    ◇ A J x x x .
    ♣ x x x

WEST	NORTH	EAST	SOUTH
1 ♣	Double	Pass	1 ◇
Pass	1 ♡	Pass	?

41. ♠ J x x x
    ♡ Q J
    ◇ K x x
    ♣ J 10 x x

NORTH	EAST	SOUTH	WEST
1 ♡	2 ♣	Pass	Pass
Double	Pass	?	

42. ♠ 10 9 x x x x
    ♡ J 10
    ◇ x x x
    ♣ x x

WEST	NORTH	EAST	SOUTH
1 ♡	Double	4 ♡	Pass
Pass	Double	Pass	?

43. ♠ Q 9 x x x
    ♡ x x
    ◇ x x
    ♣ A 10 9 x

NORTH	EAST	SOUTH	WES?
1 ♡	2 ◇	Pass	Pass
Double	Pass	?	

44. ♠ x
    ♡ Q 10 9 x
    ◇ A J x x
    ♣ A Q x x

WEST	NORTH	EAST	SOUTH
1 ♠	Double	2 ♠	?

45. ♠ A x x
    ♡ K 10 9 x
    ◇ x x x
    ♣ Q 9 x

EAST	SOUTH	WEST	NORTH
4 ♠	Pass	Pass	4 N T
Pass	?		

46. ♠ K J 9 x x x
    ♡ A Q x
    ◇ x
    ♣ x x x

WEST	NORTH	EAST	SOUTH
1 ♣	Double	Pass	2 ♠
Pass	4 ♠	Pass	?

47. ♠ A J 9 x
    ♡ Q x x
    ◇ J 10 9 x
    ♣ x x

WEST	NORTH	EAST	SOUTH
1 ♣	Double	1 ♠	?

48. ♠ K x x x x
    ♡ x
    ◇ A K J
    ♣ K J 9 x

EAST	SOUTH	WEST	NORTH
1 ♡	Double	1 ♠	Double
Pass	Pass	2 ♡	Pass
Pass	?		

49. ♠ x
    ♡ A J x x x
    ◇ A 9 x x
    ♣ K Q x

NORTH	EAST	SOUTH	WEST
1 ♠	Double	?	

50. ♠ J x
    ♡ x x x
    ◇ A Q J 9 x
    ♣ x x x

NORTH	EAST	SOUTH	WEST
1 ♠	Double	?	

51. ♠ x x x
    ♡ A x x
    ◇ K x x x
    ♣ J x x

NORTH	EAST	SOUTH	WEST
1 ♠	Double	?	

52. ♠ x x
    ♡ x x x
    ◇ K x x x x
    ♣ Q x x

NORTH	EAST	SOUTH	WEST
1 ♠	Double	?	

53. ♠ A x x x x
    ♡ 10 9
    ◇ J 10 9 x x
    ♣ x

NORTH	EAST	SOUTH	WEST
1 ♠	Double	?	

54. ♠ A K 10 x x
    ♡ x x
    ◇ A Q x
    ♣ x x x

SOUTH	WEST	NORTH	EAST
1 ♠	Double	3 ♠	Pass
?			

55. ♠ K J x x x
    ♡ Q x x
    ◇ x
    ♣ J x x x

NORTH	EAST	SOUTH	WEST
1 ♣	Double	?	

TAKE–OUT DOUBLE QUIZ—ANSWERS

1. Double. This is a good hand and need not necessarily play in Hearts. It might play in Spades or Diamonds. You may show the Hearts next round.

2. Pass. The best prospect for a gain is to let the opponents get into trouble. To double is the worst procedure. Partner will almost surely bid 2 Hearts, and then what? As for overcalling with two of a minor suit, no one has that much money.

3. 2 Diamonds. This is apparently contradictory to the answer given in Problem 1, where the double was recommended. In the present case most of your strength is in the minors. Unless partner can bid Hearts voluntarily there will be no game. So give partner a chance to bid that suit voluntarily, rather than by force.

4. Pass, despite the $3\frac{1}{2}$ honor tricks. This is not the type of hand with which to compete. The defensive possibilities are great but offensively this hand is feeble. Do not enter the auction unless the enemy stops bidding early.

5. 2 Hearts. It is better tactics not to double with a two-suiter because you may not have time to show both suits. If you overcall with 2 Hearts you can show Diamonds the next round even if the bidding reaches a pretty high level.

6. Double. If partner responds with 1 Heart you may bail out with 1 Spade.

7. Double rather than overcall with 3 Clubs, because partner might have four Hearts and game might be there.

8. Double, in preference to making a jump overcall of 2 Spades, because this hand need not necessarily play in Spades. If partner is short in Spades, Diamonds might conceivably be the spot. Double first and jump in Spades later if desirable.

9. 1 Spade, rather than double. This allows the showing of both suits more conveniently.

10. Double. Do not make the mistake of bidding 2 Hearts. The double allows for every possibility, Spades, Hearts, Clubs or penalties.

11. Double. In this sequence of bids, the enemy having shown both Diamonds and Clubs, your partner will realize that you are looking for a choice between Spades and Hearts.

12. Double. This will show Hearts and Diamonds, for the same reason as outlined in Problem 11.

13. Pass. You should not make a free raise, because you had a minimum double. Partner has another chance to bid.

14. 2 Hearts. Do not jump to three. You forced partner to bid and he may have nothing. You have no reason to be confident that you can make nine tricks.

15. Pass. There can be no reasonable chance for game and it is pointless to try one of your suits, because partner has virtually denied a holding of a four-card major. Furthermore, another bid by you would denote a very good double, with game prospects, and partner would be justified in raising on slight values.

16. 4 Spades. A good gamble. Even though partner may have no honor strength at all game is not unlikely because the missing honors will probably be favorably located. The opening bid suggests that the Heart finesse will probably succeed and that the Diamond Ace will probably be "right."

17. 2 Hearts. You dare not jump because you have no reason to feel confident you can make a nine-trick contract.

18. Double. You are prepared for Spades as well as for Hearts. If partner bids 2 Clubs you can run to 2 Hearts.

19. 2 Clubs, rather than a double to which partner would probably respond with 2 Diamonds; that would make it necessary for you to bid 3 Clubs. Your hand is not quite that good.

20. 2 No Trump. This is a hand of game proportions and a jump in No Trump is better bidding tactics than showing the Clubs.

21. 3 Diamonds.

22. Pass. You have four sure trump tricks, and the King of Diamonds besides. You expect to defeat 1 Heart. Although your side might score a game the penalty at 1 Heart doubled should be adequate compensation.

23. 1 Spade, not 1 No Trump. With this bad hand you make the cheapest bid available.

24. 1 Spade, not 1 No Trump. Partner will be more interested in knowing that you have four Spades than that you have a Heart stopper. If desirable you may show the Heart stopper later.

25. 1 No Trump. This is preferable to 2 Clubs, since you have a good hand.

26. 2 Spades, though the suit is not a good one, since you have more than 2 honor tricks.

27. Pass, not 2 Clubs. A good-sized penalty is in view.

28. Pass, not 2 Spades.

29. Pass for the penalty.

30. 2 Hearts. Your hand is unbalanced and has not sufficient defensive strength to leave in the double.

31. 1 Heart, your only four-card suit.

32. 2 Hearts. Just about enough for a free bid. You have 1-plus honor tricks and a five-card suit. This hand rates between fair and good.

33. 4 Spades. You have favorable distribution and good playing strength. East has probably tried to shut out the Spade suit.

34. 3 Spades, or, with a conservative partner, even 4 Spades. Your hand is not rich in honor strength but you have cards that are surely valuable. Partner is probably short in Diamonds and the hand no doubt fits.

35. 1 Spade. A five-card suit should be shown over the redouble. This does not denote strength.

36. 4 Hearts. East has placed you in an awkward position but you should refuse to let him shut you out. Your hand has splendid playing values. Partner is marked short of Spades and you have only one losing Diamond.

37. 3 No Trump, with a smile. You have 1½ honor tricks that partner knows nothing about.

38. 2 Hearts. Do not leave in the double. You have insufficient defense. Furthermore, partner is probably looking for the other major.

39. 3 Hearts. Partner no doubt has a good five-card Heart suit and you therefore have normal trump support.

40. 1 Spade. Partner will know you have four very weak Spades, else you would have shown them in the first place. Surely you do not wish to pass 1 Heart and a Spade bid is cheaper than bidding 2 Diamonds.

41. Pass, since you have fairly good defensive values. The penalty should be worth while. Partner's hand was:

♠ A K x　　♡ K 10 9 x x　　◇ A x x　　♣ Q 9

42. 4 Spades. Partner is obviously not doubling on Hearts but on side cards. Your hand has no defensive value at all, but you might conceivably make 4 Spades. There is too much danger that the opponents will make 4 Hearts if you pass.

43. 3 Spades. One more than is necessary, to show a near bid the first time. Partner should remember that you refused to bid 2 Spades over 2 Diamonds and must not expect too much.

44. 3 Spades. This hand, with almost three tricks and favorable distribution, holds forth promise of a slam. The best procedure is to force partner to select the suit by making a cue-bid, even though it involves a little poetic license concerning your Spade holding.

45. 6 Hearts. Partner has promised safety for an eleven-trick contract even if you may have nothing. Actually you have three important cards, much more than partner could have hoped for. Partner held:

♠ x   ♡ A Q J x   ◇ A K x x   ♣ A K x x

46. 5 Hearts. Partner's double and subsequent jump indicate a hand stronger than an ordinary opening bid. You have the playing strength of more than an opening bid. Slam is probable. You should be safe for eleven tricks. Make one try by showing your Ace.

47. Double. 1 Spade is the bid you intended to make if East had not spoken. He may be trying to talk you out of house and home. The way to make this clear to partner is to make a penalty double. If partner has a sound double East will not be able to make 1 Spade, and if East is playing horse this will show him up.

48. 3 Spades. Partner has shown that he has Spades by making a penalty double. West is obviously faking. You very likely can make game in Spades.

49. Redouble. This is routine to show a good hand, despite the singleton Spade. No other action is proper. The opponents are in hot water and you should not permit them to get away unburned.

50. 2 Diamonds. This does not denote weakness, as so many players erroneously believe. It merely says, "Partner, I have a little something, not very much, and I had better show it now."

51. 1 No Trump, for the reason stated in Problem 50.

52. Pass. There is nothing to be gained by bidding. You haven't even enough to make it worth while telling your partner about.

53. 4 Spades. First of all, you might make it, but even if you don't it's desirable to keep the opponents from getting together.

54. Pass. Remember, while partner has length in Spades he has not a good hand. If he had he would have redoubled. If partner has not a good hand you will not make ten tricks.

55. 1 Spade. Before the bidding gets too involved you had better show the Spades. You may find it desirable to support Clubs later in order to fight for the part score. Your 1 Spade bid does not show weakness, it merely says that you are not strong enough to redouble.

CHAPTER 8

THE PENALTY DOUBLE

AN OUTSTANDING SOURCE of unrealized wealth is the penalty double made when an opponent overcalls at the level of one or two. The average player never contemplates penalizing the opponents until they reach the upper levels, and appears to be completely oblivious of the fact that by far the most profitable penalties are gathered at the very low levels. The reason for this is very clear. When your opponents eventually reach a contract of four, five or six, it is usually as the result of some exploration. While they may have misjudged their strength, they have, more often than not, succeeded in finding a reasonable place to play the hand. But when your partner has opened with 1 Spade and next hand bids 2 Clubs, he has many times just tested his luck with what has come to be known as a "nuisance bid." The question of who more frequently finds him to be a nuisance has not been definitely cleared up. Penalties at this point can be devastating.

First of all, it is important to differentiate between a penalty double and one intended for a take-out. This problem we discussed in the chapter on Take-out Doubles. Here is a restatement:

Doubles of all No Trump contracts are intended for penalties. All doubles, even at the level of one, are intended for penalties if made after partner has bid. There is no such thing as a take-out double after partner has made a bid.

The question arises, how is the inexperienced player to tell when to double an adverse bid for penalties? Generally speaking, this is done on a simple arithmetic basis. You count those tricks which you may reasonably expect to win, add them to those partner is expected to deliver, and if the total is sufficient to defeat the contract, let the axe descend. In the higher brackets this calculation is not very difficult, but it is not quite so easy to judge in doubling contracts of one and two.

Perhaps the following suggestion may serve as an effective guide. At least it possesses the merit of simplicity:

When your partner opens the bidding (or in any other way shows strength, as by a take-out double) and your right-hand opponent overcalls in the suit which you wanted to bid, you should double for business. For example, you hold:

♠ K J 9 x   ♡ J 10   ◇ A J 10 x   ♣ x x x

Partner opens with 1 Heart. Opponent overcalls with 1 Spade. You should double, and your adversary isn't going to enjoy it. You are not doubling to show that you have the Spades. You are doubling to collect points. Had second hand passed you would cheerfully have responded with 1 Spade. That is the test. It is not whether you might have responded with 1 Spade. It is whether you *wanted* to. For example, in the same situation you hold:

♠ K J x x   ♡ x x x   ◇ K x x   ♣ x x x

In this case you would have responded to partner's opening bid of 1 Heart with 1 Spade, not because you had any desire to, but because you felt it was your duty. If second hand overcalls with 1 Spade, a double on this hand is not recommended.

Another simple guide: Partner opens with one of a suit and the next hand overcalls with two of some other suit. On hands which tempt you to call 2 No Trump, pause for five seconds and maybe you will change your mind. Double instead and watch your savings grow. For example, your partner opens with 1 Spade, the next hand overcalls with 2 Diamonds, and you hold:

♠ J x   ♡ A x x   ◇ Q 10 x x   ♣ K x x x

While you are seized with the temptation to bid 2 No Trump, my suggestion is that you resist it. That your hand will produce at least four tricks in defense is a reasonable assumption. These, coupled with your partner's expected three tricks, will account for a two-trick penalty. Assuming the opponents are not vulnerable, this will yield 300 points.

What, you will contend, about the situation in which you will be abandoning game, for which 300 points would not be adequate

compensation? The answer is really very simple. If your partner
has a minimum hand you will have no game. Suppose the second
hand has not overcalled. Would you have been willing to suggest
that you have a good chance for game? I think not. But if your
partner has more than a minimum and a game is probable it follows that the penalty will be correspondingly greater. In other
words, the more your partner has the more the opponents are
going to suffer.

There is this consideration of paramount importance: When
the contract which you double will yield a game if fulfilled, you
must exercise greater caution and allow yourself a trick leeway
for margin of error, or for the arrows of outrageous fortune. In
other words, don't double a contract of 2 or 3 Spades or 3 or 4
Diamonds unless you expect to defeat it two tricks. But when your
partner opens the bidding, and next hand overcalls with 2 Clubs
or 2 Diamonds, great latitude is allowed in the exercise of the
double "on suspicion." The risk is not great. The doubled contract, though fulfilled, does not yield the enemy a game. An illustration from real life:

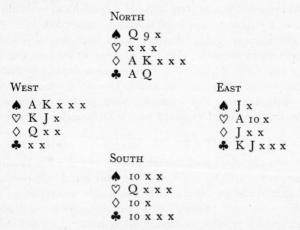

NORTH
♠ Q 9 x
♡ x x x
◇ A K x x x
♣ A Q

WEST
♠ A K x x x
♡ K J x
◇ Q x x
♣ x x

EAST
♠ J x
♡ A 10 x
◇ J x x
♣ K J x x x

SOUTH
♠ 10 x x
♡ Q x x x
◇ 10 x
♣ 10 x x x

West opened the bidding with 1 Spade. North was vulnerable
and overcalled with 2 Diamonds. East was presented with a
problem. He had what he regarded as a little too much to pass,

but after the 2 Diamond overcall the thought of a 3 Club bid could not be entertained for even a moment, and there was no other available bid for him. Reasoning that his hand would probably develop at least three tricks in defense and counting on his partner for the usual minimum of three, he elected to double, relaxing in the knowledge that even if the opponents fulfilled the contract they could not score game. The result was an 800-point penalty, and what is more remarkable about it is that East and West could not have scored game.

TRICKS FOR A PENALTY DOUBLE

In counting your expected tricks for the purpose of making a penalty double too much reliance must not be placed on the honor trick table. Common-sense methods of deduction should be resorted to.

Sometimes you may allow a greater value than that suggested by the table. Ace-Queen is regarded as 1½ honor tricks but if that suit has been strongly bid on your right you may be justified in counting on two winners. Similarly, a guarded King is regarded as ½ honor trick, but if your right-hand opponent may reasonably be expected to hold the Ace you may rely upon the King as a winner. However, when the suit has been bid on your left the Ace-Queen should not be valued at much more than a trick and a King should be discounted almost entirely.

It is rarely sound to count more than two tricks in any one suit, and if you have great length in the suit it is dangerous to rely on more than one defensive trick from that source. Occasionally none should be counted, as might be the case if you held A K Q x x x and partner has vigorously supported the suit.

Be quick to double when short in partner's suit. Be more cautious when holding as many as four of your partner's suit.

An item of value that may not appear in the honor trick table is the possession of four cards of the adverse suit. For defensive purposes this may be regarded as one trick, even though no honor card is held. The nuisance value of four small trumps should not be underestimated. It means that if Declarer is to exhaust trumps he must make four pulls, which he will rarely find it convenient to do. If Declarer is forced to ruff once, he will probably be brought down to your size in trumps.

On this basis observe the following hand. As South you hold:

♠ K Q J 9   ♡ x x x x   ◇ x x   ♣ A K J

The bidding has proceeded:

SOUTH	WEST	NORTH	EAST
1 ♠	2 ◇	Double	2 ♡
?			

What should you do? The recommendation is to double. The defensive tricks may be estimated as follows: Since partner doubled 2 Diamonds it is unlikely that he has any length in Spades, which makes it probable that two tricks will be cashed in that suit. At least two tricks may be counted in Clubs and one trick should be counted for the possession of four Hearts. This brings the tally up to five tricks, or book. Anything partner produces will be velvet. You may contend, what if partner has nothing but Diamonds and produces no tricks against a Heart contract? The answer is, your partner has made a very unsound business double if that is the situation.

In doubling the opponents one must always be conscious of the question, "Is there apt to be a rescue, and if so can I do any damage to that rescue bid?"

When counting on partner's expected tricks to defeat the contract, one must have regard for the type of action that partner has previously taken. If he has opened the bidding with one of a suit it is reasonable to expect him to produce about three tricks in the play of the hand. If he has opened with 1 No Trump he may be depended on for four tricks. If he has made a take-out double he may be relied upon to take at least three tricks. When partner has merely overcalled he should not be counted on for more than one trick defensively. Similarly, when partner has raised your suit his raise may be based to a certain extent on distribution and he should not be counted on for more than one trick.

And when partner has opened with a preëmptive bid you must base no business double on his action. Do not count on him for much of anything. Any business double must be based on your own hand.

TAKING PARTNER OUT OF A BUSINESS DOUBLE

One of the most popular cartoons of the day holds up to ridicule the player who takes his partner out of a business double. This has come to be regarded in many circles as contract's outstanding crime. I fear that this is somewhat in the nature of subversive activity. Since ignorance of the law is no excuse, it is of course a crime, and sometimes of major proportions, to take partner out of a business double from ignorance that it was intended for penalties. But the refusal to stand for partner's penalty doubles in the interest of the partnership is a matter involving the exercise of good judgment, without which no player can succeed at the card table.

Even though you make a business double your partner may still be entitled to his opinion, though little toleration is to be held out for his whims. If a player's hand is completely unsuitable for defensive purposes he is at perfect liberty to decline to stand for the double. However, the burden of proof is on the person who overrides his partner's judgment. Let us observe an illustration or two. As South you hold:

♠ x x   ♡ K Q J 10 x x   ◇ A x x x   ♣ x

The bidding has proceeded:

SOUTH	WEST	NORTH	EAST
1 ♡	2 ♣	Double	Pass

What should you do? Of course partner has made a business double, but your hand is bound to be a disappointment to him in defense against 2 Clubs. Actually, your hand may develop only one trick. You should therefore issue a warning by bidding 2 Hearts, at which contract you should be in no serious danger. However, on the same sequence of bidding, if you hold:

♠ x   ♡ K Q J x x   ◇ A K x x   ♣ J x x

you would naturally pass the double and start clipping coupons. Your hand is very well suited for defensive play. You should not be concerned about the possible loss of a game, because your penalty will be adequate to repay you.

If your hand is unsuited to defense at a contract which partner has doubled, but is a very fine hand from the offensive standpoint, you should, in refusing to stand for the double, jump the bid to make this point clear to partner. For example, as South you hold:

♠ x   ♡ A Q J 10 x x   ◇ A K J x x   ♣ x

The bidding has proceeded:

South	West	North	East
1 ♡	2 ♣	Double	Pass

What do you do? In this hand you have good defensive values despite your shortage in Clubs, and you do not fear the fulfillment of the adversaries' contract, but there is a question in your mind whether it will be adequate compensation, inasmuch as your prospects for scoring a game are very bright. It is not recommended that you stand for the double, but in taking out the double you should make a jump—you should bid 3 Diamonds— to indicate to your partner that you are bidding aggressively and not merely because your hand is not suitable for defensive play.

It will be seen, therefore, that the mere circumstance that the enemy can be defeated is not always sufficient justification for doubling. You must always inquire, will it be worth while? If you can score more points by going on with the bidding, naturally the double should be eschewed; but in doubtful cases lean towards the double on the theory that you will never go broke by taking sure profits.

CLOSE DOUBLES

Occasionally we must desist from doubling the adversaries in a close situation where it is feared that our double will locate certain strength for the Declarer and permit him to play the hand in a somewhat unnatural manner. It is a good principle not to double a close contract if your double is apt to cost you a trick. When your trump holding is something like Q 10 x x, for example, a double may warn the Declarer of the adverse trump distribution and may permit him to play that suit unnaturally on the basis of your warning.

On the same line of reasoning, close doubles of slams should never be made. There is not enough profit in them compared to the risk of affording Declarer an occasional clue to the successful fulfillment of the contract.

Sometimes a doubtful double must be made in the competitive situation when it is definitely wise for your side to discontinue bidding. In such cases if you pass the bid to your partner there is a mild suggestion that you are willing to have him go on.

DOUBLES OF SLAM CONTRACTS

It has been pointed out that few points are gained above the line by doubling slam contracts. As a result of this experience a convention has been developed in modern times, relating to the double of a slam contract by a player who does not have the opening lead. The purpose of the convention is to guide the opening leader in the selection of his attack.

When partner doubles a slam you must not make your normal opening lead. If you and your partner have bid any suit or suits these suits should not be led, and obviously a trump lead is out of the question. The convention makes the following provisions:

1. If Dummy has bid any suit or suits (other than trump) the double demands the lead of the first suit bid by Dummy.

2. If Dummy has bid no side suit, but Declarer has bid another suit, the double demands the lead of the first side suit bid by Declarer.

3. If neither Dummy nor Declarer has bid any side suit, but the defensive side has, the double demands the lead of one of the unbid suits.

In other words, the opening leader must not lead his own or his partner's suit. It follows, therefore, that you must not double a slam contract if you are anxious to have your partner make his normal lead. Of course, if the opponents have stepped so far out of line that the opening lead will not matter very much you might as well strike and collect a bonus. But where it is a question of just another 50 or 100 points you must forego the luxury.

For example, as South you hold:

1 ♠ A x x   ♡ K Q J 10 x x   ◇ x x x x   ♣ ——

2 ♠ Q J 10   ♡ A Q J x x x   ◇ x x   ♣ x x

The bidding has proceeded:

WEST	NORTH	EAST	SOUTH
1 ♠	Pass	3 ♣	3 ♡
3 ♠	Pass	4 ♠	Pass
6 ♠	Pass	Pass	?

What should you do?

With No. 1 you should double. This demands the lead of Dummy's first suit, Clubs, which you ruff and defeat the contract.

With No. 2 you must not double. If you do, partner has instructions not to lead a Heart, which is the lead you want to get.

An illustration of an unwise double of a slam contract follows:

NORTH
♠ A Q
♡ 10 x x
◇ K J 10 9
♣ A Q 10 x

WEST
♠ 10 9 8 x x x
♡ ——
◇ x x x x
♣ J x x

EAST
♠ K x
♡ x x
◇ A Q x x
♣ K 9 x x x

SOUTH
♠ J x x
♡ A K Q J x x x x
◇ x
♣ x

The bidding:

NORTH	EAST	SOUTH	WEST
1 ♢	Pass	1 ♡	Pass
1 N T	Pass	5 ♡	Pass
6 ♡	Double	Pass	Pass
Pass			

West dutifully led a Diamond and Declarer had no difficulty in fulfilling his contract. East was in with the Queen of Diamonds on the opening lead and had no satisfactory continuation. It was a simple matter now for Declarer to establish Dummy's Diamonds for the necessary Spade discards. Had East not doubled, West would no doubt have led a Spade, which would probably have defeated the contract.

Tempting though the double might appear, East should have refrained from doubling because the Diamond lead is not desired. From the texture of East's hand it is quite apparent that there will be no reasonable way for the Declarer to get rid of his Diamonds. East should prefer to have either a Spade or a Club trick established while he still controls the Diamond suit.

DOUBLES OF 3 NO TRUMP CONTRACTS

The double of a 3 No Trump contract by a player not on lead carries with it certain inferences regarding the opening lead.

1. If the doubler has bid a suit, his partner must unconditionally lead that suit, even though he may have but a singleton in it and a very fine suit of his own.

2. If the opening leader has bid a suit, partner's double requests him to lead that suit.

3. When neither the leader nor the doubler has bid, the double is a suggestion to partner to lead the Dummy's first bid suit, unless he has a very fine opening lead of his own. But bear in mind, this is only a suggestion, *not a demand*. The leader may exercise his own judgment and if Dummy's suit has been rebid it is doubtful that he should lead it.

PENALTY DOUBLE QUIZ

ANSWERS BEGIN ON PAGE 238

You are South and hold the following hands. The bidding has proceeded as indicated. What do you do in each case? Opponents are vulnerable.

1. ♠ K x x
   ♡ 10 x x x
   ◇ K J
   ♣ 10 x x x

NORTH	EAST	SOUTH	WEST
1 N T	2 ♣	?	

2. ♠ x x
   ♡ K J 9 x
   ◇ K x x
   ♣ K J 10 9

NORTH	EAST	SOUTH	WEST
1 ♠	1 N T	?	

3. ♠ A J 9 x
   ♡ x
   ◇ A Q 9 x
   ♣ K x x x

SOUTH	WEST	NORTH	EAST
1 ◇	Pass	1 ♡	1 ♠
?			

4. ♠ J x
   ♡ A x x
   ◇ Q 10 9 x
   ♣ K 10 x x

NORTH	EAST	SOUTH	WEST
1 ♠	2 ◇	?	

5. ♠ x
   ♡ Q 10 x x
   ◇ K J x x x
   ♣ J x x

EAST	SOUTH	WEST	NORTH
1 ♠	Pass	Pass	2 ♣
2 ♠	Pass	Pass	Double
Pass	?		

6. ♠ K Q J 9 x x
   ♡ x
   ◇ x
   ♣ J x x x x

EAST	SOUTH	WEST	NORTH
1 ♡	1 ♠	4 ♡	Double
Pass	?		

7. ♠ x x x
   ♡ A K Q x x
   ◇ K x x
   ♣ x x

SOUTH	WEST	NORTH	EAST
1 ♡	1 ♠	Double	Pass
?			

8. ♠ x
   ♡ A Q x x
   ◇ A J 10 x
   ♣ K Q x x

EAST	SOUTH	WEST	NORTH
4 ♠	?		

9. ♠ Q J x x
   ♡ x x
   ◇ A 10 9 x
   ♣ x x x

NORTH	EAST	SOUTH	WEST
1 N T	2 ♠	?	

10. ♠ K J x x x
    ♡ A J x x
    ◇ x x x
    ♣ x

NORTH	EAST	SOUTH	WEST
1 ♡	1 ♠	?	

11. ♠ x
    ♡ Q 10 x x
    ◇ A Q 10 9 x
    ♣ 10 x x

You are vulnerable.

NORTH	EAST	SOUTH	WEST
1 ♠	2 ♡	?	

12. ♠ 10 x
    ♡ 10 9 x
    ◇ K Q 9
    ♣ A J x x x

The opponents are vulnerable.

NORTH	EAST	SOUTH	WEST
1 ♠	2 ◇	?	

13. ♠ K Q 10 x x
    ♡ x
    ◇ A K x x
    ♣ J 9 x

The opponents are vulnerable.

NORTH	EAST	SOUTH	WEST
1 ♡	2 ♣	?	

14. ♠ A x x
    ♡ x
    ◇ K 9 x x
    ♣ A K 9 x x

The opponents are vulnerable.

NORTH	EAST	SOUTH	WEST
1 ♠	2 ◇	?	

15. ♠ A J 10
    ♡ K x x x x x
    ◇ ——
    ♣ A K x x

SOUTH	WEST	NORTH	EAST
1 ♡	2 ◇	Double	Pass
?			

16. ♠ A K Q
    ♡ A 10 x
    ◇ A K Q x x x
    ♣ x

SOUTH	WEST	NORTH	EAST
2 ◇	3 ♣	Double	Pass
?			

17. ♠ A Q x x x x
    ♡ Q x x
    ◇ K
    ♣ K x x

SOUTH	WEST	NORTH	EAST
1 ♠	2 ♣	Double	2 ♡
?			

18. ♠ x x
    ♡ x
    ◇ K J x x x x
    ♣ Q x x x

NORTH	EAST	SOUTH	WEST
1 ♠	2 ◇	?	

19. ♠ x ♡ A Q 9 x ◊ 10 x x x ♣ K 9 x x

The opponents are vulnerable.

NORTH	EAST	SOUTH	WEST
1 ♠	2 ◊	?	

PENALTY DOUBLE QUIZ—ANSWERS

1. Double. You may reasonably expect to take a Spade, a Diamond and a Club, which combined with partner's four tricks should result in a two-trick penalty. 500 points are not to be sneered at, particularly when you have no sound raise for partner.

2. Double. You have a reasonable expectation of winning about five tricks in the play, which with partner's expected three tricks spell a two-trick set. If partner has more, so much the merrier.

3. Double. You can probably win the "book" in your own hand. Any tricks partner produces will be "pay-off" tricks. If he has no defensive values he need not stand for the double. Don't bid No Trump.

4. Double. You can count on winning four tricks, partner the usual three. Don't bid 2 No Trump. If partner has a minimum you will have no game. If he has more the penalty may be enormous.

5. Pass. Partner's double is for penalties. If he wanted you to bid he would have doubled 1 Spade. He has Declarer where he wants him. Dummy must have nothing and East has no doubt committed a social error.

6. 4 Spades. True, partner's double is for penalties, but his action is no doubt not based on Heart strength but on side cards, which should give you a fair chance to make 4 Spades. Besides, you have no defense at all.

7. Pass. You have a normal hand and the advantage of possessing three cards in the adverse suit.

8. Double. You can no doubt defeat 4 Spades. If partner has a very long suit he may decide to bid, in which case you can play the hand offensively. This is not strong enough for a 4 No Trump overcall, since that would automatically force your partner into a five-bid.

9. Double. You can develop at least three tricks, which with partner's four will spell a two-trick penalty. Furthermore, it is unlikely that your

side has a game. In fact, had second hand passed you would not have a good raise to 2 No Trump.

10. 2 Hearts. A double is not recommended; first, because you have too many of partner's suit, and secondly, because your hand has great offensive possibilities. By doubling you may give up a game.

11. Double. You can probably win four tricks. Don't bid 2 No Trump. There is no reason to visualize a game. What if East had passed? Would you have thought much of your hand?

12. In view of the vulnerability the double is superior to bidding 2 No Trump. If it should turn out that you can make game the chances are good that you will beat the enemy two tricks for 500 points, more than the value of your game.

13. Double. You can count on taking at least four tricks. With partner's three, a score of 500 points is in sight. Unless partner is satisfied with Spades you may have no game. If partner's principal strength is Hearts you are well out of the hand.

14. Double. You have a reasonable expectancy of taking five tricks, which with partner's three tricks should yield a penalty of 800 points, possibly 1,100 points if partner has more than a minimum. This will take care of a lost slam in the event that you have one.

15. Pass. While you should normally be reluctant to pass a penalty double at a low level when void of the adverse suit, nevertheless this hand contains splendid defensive values in the black suits and will not be a disappointment to partner. This looks like a misfit, since partner is probably short in Hearts.

16. Pass. There is no reason why you should override partner's decision to play for penalties. You have done justice to your hand by the 2 Diamond bid. Partner knows best.

17. Pass. Your hand is not strong defensively. The value of your King of Clubs has vanished. East may have none. Don't rebid 2 Spades. Partner may not like that suit at all. Leave the decision to him.

18. Pass. This is too good to be true. A double would not be good strategy because there is bound to be a rescue bid by either West or your partner. If partner should double a rescue bid of 2 Hearts, for example, it would probably be disastrous, since you will not be able to contribute to the defense.

19. Double. You have a good chance to win two tricks in Hearts, since either partner or East probably holds the King. For similar reasons you may count the King of Clubs as a winner. Count one trick for possession of four trumps. That gives you at least four tricks.

CHAPTER 9

ADVANCED BIDDING
SITUATIONS

MISFITS

RIFTS IN FRIENDSHIPS of long years' standing, as well as sizable financial disasters, are frequently brought about on hands in which each partner is short of the other's suit. One denies the other for round after round, until one of the opponents finds it high time to enter the auction with a resounding double.

Success at the bridge table involves not only making the most of your good cards but holding your losses to a minimum on hands that were not destined to show a profit. A willingness to take a short loss on hopeless hands is one of the distinguishing features of the experienced player.

In cases of misfits, which one of the partners should quit? You have all listened at one time or other to bidding like this:

OPENER	RESPONDER
1 ♠	2 ♡
2 ♠	3 ♡
3 ♠	4 ♡

and so on ad infinitem.

Now, who should quit in this case? I have sought for some time to hit upon a practical solution. At one time I recommended that it be done on a priority basis. The younger of the two partners, it was suggested, should be the first to resign. This practice was not endorsed by the Bureau of Vital Statistics, which was burdened by too heavy a demand for birth certificates. So that possible solution had to be abandoned.

In any such case the exercise of good judgment is called for. A few general principles, however, may be laid down.

1. The player who can buy the hand at the cheapest price should, as a rule, be given the courtesy of the road. It is not always wise in these cases to look for the best possible contract. In case of a storm an inferior contract, undoubled, is better than a superior one that is doubled and down. When it is probable that a loss must be taken, a player with Spades should have priority over a player with Hearts, for the one holding Hearts must bid to a new level to buy the hand.

2. The player with high cards should be willing to become Dummy, permitting the player with the long suit to be Declarer. Let us see how this applies to a case from real life.

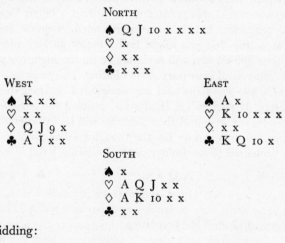

NORTH
♠ Q J 10 x x x x
♡ x
♢ x x
♣ x x x

WEST
♠ K x x
♡ x x
♢ Q J 9 x
♣ A J x x

EAST
♠ A x
♡ K 10 x x x
♢ x x
♣ K Q 10 x

SOUTH
♠ x
♡ A Q J x x
♢ A K 10 x x
♣ x x

The bidding:

SOUTH	WEST	NORTH	EAST
1 ♡	Pass	1 ♠	Pass
2 ♢	Pass	2 ♠	Pass

What should South do? When I saw this hand played, South went on. In fact, he went on indefinitely, as is the tendency of most players who hold two five-card suits. That holding seems to instill in them some pride of possession.

South should have realized that game was hopeless when North failed to support one of his red suits and also was unable to bid

No Trump. Despite his shortage in Spades, South should have passed the 2 Spade bid, realizing that game was hopeless. South's hand makes a good Dummy because of its high card content. North must have length in Spades to repeat them in the face of an announced two-suiter. North's hand will probably be a useless Dummy, so South should be inclined to permit North to be Declarer.

Another type of hand on which a checkout is recommended is the following. Your partner opens with 1 Heart, and you hold:

♠ J x x x x   ♡ ——   ◇ x x   ♣ A J x x x x

You respond with 2 Clubs. Partner bids 2 Hearts. Most players become panicky at this point and try to find a better "spot" by bidding 2 Spades. This is not recommended. A quick pass is in order. It is true that you might find a better parking place, but by the time you do you will probably be up too high, for partner will misunderstand your purpose in bidding. This must be marked down as a hopeless hand and any undoubled contract should be satisfactory. If partner's 2 Hearts are doubled for penalties it is quite another matter and then a rescue will be in order.

A splendid opportunity for the thoughtful handling of a misfit was presented to the holder of the following hand:

♠ A K J x   ♡ A Q x x x   ◇ ——   ♣ A 9 x x

He opened with one Heart and partner responded with 2 Diamonds. His rebid was 2 Spades and partner bid 3 Diamonds. What should he do? He knows that his partner has a maximum of two Hearts, since with three it would have been his duty to return to the opener's first suit, the opener having shown a 5-4. The responder is known to have a maximum of three Spades, since with four he would not have gone out of that suit into another Diamond bid. Responder cannot have anything very good in Clubs, else he would have tried No Trump on opener's display of great strength. It is evident that responder has a long string of Diamonds and nothing else and that it is a hopeless hand. Opener therefore made a very fine pass. His mate held:

♠ x x   ♡ x x   ◇ K Q 10 x x x x   ♣ x x

THE FORCING PASS

A pass is not always a confession of weakness. It may be a definite sign of strength. When in a competitive auction you and your partner have shown great strength and have bid up to 4 Hearts and your right-hand opponent now makes an obvious sacrifice bid of 4 Spades, a pass by you does not indicate fear, because it is quite apparent that you could double a 4 Spade bid if you chose. If you double you are in effect saying to your partner that you do not care to go on to 5 Hearts. If, however, you feel that the penalty may not be adequate compensation and you believe that you may have a fair chance to make 5 Hearts, you pass and permit partner to make the decision.

In such a sequence of bids, of course, partner is obliged to act. If he does not choose to bid 5 Hearts he must without reference to the merits of his own hand automatically double, which you would have done yourself had you been quite sure there was no chance for 5 Hearts. A pass by you at this point is known as a forcing pass. It forces partner either to double the opponents or to go on with the bidding.

It is not always easy to identify a forcing pass. Not every pass in a competitive auction is forcing. A pass becomes a force when it is quite evident from the common sense of the situation that your side has the best holding and that the opponents are trying to wrest it from you. Let us take an illustration or two.

You are South and vulnerable. The opponents are not. You hold:

♠ A x x x   ♡ x x   ◇ K Q x x   ♣ x x x

The bidding has proceeded:

NORTH	EAST	SOUTH	WEST
1 ♠	2 ♡	2 ♠	3 ♡
4 ♠	5 ♡	?	

What should you do?

You are quite convinced that the opponents cannot make 5 Hearts. Should you double? Since you have a very fine raise, should you try 5 Spades? You are not sure. In that case, why not let partner decide? You should pass. This is not a confession of weakness; you made a free raise early in the auction, and thus showed strength. On the contrary it is an announcement of strength. Your pass says, "Partner, I think we have a fair chance to fulfill a contract of 5 Spades. What do you think?" If partner does not think so he will double the 5 Heart bid.

Another case. The opponents are vulnerable. You are not. As South you hold:

♠ x x   ♡ A K Q x   ◇ 10 x x x   ♣ A Q 10

The bidding has proceeded:

South	West	North	East
1 ♡	Pass	3 ♡	3 ♠

What do you do?

Had East passed you would have bid 4 Hearts in routine manner. It is true that East's 3 Spade bid does not prevent you from bidding 4 Hearts if you choose to. Should you so choose? The answer is No. Your partner has made a bid that is forcing to game. Each of you is committed to a final game contract (unless the opponents pay an adequate price for taking it from you). Your proper procedure is to pass it around to your partner. He will do one of three things, whichever is most suitable to his hand. He may go on to 4 Hearts, which he announced the partnership could make. He may decide to play for 3 No Trump, to which you will have no objection. Or, and this is the important consideration, he may be able to double a 3 Spade bid, and if he wishes to do so you would find it quite delectable.

In the actual case the 3 Spade bid was doubled by North and defeated 1,100 points.

In the next case it is you who have made a game-forcing bid. You are South and hold:

♠ x   ♡ A K Q 10 x x   ◇ A K x   ♣ A Q x

The bidding has proceeded:

South	West	North	East
2 ♡	Pass	2 N T	3 ♠
?			

What should you do?

In my opinion there is only one proper call at this point, and that is a pass. Your opening two-bid was forcing to game and remains so. You should not crowd the bidding by calling 4 Hearts, for three reasons. First, partner may wish to show one of the minor suits at the level of four and a 4 Heart bid will make it impossible for him to do so. Secondly, partner may wish to double the 3 Spade bid if he considers that profitable. Finally, he may have a Spade stopper and desire to play the hand at 3 No Trump. He will be in a better position to judge than you. You have announced the approximate strength of your hand by your original 2 Heart bid and no further announcements from you are necessary.

Another interesting example:

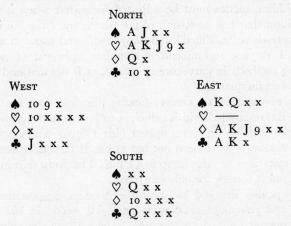

NORTH
♠ A J x x
♡ A K J 9 x
◊ Q x
♣ 10 x

WEST
♠ 10 9 x
♡ 10 x x x x
◊ x
♣ J x x x

EAST
♠ K Q x x
♡ —
◊ A K J 9 x x
♣ A K x

SOUTH
♠ x x
♡ Q x x
◊ 10 x x x
♣ Q x x x

With North and South vulnerable, the bidding has proceeded:

North	East	South	West
1 ♡	2 ♡	Pass	3 ♣
3 ♡	?		

What should East do at this point? Only one call may be re-garded as correct, and that is a pass. A bid of 4 Diamonds or a raise of the Clubs would be little short of an atrocity. There is no need for East to act when his previous cue-bid committed the partnership to game, and West in his next turn is in duty bound to take some action, either by doubling the enemy or by going on with the bidding as best he can.

In the actual case West doubled and East passed. As the cards lay, it may be seen, East and West could not even have gone game. We pass lightly over North's bid of 3 Hearts. Those things will happen and no one will ever completely stamp out such practices.

PART–SCORE BIDDING

A number of the bidding principles which we have discussed in the preceding pages must be modified to a certain extent when the bidding side has the benefit of a part score. Similarly, defen-sive bidding tactics must be adjusted somewhat when it is the opposition that has possession of the part score. Note the use of the expressions "modified" and "adjusted," and those in a mild sense. I do not recommend a complete upheaval of normal bidding methods in part-score situations, as is the unsound prac-tice in certain quarters.

The new-suit(by responder)-forcing principle does not apply where the responder's bid is sufficient to complete the game. For example, with 60 on score, opener bids 1 Spade and responder bids 2 Clubs. Opener need not bid again. If responder has mild slam aspirations he must jump to 3 Clubs. The jump shift in these conditions is forcing for only one round.

An opening demand bid is still a demand, despite the part score, and responder must reply once. He need not bid again unless opener jumps in a new suit, in which case the obligation to speak once more arises.

When an advanced score of 60 is held, responder should be willing to stretch a point to keep the bidding alive, since a con-tract of 1 No Trump will complete the game.

The possession of a part score by either side will frequently influence decisions as to opening bids. Part scores of 20 and 30 should, for practical reasons, be disregarded, and the bidding should proceed, except for the final call, as though such a score did not exist. But when an advanced score is held such a consideration as preparing for a rebid disappears entirely. For example, you hold:

♠ A K x x ♡ A x x ◇ x x x ♣ x x x

With a clear score a pass is recommended on this hand, because of the difficulty of finding a convenient rebid. However, with a part score of 60 this hand should be opened with 1 Spade, since any response of two by partner may be dropped.

Similarly, holding:

♠ A K 10 x ♡ x x x ◇ x x x ♣ A J x

With a clear score it is recommended that this hand be opened with 1 Club, but with a part score such action is unthinkable. The proper procedure is to open with 1 Spade.

When the opponents have a part score and it is to be presumed that they will try to "sneak out," doubtful hands must be opened against them. Holding:

♠ A K x x ♡ A x x x ◇ x x ♣ x x x

you should open against a part score, because otherwise you may expect the opponents to open and it will be difficult for you to compete at a later stage.

It is good practice with a 60 part score to vary your tactics in No Trump openings. The requirements should be relaxed and a hand such as this:

♠ K x x ♡ A x x ◇ J 10 x ♣ A Q x x

should be opened with 1 No Trump rather than 1 Club. In the first place, if partner has scattered values this contract completes a game. Secondly, if he has length of suit without any high card values he is at liberty to take you out into two of his suit, which also completes a game.

Such a bid has the added advantage of keeping the opponents guessing. If they stay out of the bidding they may lose. If they come into the bidding your partner may be waiting to administer a crushing blow.

Since slams are available even to people with part scores, our tactics must be adjusted to this condition. An opening demand bid is permissible with one playing trick less than is normally required. For example, either of the following hands should be opened with a demand bid when you have a part score of 40 or 60:

1.   ♠ A x x   ♡ A K Q J x x   ◇ A x x   ♣ x
2.   ♠ A x   ♡ K Q J 10 x x   ◇ A x x x   ♣ x

When you have an advanced score of 70 or 80 and partner opens with one of a suit, you should not pass simply because the bid completes game. You should give partner a mild chance if you have a good hand. For example, with a 70 part score partner opens with 1 Spade and you hold:

♠ A 10 x   ♡ K x   ◇ A K x x   ♣ x x x x

If partner has a very fine hand you may have a chance for big things. Your proper procedure is to bid 2 Spades. This is over-bidding the game and suggests that you are interested in going places if partner chooses to act. If he does not, 2 Spades will surely be safe. You must not make the mistake of responding with 2 Diamonds, which partner, in view of the part score situation, may pass.

Similarly, under the same conditions you hold:

♠ A x x x   ♡ Q x x   ◇ A K Q x x   ♣ x

With a clear score you would have responded with 2 Diamonds, intending to jump in Spades on the next round, but in this case you dare not bid 2 Diamonds, and it is suggested that you do one of two things, either overbid the game with 3 Spades or, pref-erably, make a jump shift to 3 Diamonds. This forces partner for one more round. You will show Spade support subsequently.

FOUR OPPOSITE FOUR

"The more the merrier" does not always apply to the trump suit. Nine trumps are not necessarily better than eight. This sounds cryptic so let us examine a hand from a tournament:

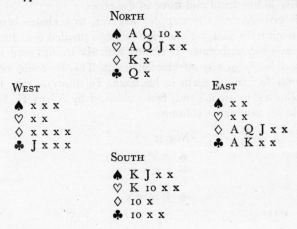

NORTH
♠ A Q 10 x
♡ A Q J x x
♢ K x
♣ Q x

WEST
♠ x x x
♡ x x
♢ x x x x
♣ J x x x

EAST
♠ x x
♡ x x
♢ A Q J x x
♣ A K x x

SOUTH
♠ K J x x
♡ K 10 x x
♢ 10 x
♣ 10 x x

The bidding actually proceeded:

NORTH	EAST	SOUTH	WEST
1 ♡	2 ♢	2 ♡	Pass
4 ♡	Pass	Pass	Pass

East cashed the Ace and King of Clubs and gave up the lead and just waited for his two Diamond tricks to defeat the contract. At one table the bidding proceeded in the following manner:

NORTH	EAST	SOUTH	WEST
1 ♡	2 ♢	2 ♡	Pass
2 ♠	Pass		

and South, realizing that his partner had five Hearts and four Spades, nevertheless elected to support the Spades, whereupon North contracted for game in that suit. It will be noted that the contract of 4 Spades by North could not be defeated, because one of South's Diamonds was discarded on North's fifth Heart.

It is apparent, therefore, that provided each of the partners has four trumps the five-card suit is much more desirable as a side suit than as trump, because the long suit will provide discards for losers in the other hand. If you have eight trumps between you it is much better to have four in each hand, than to have five in one hand and three in the other.

This principle does not apply, however, to a choice between eight trumps divided 5-3 and eight trumps divided 6-2. *The 6-2 division is better,* because Declarer, with six trumps, can stand repeated forces in any adverse long suit. This he could not do with only five trump cards in his hand. To illustrate this, I cite the following unusual hand, first published by Albert H. Morehead in his newspaper column.

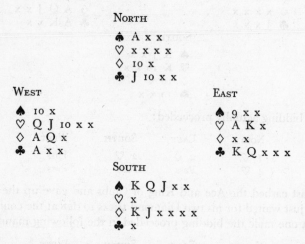

NORTH

♠ A x x
♡ x x x x
♢ 10 x
♣ J 10 x x

WEST

♠ 10 x
♡ Q J 10 x x
♢ A Q x
♣ A x x

EAST

♠ 9 x x
♡ A K x
♢ x x
♣ K Q x x x

SOUTH

♠ K Q J x x
♡ x
♢ K J x x x x
♣ x

East opened with 1 Club and South overcalled with 1 Diamond. South thereafter bid Spades twice, showing that he had 6-5 distribution (see page 13). When East and West got to 4 Hearts, South chose to sacrifice, bidding 4 Spades and thus giving North a choice between Spades and Diamonds.

Though he had three Spades as against two Diamonds, *and though Diamonds required a contract one trick higher,* North should have preferred Diamonds, the 6-2 suit, as a safety measure.

At Spades, South would be forced on the second trick by a Heart opening and continuation. He could play safe for down four, but would probably go over to the trump Ace and try a finesse for the Diamond Queen, after which he would be forced in Hearts again. Now he could not both draw trumps and establish his Diamonds, and he would probably win only five tricks, going down 900. At Diamonds, however, South would have plenty of trumps for Heart ruffs, and would lose only his two singletons and two trump tricks, going down 300 points even at a higher contract. (Even the double-dummy defense of a Spade opening and continuation by West, without touching Hearts, could beat South only 500 points).

In this case, therefore, the 5-3 Spade suit produced only five tricks as against nine tricks for the 6-2 Diamond suit, a difference of four tricks; and it will be noted that neither suit broke badly.

SLAM TRIES ON WEAK HANDS

When your partner makes one of the powerhouse opening bids like an opening two-bid or an opening 3 No Trump bid, you have to perform a sort of mental gyration to remind yourself that a weak-looking hand may represent just the added measure of strength necessary to make a slam. For example:

OPENER	RESPONDER
♠ A K x	♠ x x
♡ K Q 10 x	♡ x x
◇ A K x	◇ x x x
♣ A Q x	♣ K x x x x x

Opener bids 3 No Trump, for which he has the precise values. Responder bids 4 Clubs. Opener rebids 5 Clubs, showing a fit with Clubs. Responder should bid 6 Clubs. Opener can hardly have 6½ honor tricks, lacking the King of Clubs, unless he has at least three Aces. Even if opener has the minimum of 6½ honor tricks, as he has in this case, the combined hands have at least eleven tricks in top cards and trumps, and should have at worst a finesse for a twelfth trick. If opener has anything extra, there will be twelve sure tricks.

In the example shown, a trick must be lost to the Ace of Hearts, but if the Ace is under the King-Queen an extra Heart trick can be set up for a discard of one of responder's Diamonds; and if either opponent has the Jack of Hearts no more than twice guarded, it can be ruffed out and an extra trick established in that way. The result is a far better than fifty per cent chance of making six.

Another case, in which the responder must take the initiative in slam bidding after a two-bid:

OPENER	RESPONDER
♠ A K Q J x x	♠ x x x
♡ A x	♡ K 10 x x
◊ A K Q 10	◊ J x x
♣ x	♣ x x x

The bidding:

OPENER	RESPONDER
2 ♠	2 N T
3 ◊	3 ♠
4 ♡	5 ♡
6 ♠	

The opening bid of 2 Spades requires no comment, nor does the response of 2 No Trump. West shows the Diamonds merely for the purpose of eliciting some further information from responder. When responder merely returns to 3 Spades, he has so far shown absolutely nothing. So when opener bids 4 Hearts, obviously a "fishing" bid, responder must show that he has the King of Hearts, for he could have made his previous bids without any high cards. The opener is now able to contract for the slam. Note that responder had the right King. The King of Clubs would have been a useless card.

CHAPTER 10

DUPLICATE BRIDGE BIDDING

THE POINTS OF VARIANCE between duplicate contract and rubber bridge are fewer than is commonly supposed. There are, to be sure, certain fundamental differences in the philosophy of the two games. In rubber bridge it is the big hands (or those involving big penalties) that really matter. In duplicate bridge with match-point scoring, every hand counts. In fact, every hand counts exactly as much as every other hand, and one producing a contract of 2 Clubs weighs just as heavily in the scales as one that produces 7 No Trump.

Each deal in a match-point duplicate game is a separate contest. The purpose of each pair is to do better than the other pairs. *How much* better is not really important, as examination of the following "travelling score slip" (that is, the record of all the times a certain deal was played) will indicate:

BOARD 4

N–S vs. Pair No.	E–W Pair No.	Contract	N–S +	N–S —	N–S Match-Points
1	1	4 ♠	620		3
2	3	3 N T	600		1½
3	5	3 N T	600		1½
4	2	3 N T	630		4
5	4	5 ♡ x	1400		5
6	6	5 ♠		100	0

Match-point scoring is accomplished in this manner: The scores of the pairs which played the same cards are compared. Each pair receives 1 match-point for each other pair with a lower score, and ½ match-point for each other pair with the same score.

Observe the results of the North-South pairs on the deal (designated as Board 4) which is scored above. Pair 5 was able to double an opposing 5 Heart contract and to defeat it 1,400 points. This score beat the results obtained by the other five North-South pairs, whereupon Pair 5 gets 1 match-point from each of them, a total of 5 match-points. Pair 4 had the next-best North-South score; it beat four other pairs and receives 4 match-points. Pair 1 beat three other pairs and receives 3 match-points.

The +1,400 score of Pair 5 was 770 points better than the score of Pair 4, yet Pair 5 receives only 1 match-point more than Pair 4. And Pair 4 has the same 1-point advantage over Pair 1, whose score it beat by only 10 points.

OPENING BIDS

My tactics in the matter of opening bids at match-point duplicate do not vary widely from those employed in rubber bridge. A slight relaxation of the requirements has been found profitable when the prospective opener holds a suit headed by the Ace and King. The advantage is to be found in the assurance that the best opening lead will be obtained should the final contract fall to the adversaries.

The importance of the opening lead can hardly be overestimated at match-point play.

And in third position, whether vulnerable or not, I never pass holding a biddable suit headed by the two top honors.

IT DOESN'T PAY TO "SHOOT"

Although the objective in match-point duplicate is to beat the other pairs, this does not mean that you should make a direct effort to make a big score on every hand. Such tactics may yield a few "tops," when you have the best score on the board, but gambling bidding will inevitably lead to an even greater number of "bottoms," when you have the worst score. A "top-or-bottom" style of bidding is losing play in duplicate bridge.

For example, you are South and hold this hand:

♠ A J x ♡ A Q 10 x x ◇ J 10 x x ♣ J

The bidding has proceeded:

SOUTH	WEST	NORTH	EAST
1 ♡	Pass	1 N T	Pass
2 ♡	Pass	2 N T	Pass
?			

At rubber bridge, you might decide to push on to 3 No Trump. You realize that this is a gambling bid, but the gamble is worth while. Making a game is worth 500 to 600 points; making a part score is worth no more than 150 points. For the chance for increased profit you can risk going down a trick, or perhaps going down an additional trick.

But in duplicate this gamble is not a good one. If you stop at 2 No Trump, the mere fact that you are in a No Trump contract, in which the first trick counts 40 points, will give you a better score than pairs which stop at a Heart or other suit contract and take the same number of tricks that you do. If you gamble on 3 No Trump and go down, these pairs will automatically beat you. The fact that a successful game contract might add several hundred points to your total-point score does not influence you; in match-point scoring you are not interested in the extent of your advantage over other pairs. Any advantage at all is sufficient.

This point was first forcibly brought home to me in the Great Lakes Championship the year that tournament was held in Buffalo. On the hand which comes to mind the bidding had progressed to 2 No Trump, at which point it was clearly indicated that I should pass. However, it was near the end of the session, and feeling, as I did, that drastic measures were in order, I stretched to 3 No Trump, which, due to an error in the defense, I was permitted to make for a score of plus 600. There were 24 tables in play and when the scores were posted, I observed that I had attained a complete top score of 23 points. I also noted, however, that had I been content to pass at 2 No Trump a score of plus 150 would have yielded 22 points. It occurred to me, therefore, what a "sucker" I had actually been. I had risked perhaps 20 points in order to gain an additional 1.

On the same reasoning, you should not bid doubtful slams in a duplicate game. When a slam is at all close, at least half of the other pairs, and possibly two-thirds of them, will fail to reach it.

If you gamble on a slam, you risk losing to all these pairs in order to tie the minority who will bid the slam.

In an effort to obtain the maximum score, many players will strain to play a slam at No Trump instead of a major suit, or to play in a doubtful major instead of a minor suit. If the higher-ranking contract is just as safe as the lower, naturally it should be selected. It has been my observation, however, that in the long run it will prove more profitable to select for the final slam contract that suit which offers the greatest safety. In this respect, the leaning should be more in the direction of rubber bridge tactics. The reason is that a vast majority of slam contracts, though they are not played in the maximum contract, will yield an above-average score. The risk entailed in seeking a higher-ranking contract is frequently not commensurate with the increase in the number of match points that the higher contract yields.

WATCHING THE VULNERABILITY

For making a vulnerable game in duplicate, you add 500 points to your score. Since the trick-score must be at least 100 points, a vulnerable game contract bid and made must total at least 600.

When you have a choice between doubling the opponents and making a game of your own, vulnerability decides the issue far more often than it does in rubber bridge. Suppose you are vulnerable and your opponents are not, and you hold:

♠ J x   ♡ A J x   ◇ K 10 x x   ♣ K J x x

Your partner is the dealer and bids 1 Spade. Next hand overcalls with 2 Diamonds. In rubber bridge, you would double. In duplicate, if you were not vulnerable, or if your opponents were vulnerable, you would double. The 2 Diamond overcaller is getting a very bad trump break, and should go down three tricks even if he had a sound overcall.

Inasmuch as you are vulnerable against non-vulnerable opponents, there is some doubt as to the wisdom of doubling. There is a strong likelihood that you can make game, for a score of 600 or more. Now, should it develop that you can punish the adverse contract to the extent of only three tricks, for 500 points, your action will prove disastrous. However, if a four-trick sting can be inflicted, the 700 points should yield a top score or close to it. The conservative procedure is to go for game, the aggressive step is to try for the four-trick penalty.

In rubber bridge, no such anxious moment is presented. A sure profit of at least 500 points is there to be taken. And the double is the proper procedure in order to "sweeten the kitty." After this hand the odds will still remain 3 to 1 in favor of your winning the rubber.

While taking sure profits in rubber bridge is sound business it is not necessarily so in duplicate because all profits are comparative.

In rubber bridge, you make a preëmptive bid when you are sure you cannot go down more than 500 points. In duplicate, you cannot do this against non-vulnerable opponents. Making a non-vulnerable game adds a bonus of only 300 points to the trick-score, so that the maximum score for bidding a game (and making less than a slam) is 460. You cannot risk a loss of 500 points to keep your opponents from making a score of 400 to 460 points.

As a matter of fact, preëmptive bids in general are not so sound in duplicate as they are in rubber bridge. When the strength is evenly divided between the two sides, making a part score of 2 Spades may be the best either side can do. If you make a preëmptive 3 Spade bid and go down one, you will have a very bad score.

FREE RAISES

Free raises when partner's opening bid has been overcalled should still be sound, though somewhat more shading is permitted in duplicate bridge. However, the shading must not be carried too far.

For example: As South you hold:

♠ Q 10 x x x x
♡ x
♢ 10 x x
♣ J x x

The bidding has progressed:

NORTH	EAST	SOUTH
1 ♠	2 ♡	?

A raise to 2 Spades is not recommended. Better procedure is to pass and await developments. If the opponents should reach a 4 Heart contract, you will naturally wish to sacrifice at 4 Spades, but if you make an immediate free raise, you may find yourself in a position where you are called upon to make a very difficult decision later on in the auction. If you pass first and compete violently in Spades thereafter, partner knows that you have trumps and distribution but no honor strength.

CHOICE OF CONTRACTS

The fact that Spades and Hearts count 30 per trick, as against 20 per trick for Diamonds and Clubs, often makes it wise to choose a higher-scoring contract in preference to a safer one. Suppose you hold:

♠ J x x   ♡ A 10 x x   ◇ J x x x   ♣ x x

Partner opens with 1 Diamond. In rubber bridge you would respond by raising to 2 Diamonds. It is a safe contract, and unless partner can rebid over 2 Diamonds there is no possible hope of game. At duplicate, your response would be 1 Heart; you cannot surrender the opportunity of getting into a major suit.

Now partner rebids 1 Spade. At rubber bridge you would return to the safer 2 Diamond contract; partner probably has only a four-card Spade suit and may have a five-card Diamond suit, and even if he has only four Diamonds, your added length in that suit would make it safer. But at duplicate, you pass 1 Spade. If by chance you can make the same number of tricks in Spades and Diamonds, the 2 Spade contract will be far better. If you can make one more trick at Diamonds, a 2 Spade contract fulfilled will still be as good as a 3 Diamond contract.

OVERCALLS

Everything that has been said in the previous chapter on over-calls applies with almost equal effect to duplicate. A slight modification is to be noted in the direction of the freer use of overcalls. At rubber bridge, one bad bid might cause you the afternoon's profits. At duplicate, an error in judgment will result at most in the loss of that particular hand.

Any reasonable risk should be assumed in making overcalls in a suit in which the lead is desired. The importance of obtaining the best lead from partner can hardly be exaggerated in duplicate play, since countless numbers of match points are won and lost in the scoring of extra tricks. If a defense holds a suit headed by A K Q, it is almost obligatory to overcall even though a risk of being set for more than the value of game is thereby incurred. It will be seen that where such a trump suit is held, the likelihood of being doubled is reduced considerably, inasmuch as the highest outstanding trump is the Jack.

Where the lead of a suit is not especially desired, caution should be exercised in making overcalls of two in a minor suit, especially when vulnerable. Such overcalls are a frequent target for severe penalty doubles. The making of such a bid many times provides the opponents with "fielder's choice." That is to say, they have the choice of doubling, if that appears more profitable to them; or if you can make the contract, they simply go on with their bidding and your overcall has not served as very much of an obstruction, since it is made at a reasonably low level.

It is to be borne in mind that when you enter the auction with an overcall, you are apt to induce your partner to enter the fight with a suit of his own. Consequently, one should be very careful in making overcalls on a hand which contains a singleton in some unbid suit which partner may choose to name.

For example:

♠ 10 x x x   ♡ 10   ◇ A Q x x x x   ♣ K x

If the opening bid is 1 Heart, a 2 Diamond overcall is a reasonable step in duplicate. If partner elects to compete either by raising or by mentioning Spades or Clubs you should not be in difficulty, but if the opening bid happens to be 1 Spade, an overcall of 2 Diamonds would be of very doubtful wisdom, since partner may elect to compete in Hearts and you have no safety in a return to 3 Diamonds. That is another way of saying that one should beware of overcalls when he has length in the suit bid by the opponent.

♠ A K J x   ♡ x x x   ◇ x   ♣ K J 10 x x

The adversaries' opening bid has been 1 Heart. The orthodox overcall of 2 Clubs is recommended. If partner desires to bid 2 Diamonds, you will have a convenient retreat to 2 Spades and your distribution will have been shown. In duplicate, competition from partners in part score hands is more to be expected than in rubber bridge. Then there is the further consideration that if the opponents stop at 2 of their suit, you will be able to compete conveniently with a further overcall of 2 Spades.

♠ x   ♡ A K J x   ◇ x x x   ♣ K J 10 x x

Over an adverse opening bid of 1 Diamond, the recommended overcall is 1 Heart. If partner competes with 1 Spade, a convenient return bid by you of 2 Clubs is available.

Early raises of partner's overcall should be given more freely in duplicate than in rubber bridge, particularly if a high card is held in his suit. This will permit him safely to lead away from a doubtful holding such as A Q or K J against a final contract.

Furthermore, it will provide him with information which should be helpful to him in determining whether or not to make a sacrifice bid against the opposing contract. This is especially true where your side holds the Spade suit. For example:

As South you hold:

♠ K x x x   ♡ x x x   ◇ Q x x x   ♣ x x

The bidding has proceeded as follows:

WEST	NORTH	EAST	SOUTH
1 ♡	1 ♠	2 ♡	?

A raise to 2 Spades is recommended. Such a bid accomplishes the dual purpose of permitting partner to open Spades safely should the opponents play the hand and also permits him to take a sacrifice at 4 Spades should such action appear judicious to him.

In the pages on Responses to Overcalls it has been pointed out that the partner of the overcaller should never strain to make a bid, inasmuch as overcaller has failed to double, and consequently is not inviting voluntary action from partner. This principle should be relaxed somewhat in duplicate bridge. For example:

As South you hold:

♠ A Q 10 x x   ♡ x x   ◊ 10 9 x   ♣ 9 x x

The bidding has proceeded as follows:

WEST	NORTH	EAST	SOUTH
1 ◊	2 ♣	Pass	?

In rubber bridge a bid of 2 Spades at this point is doubtful strategy, but in duplicate bridge a bid of 2 Spades is recommended inasmuch as it is highly unlikely that opener will permit your partner to buy the contract at 2 Clubs, and you may feel disposed to compete on a later round when it will be less safe to do so. Furthermore, a bid of 2 Spades at this point may inhibit the opener from taking further action which from your standpoint appears to be not especially welcome. The actual hand to which I refer was played in a recent national championship and the complete deal was as follows:

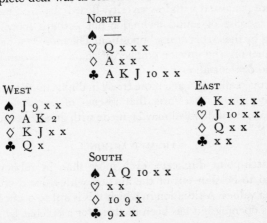

```
                    NORTH
                    ♠ —
                    ♡ Q x x x
                    ◊ A x x
                    ♣ A K J 10 x x
     WEST                             EAST
     ♠ J 9 x x                        ♠ K x x x
     ♡ A K 2                          ♡ J 10 x x
     ◊ K J x x                        ◊ Q x x
     ♣ Q x                            ♣ x x
                    SOUTH
                    ♠ A Q 10 x x
                    ♡ x x
                    ◊ 10 9 x
                    ♣ 9 x x
```

The bidding actually proceeded as follows:

WEST	NORTH	EAST	SOUTH
1 ◇	2 ♣	Pass	Pass
Double	3 ♣	3 ♡	3 ♠
Pass	4 ♣	Pass	Pass

The contract was defeated 1 trick.

It will be observed that if South had bid 2 Spades immediately, West would have been obliged to pass. North would have bid 3 Clubs and East would very likely have passed, permitting the fulfillment of contract. If, however, East decided to act, South would be able to pass with perfect ease. He would have done his duty, permitting North to take appropriate action, which in this case would be a profitable penalty double.

I recognize that in the game of bridge generalizations have little value, but for what it may be worth I offer the following: If it is true that at rubber bridge where a doubt exists the pass is usually superior, it is my belief that in duplicate bridge, where a genuine doubt exists, aggressive action will be more profitable The reason is that there are different goals at stake. In rubber bridge, it is the attainment of total points. In duplicate, it is dog-fight for the particular hand. It has been my observation that in match-point duplicate enterprise is rewarded more highly and errors are penalized with less severity. Boards are won not merely by the exercise of sound technique but perhaps more often in profiting by the errors of the opposition. The more you participate in the auction, the greater number of chances do you afford the enemy to commit an error.

Since overcalls are made more freely in duplicate than in rubber bridge it follows, therefore, that rescues of partner's overcalls which have been doubled may be made with greater frequency.

PROMPT ACTION

In match-point duplicate, even more than in rubber bridge, it is fatal to be shut out of the auction with a hand containing moderate values. A situation in which this is apt to occur is where partner's opening bid has been doubled for a takeout by the next opponent. Where you lack sufficient strength for a redouble, it may be vital for you to act at once, especially where participation on a later round may be fraught with danger; or where you may not have time to describe two salient features of your hand.

As South you hold:

♠ x x   ♡ A Q 10 x   ◇ x x x   ♣ Q 10 x x

The bidding has proceeded:

NORTH	EAST	SOUTH
1 ♣	Double	?

What do you do?

I have found it profitable in situations of this type to make an immediate bid of 1 Heart. On the next round I am in a position to make a competitive bid in Clubs, and partner should realize that my hand is of only moderate strength inasmuch as I had not seen fit to redouble. The bid of 1 Heart has the advantage (a) of suggesting what appears to be a good lead should the opponents win the auction; (b) of insuring against being shut out of the Heart suit, should partner have four mediocre Hearts.

CLOSE DOUBLES

At rubber bridge you would not dream of making a close double of a contract such as 3 Clubs, which if fulfilled will give your opponents game. But in duplicate you may have to risk a doubtful double now and then, as in such bidding as this:

SOUTH	WEST	NORTH	EAST
1 ♠	Pass	2 ♣	2 ◇
Pass	Pass	2 ♠	Pass
Pass	3 ◇	Pass	Pass
?			

Both sides are vulnerable. You are South and hold:

♠ A Q x x x   ♡ x x x   ◇ K 10 x   ♣ K x

Your side should be able to win five tricks against 3 Diamonds, but unexpected breaks might permit East to make the contract. You would never double in rubber bridge and risk having a game made against you, just for the chance of increasing the expected penalty from 100 to 200. But at duplicate you should think of this: You could probably have made the 2 Spade contract, which would score 110. If you defeat 3 Diamonds one trick undoubled, it will give you only 100 points and you will lose to all the North-South pairs whose opponents did not choose to go to 3 Diamonds against them. So you must double to protect your chance to get better than the 110-point score you could have made at 2 Spades.

If I were asked what single score produces more swings than any other, when match points are computed, I would unhesitatingly reply: minus 200. While minus 100 many times proves to be a good score (in cases where the adversaries could have made 110, 120, 130, or 140), 200 points exceeds the value of any part score contract and is apt to be disastrous, unless the loss is incurred as a save against a game.

Conversely it follows that plus 200 is one of the best scores attainable and is the figure upon which the duplicate player must frequently fix his aim.

In a dogfight for part score, by two non-vulnerable teams, where you have reached the conclusion that your side can go no farther than 3 Hearts and the opposition competes at 3 Spades, a double, when only a one-trick set is in view would be unthinkable at rubber bridge, for the extra 50 points thus scored are inadequate compensation for the risk incurred. Even when the opponents are vulnerable and the additional revenue is increased by 100 points, such close doubles should be eschewed when the coin of the realm is the prime objective.

At match-point duplicate entirely different considerations prevail. When the opposition has deprived you of the opportunity to score 140 points, an effort should be exerted to make them pay for their trespass. If they are not vulnerable and you succeed in defeating them only one trick, the compensation of 100 points will be inadequate and your match-point score will probably still be bad. The difference between 50 and 100 points will not be very decisive and such doubles should therefore not be made on suspicion, since a fulfilled doubled contract will surely result in a bottom for you.

Where you are quite confident that you can defeat them one trick, you should double because occasionally you will defeat the contract a trick more than was expected and the 300 points thus attained should land you close to the top.

Where the opponents are vulnerable, regardless of whether or not you are, a somewhat different attitude should be assumed. Since a set of one trick doubled will yield you 200 points, you should be quicker to wield the ax, despite the fact that such practice will occasionally result in a bottom score when the adverse contract is fulfilled. In most such cases it will be found that the "zero" thus incurred was not quite the disaster that it would seem to be at first blush, for in most of these cases you will discover that had the opposition been permitted to play the hand at 3 Spades undoubled and scored 140 points, your score would have been well below average, anyhow; so that your loss by doubling was only a few points. Whereas the gain where the double succeeds is much more than just a few points. The percentages, therefore, favor close doubles of vulnerable opponents.

SACRIFICING

There is much more sacrifice bidding in duplicate than in rubber bridge. In rubber bridge, a non-vulnerable pair does not deliberately take a 500-point set to keep its opponents from winning the rubber. At best the 500 loss would give it approximately an even break, and perhaps the opponents can be defeated.

In duplicate, a non-vulnerable pair must not overlook an opportunity to stop a vulnerable game by taking a sacrifice of 500, provided it is a fairly sure thing that the opposing game can be made. It doesn't pay, in duplicate, to hope for miracles.

My advice, however, is never to take a doubtful sacrifice. Once you do so you commit yourself to a minus score. If the opponents are permitted to play the hand, there is still the chance that you will be plus. It is my practice never to move deliberately minus

while there still remains a chance to be plus. Nor is it my policy
to take it for granted that the opponents always make what they
have bid.

As a matter of fact, a premature sacrifice bid may prove very
effective. For example: the adversary are bidding strongly and
appear to be headed for a final contract of 4 Hearts. You and
partner have participated in Spades. If it is your intention to sacrifice at 4 Spades, when the adversary arrives there, it might be
a good policy to bid 4 Spades before they actually reach game.
The psychological effect of such procedure is at times surprising.
The opposition will sometimes feel from your apparent show of
confidence that it is necessary for them to sacrifice at 5 Hearts
instead of doubling you (don't try this too often).

Sacrifices against slams should be engaged in very sparingly,
where the penalty will exceed the value of the adverse game. The
reason is that any penalty in excess of the game value will more
often than not mean a below-average score for the defender and
he will be salvaging very few match points by the "save." These
will be made up for by those hands in which the slam is, surpris-
ingly enough, defeated.

The bidding on this deal is fairly typical:

NORTH

♠ 10 x x x
♡ x x x
♢ K 9
♣ 9 x x x

WEST

♠ x
♡ A 9 x x
♢ Q 10 x x x
♣ A K Q

EAST

♠ Q x x
♡ K Q J 10
♢ J x x x
♣ J x

SOUTH

♠ A K J 9 x
♡ x x
♢ A x
♣ 10 x x x

Both sides were vulnerable. The bidding:

NORTH	EAST	SOUTH	WEST
Pass	Pass	1 ♠	Double
2 ♠	3 ♡	Pass	4 ♡
Pass	Pass	4 ♠	Double
Pass	Pass	Pass	

South, vulnerable, would never have bid 4 Spades in rubber bridge. The chance of beating 4 Hearts is a doubtful one, but enough of a possibility to hope for. South fully realizes that there is no chance of making 4 Spades. But at duplicate, knowing that he is most unlikely to go down more than two tricks (500 points) at Spades, South considers sacrifice bid a better chance.

The play of this hand, too, was typically in duplicate style. West started off by cashing three Club tricks, then East-West took two Heart tricks and South was already down two. He had lost the maximum of 500 he had expected. He had to win all the rest of the tricks or he would be down 800 and could not possibly get a good score, whether the opponents could make a vulnerable game or not.

Now South got in by trumping a third round of Hearts. He took the Ace of Spades. Then he entered dummy with the King of Diamonds, led a low Spade, and finessed for the Queen. By winning the finesse he held the set to 500 points.

There was no "guessing" connected with South's decision to finesse for the Queen of Spades. If the Queen of Spades could be dropped by leading the King, North-South could have won two Spades and two Diamonds against 4 Hearts, so the 4 Heart contract could not have been made. In that case, even the score of down 500 would be a bad one. South had to assume that 4 Hearts could have been made, in which case West had to have a singleton Spade and the finesse would work.

FOURTH-HAND OPENINGS

Certain holdings which might be "tossed in" at rubber bridge by the player in the fourth seat are justifiable openings in duplicate. However, the range of difference is very narrow, and liberties should be taken, as a rule, only with hands that have some values in the Spade suit, to guard against painful competition from the adversaries in that direction.

My observation has been that sub-minimum openings, fourth hand, are a losing practice. While an occasional good score will be obtained by such ventures, I am convinced that on balance the net result will be below average. When such openings are made, you are more apt to run into adverse competition, and you will be at a psychological disadvantage in exercising your judgment in making future decisions. Any further action on your part will be colored with the apprehension induced by your doubtful opening.

CHAPTER II

MODERN EXPERT VARIATIONS

EXPERT PLAYERS have their individual preferences in bidding conventions and are always likely to be experimenting with "something new." In this chapter I outline a few methods which I do not use myself, but which have the support of certain groups of good players. You may want to try them; and at least you will want to be prepared to play against them.

ACE-SHOWING RESPONSES TO TWO-BIDS

Some players play that the first response to an opening (game-forcing) two-bid should show an Ace if possible. If the responder holds an Ace, he must respond in the suit in which he has the Ace.

Suppose your partner opens with 2 Hearts, as described on page 22. Playing the Ace-showing responses, you respond as indicated on the following hands:

♠ K Q x x x   ♡ x x x   ◇ A x   ♣ x x

Bid 3 Diamonds; not 2 Spades, which would show the Spade Ace.

♠ K Q J 10   ♡ J x x x   ◇ x x x   ♣ x x

Bid 2 No Trump; a raise to 3 Hearts would show the Heart Ace.

♠ Q x x x x   ♡ x x x   ◇ ——   ♣ K x x x x

Bid 2 No Trump; void suits are not shown on the first response.

With any two Aces, the responder jumps to 4 No Trump over partner's two-bid. For example, he would bid 4 No Trump over partner's 2 Hearts with this hand:

♠ A x x x   ♡ A x   ◇ J x x x   ♣ x x x

Other jump responses are used to show strength without Aces. Therefore, when playing the Ace-showing responses, the weak double raise to four (described on page 25) is not used. For example, partner opens with 2 Hearts and you hold:

♠ x   ♡ x x x x   ◇ K J x x   ♣ Q x x x

Bid 4 Hearts; a 3 Heart bid would show the Heart Ace, while on a weak hand you would first respond 2 No Trump, even with good trump support.

♠ K Q J 10 x x   ♡ x   ◇ x x x   ♣ x x x

Bid 3 Spades, denying any Aces but showing a near-solid suit.

♠ K x x   ♡ x x   ◇ K Q x x   ♣ x x x x

Bid 3 No Trump, denying any Aces but showing 1½ honor tricks.

The use of the Ace-showing responses puts the opening two-bid in the class of the famous Sims three-bids which were popular back in 1932 but which could be used so rarely that their use was soon discontinued. However, the players who now use Ace-showing responses to two-bids get frequent opportunities to use them, because they open with two-bids on many hands of considerably less than 4 honor tricks and no sure game. For example, I have seen one of these players make an opening two-bid on a hand like this:

♠ A K Q J x x   ♡ x   ◇ K Q 10 x x   ♣ x

He figured that if his partner had two Aces and could respond 4 No Trump, he had a good gambling slam bid; and if his partner had a weaker hand his two-bid might scare the opponents out of bidding. However, I think it is more important to show a definite minimum strength with a two-bid, for slam-bidding purposes (see page 251), and that it is more valuable to find the best trump suit than to locate the Aces immediately. Aces can be shown later.

THE FOUR ACES "WEAK" TWO–BID

There is a small school of players, including members of the Four Aces team, who have in recent years been using an opening bid of 2 Diamonds, 2 Hearts or 2 Spades to indicate a hand that contains a good suit but lacks the 2½ honor tricks required for a standard opening one-bid.

The term "weak" in this connection refers to the high-card strength. The hand is not weak in playing strength. In fact, the bidder guarantees that he will take at least five tricks in the play and possibly as many as seven. While he denies holding 2½ honor tricks, he indicates the type of hand on which you "feel like bidding" although you have only 1½ to 2 honor tricks. The weak two-bidder promises to take one trick defensively.

The purpose of the weak two-bid is to deprive the opponents of one level of bidding, which may keep them from their best contract when they have the stronger hands. When the two-bidder's side has the stronger hands, the weak two-bid does not interfere with its reaching its best contract, because the two-bidder shows precise values and his partner therefore knows exactly how far to go. Such, at least, is the argument of those who use this bid. It has not really been tested widely enough for any final verdict to be in order. While the weak two-bid has produced good results so far, it must be remembered that it has been used only by very strong players, who are usually able to make any bidding convention seem good.

The following are examples of "weak" opening two-bids. On each of the following hands 2 Spades would be bid originally:

1. ♠ K Q J 9 x x   ♡ x   ◊ K x x   ♣ x x x
2. ♠ Q J 10 9 x x   ♡ x   ◊ A x x x   ♣ x x
3. ♠ K Q 10 x x x   ♡ x x   ◊ A x x   ♣ x x

The following hand does not qualify as an opening two-bid because it lacks one defensive trick.

♠ Q J 10 9 x x x   ♡ x x   ◊ Q J x   ♣ x

If not vulnerable the above hand may be opened with a preëmptive bid of 3 Spades.

There are certain hands of the same type which should not be opened with a weak two-bid because they might impede partner in his effort to reach a game contract. For example:

♠ K J 10 9 x x   ♡ A J 9 x   ◇ x x   ♣ x

This hand meets with the requirements for a weak two-bid but it would be bad strategy to make the call because it might prevent your side from reaching a game in Hearts if your partner has that suit with a smattering of high cards. If the Heart holding were in one of the minor suits instead, the hand would qualify as a weak 2 Spade bid.

When partner has already passed and game is doubtful, a strategic weak two-bid may be made with 2½ or more honor tricks, with the hope of trapping the opponents.

RESPONSES TO THE WEAK TWO-BID

There is no point in responding unless you have about the equal of an opening bid, for otherwise there can be no hope of game. If the responder bids 2 No Trump or takes out into another suit the opener must bid once more. If the responder raises from two to three the opener may bid again or pass, as he chooses.

THE ARTIFICIAL 2 CLUB BID

When the opening bid of 2 Spades, 2 Hearts or 2 Diamonds is used to designate a particular type of hand, some other method must be adopted to take care of hands on which an opening demand bid is in order. The substitute method is the artificial 2 Club bid. This is employed on all hands which would ordinarily be opened with a demand two-bid.

The weakness response is 2 Diamonds. It is made when the response to the ordinary demand two-bid would have been 2 No Trump. After the 2 Diamond response the bidder starts over and proceeds in the normal manner, as though a regular two-bid were now being made.

If the responder has a hand on which he desires to make a positive response he bids 2 Hearts, 2 Spades, 2 No Trump, 3 Clubs or 3 Diamonds. The 3 Club bid in this sequence denotes a real Club suit and not merely a raise for Clubs, since the opening 2 Club bidder may not have any of that suit at all.

(1)	(2)	(3)
♠ x x x	♠ x x	♠ x x x x
♡ x x	♡ x x x x	♡ x x x
◇ x x x x	◇ x x	◇ K x x
♣ x x x x	♣ J x x x x	♣ A x x

NORTH	NORTH	NORTH
	SOUTH	

♠ A K Q x x
♡ A K x x x
◇ A x
♣ x

The bidding:

	(1)			(2)			(3)	
SOUTH	NORTH		SOUTH	NORTH		SOUTH	NORTH	
2 ♣	2 ◇		2 ♣	2 ◇		2 ♣	2 NT	
2 ♠	2 NT		2 ♠	2 NT		3 ♠	4 ♠	
3 ♡	3 ♠		3 ♡	4 ♡		6 ♠		
4 ♠	Pass		Pass					

In hand 1 North makes the negative response of 2 Diamonds. South then shows his Spade suit in orthodox manner, North's second bid of 2 No Trump, is the accepted bust response. When South shows his second suit North indicates a preference for Spades.

In hand 2 the sequence is similar but North eventually shows a preference for Hearts.

In hand 3 North's response shows an Ace and a King. His next bid shows Spade support.

NORTH
♠ x x x
♡ K x x x x
♢ A x
♣ x x x

SOUTH
♠ A K x
♡ A Q J x
♢ K Q J x
♣ A K

The bidding:

SOUTH	NORTH
2 ♣	2 ♡
7 NT	

North's response of 2 Hearts shows a five-card (or longer) Heart suit headed by at least the King and an Ace, which permits South to count thirteen tricks.

FORCING TAKE-OUTS OF NO TRUMP BIDS

Another variation recently adopted by the Four Aces is a forcing use of minor-suit take-outs of opening 1 No Trump bids.

Suppose you hold:

♠ Q x x x   ♡ J 10 x x   ♢ A J x x   ♣ x

Your partner opens with 1 No Trump. You have enough strength to raise, but you feel that a major-suit contract may be a better play for game than a 3 No Trump contract if partner has four cards in either major suit. You therefore respond 2 Diamonds. This is forcing for one round, as the Four Aces are playing it, and calls upon partner to name a fair four-card major (say, Q x x x or better) if he has one. If he has no four-card major, he rebids 2 No Trump (or may raise your minor suit to three if he lacks a stopper in one of the other suits).

The Four Aces do not recommend that this be used as an artificial bid; that is, if you respond with 2 Diamonds you must have Diamond strength and if you respond with 2 Clubs you must have Club strength.

This type of response is very much like other conventional responses to No Trump bids which have been offered from time to time. Practically all these methods have their merits, but the fact remains that the introduction of arbitrary bidding conventions leads to partnership misunderstandings and it is wise to use only such conventional bids as you really need, and then only when you are sure you can handle them without difficulty.

CHAPTER 12

REVIEW QUIZ

IN EACH OF THE FOLLOWING questions you are South. The bidding is indicated. What action do you take? (Answers begin on page 279.)

1.	♠ A K x x
	♡ A x x
	◇ x x x
	♣ x x x

NORTH	SOUTH
Pass	1 ♠
3 ♠	?

2.	♠ A K x x
	♡ A x x
	◇ x x x
	♣ x x x

SOUTH	NORTH
Pass	1 ♣
?	

3.	♠ J x
	♡ K 10 x
	◇ Q J x x
	♣ J x x x

NORTH	SOUTH
1 ♠	1 N T
2 N T	?

4.	♠ Q x
	♡ A J x
	◇ A J 9 x
	♣ K 10 x x

SOUTH	NORTH
1 ◇	1 ♠
1 N T	2 ♠
?	

5.	♠ K x x
	♡ J x x
	◇ Q x x
	♣ A K J x

SOUTH	NORTH
1 ♣	1 ♡
1 N T	2 ♣
?	

6.	♠ A K x x
	♡ x
	◇ K Q x x x
	♣ J x x

SOUTH	NORTH
1 ◇	1 ♡
1 ♠	1 N T
?	

7.	♠ A K x x x
	♡ x
	◇ K x x
	♣ J x x x

SOUTH	NORTH
1 ♠	2 ♡
2 ♠	2 N T
?	

8.	♠ J 10 x
	♡ K J x x
	◇ x x x
	♣ Q J x

NORTH	SOUTH
1 ♡	1 N T
2 ♠	?

9.	♠ J x
	♡ x
	◇ K J 10 x x x x
	♣ Q x x

NORTH	SOUTH
1 ♠	2 ◇
2 N T	3 ◇
3 N T	?

10. ♠ K x x x x
    ♡ —
    ◇ x x x
    ♣ Q J x x x

NORTH	EAST	SOUTH	WEST
1 ♠	Double	?	

11. ♠ Q x
    ♡ 10 x x x
    ◇ Q x
    ♣ K J x x x

WEST	NORTH	EAST	SOUTH
1 ♣	Double	Pass	?

12. ♠ K x x
    ♡ K Q J x x
    ◇ Q x
    ♣ J x x

WEST	NORTH	EAST	SOUTH
1 ♣	1 ◇	Pass	1 ♡
Pass	1 N T	Pass	?

13. ♠ —
    ♡ K Q 9 x
    ◇ Q J 10 x
    ♣ Q J 9 x x

SOUTH	WEST	NORTH	EAST
Pass	1 ♠	Double	4 ♠
Pass	?		

14. ♠ A J x x
    ♡ A Q x x x
    ◇ x
    ♣ A x x

SOUTH	NORTH
1 ♠	2 ◇
2 ♡	3 ♠
?	

15. ♠ K x x
    ♡ J x
    ◇ Q 10 x
    ♣ A Q x x x

NORTH	SOUTH
1 ♡	2 ♣
2 ♡	2 N T
3 ♠	?

16. ♠ x x
    ♡ Q x
    ◇ K Q 10 x x x
    ♣ x x x

NORTH	SOUTH
1 ♡	2 ◇
2 ♠	3 ◇
4 ◇	?

17. ♠ x x
    ♡ Q 9
    ◇ Q J 10 x
    ♣ A Q 9 x x

NORTH	SOUTH
1 ♡	2 ♣
3 ♣	?

18. ♠ A x x x
    ♡ A x x
    ◇ x x
    ♣ A x x x

NORTH	SOUTH
1 ♣	1 ♠
2 ♣	?

19. ♠ A J x x x
    ♡ A J x x
    ◇ A x
    ♣ Q x

SOUTH	NORTH
1 ♠	2 ♠
?	

20. ♠ A K 9 x
    ♡ 10 x x
    ◇ Q J x
    ♣ A J x

21. ♠ K 10 x x x
    ♡ K J
    ◇ K x
    ♣ A K x x

22. ♠ A K 10 x
    ♡ x x x
    ◇ x x x
    ♣ A J x

SOUTH	NORTH		NORTH	SOUTH		SOUTH	NORTH
1 ♠	2 ♡		Pass	1 ♠		1 ♣	2 ♣
2 N T	3 ◇		2 ♡	2 N T		?	
?			3 ◇	?			

23. ♠ x x
    ♡ A K 9 x x
    ◇ J x x
    ♣ K Q x

24. ♠ x
    ♡ A 10 x x
    ◇ J 10 x
    ♣ A J 9 x x

SOUTH	WEST	NORTH	EAST		NORTH	EAST	SOUTH	WEST
1 ♡	Pass	3 N T	4 ◇		1 ◇	1 ♡	2 ♣	2 ♠
?					3 ◇	Pass	?	

25. ♠ Q x
    ♡ 9 x x x
    ◇ A 9 x
    ♣ K Q x x

26. ♠ K Q x x
    ♡ x x x
    ◇ K x x
    ♣ x x x

27. ♠ A J x x x
    ♡ J x
    ◇ A Q x x
    ♣ 10 x

NORTH	SOUTH		NORTH	SOUTH		NORTH	SOUTH
1 ♣	?		1 ♠	2 ♠		Pass	1 ♠
			3 ♠	?		2 ♡	?

28. ♠ J 9 x
    ♡ x
    ◇ K Q x x x
    ♣ K x x x

29. ♠ A 9 x x
    ♡ —
    ◇ A K x x x
    ♣ A x x x

NORTH	EAST	SOUTH	WEST		NORTH	EAST	SOUTH	WEST
1 ♠	2 ♡	2 ♠	3 ♡		1 ♡	Pass	2 ◇	Pass
4 ♠	5 ♡	?			3 ♡	Pass	3 ♠	Pass
					4 ♡	Double	?	

30. ♠ A 10 9 x ♡ K x x ◇ K x x ♣ x x x

NORTH	SOUTH
1 ♡	?

REVIEW QUIZ—ANSWERS

1. Pass. Partner's previous pass makes it evident there cannot be a game in the hand.

2. 1 Spade. Do not make a jump response, despite your previous pass. If partner fails to bid again you need not fear the loss of a game. This is really not a big hand.

3. 3 No Trump. You have more than you promised when you responded 1 No Trump. Adding a plus value for the possession of six honor cards, you have about 1½ honor tricks. You have a point count of 8, whereas you might have had only 6.

4. 2 No Trump. You have more than a minimum. The Queen of Spades has become promoted in value and partner has refused to give up at 1 No Trump, showing that he has a fairly good hand.

5. 2 Hearts. Partner apparently has a good hand because he refused to quit at 1 No Trump. Therefore make a courtesy bid of 2 Hearts. He cannot expect too much because you failed to raise the first time.

6. Pass. You have already shown the full strength of your hand and partner has not done anything of an enthusiastic nature. You have no reason to assume that 2 Diamonds would be a better contract.

7. Pass. You have an absolute minimum and have run into a partial misfit. If this hand will produce 3 No Trump your partner should have bid it. The 2 No Trump rebid (not being a jump) is not a force.

8. 4 Hearts. A raise instead of a preference. Partner has five Hearts and four Spades and a very strong hand. If partner had only a fair hand he would have opened with 1 Spade rather than 1 Heart.

9. Pass. You have warned partner that your hand may not be good for No Trump. He has proceeded in the face of your warning. He should have something good in Diamonds. Don't bid 4 Diamonds. Partners should be warned, not nursed.

10. 4 Spades. You may not be able to make it, but you have no defense against the enemy. Try to make it as difficult as possible for them to get together.

11. 1 Heart. Do not pass. You cannot promise to defeat 1 Club, because you are under the disadvantage of having the Club bidder over you. Don't respond with 1 No Trump. If partner acts you may try No Trump later.

12. 2 No Trump. Do not rebid Hearts. Your hand is well suited for No Trump. Partner has shown a fairly good hand but apparently re-

fused to double the opening bid because he was anxious to see if you could make a voluntary bid.

13. 4 No Trump. A peculiar bid, but the language is plain. "Partner, please name your best suit. I like them all and believe we should try for five. It couldn't mean a willingness to play No Trump, else I would have doubled 4 Spades."

14. 4 Hearts. 3 No Trump is not a good bid with only one Club stopper. 4 Spades is not recommended because partner does not know you have 5 Hearts. The rebid will make it clear that you have 5 Hearts and probably only 4 Spades. Partner's hand was:

♠ K 10 x   ♡ K J x   ◊ A 10 x x x   ♣ x x

15. 4 Hearts. Partner has shown a holding of six Hearts and four Spades. Do not make the mistake of supporting the Spades, of which the partnership has only seven as compared with eight Hearts.

16. 5 Diamonds. Partner has shown five Hearts, four Spades and probably three Diamonds, and therefore should be read for a single Club. The Heart Queen is the determining factor. Partner has a minimum of 4 honor tricks.

17. 3 Diamonds. In view of the promoted value of the Queen of Hearts your hand is the virtual equal of an opening bid. You should make an effort to get to game. A 3 Diamond bid may enable partner to try for 3 No Trump if he has a Spade stopper. Otherwise 4 Clubs should be safe.

18. 3 Clubs. While you have the values for a double raise you should avoid getting beyond 3 No Trump.

19. 3 Hearts. You have just enough to try once more and should give yourself an additional chance. Partner might have three Spades and four Hearts.

20. 3 Hearts. Resist the temptation to bid 3 No Trump. When partner has shown a two-suiter it is almost always good policy to show a preference for one of his suits, particularly when it happens to be a major. You have already told your partner that you prefer No Trump. Do not repeat the story. Partner must not expect good Heart support when you failed to make an immediate raise. Partner's actual hand was:

♠ x x   ♡ K Q x x x   ◊ K 10 x x x   ♣ x

21. 3 Hearts. Do not bid 3 No Trump. The bidding makes it clear that partner's suits are not good, else he would not have bothered to bid

3 Diamonds, but would have taken you to 3 No Trump. The 3 Heart bid permits partner to "get off the hook" should he desire to do so.

22. Pass. Do not make the mistake of bidding 2 Spades. There is no possible future to this hand and a 2 Spade bid would be interpreted as an effort to get to game.

23. Pass. Not because you are scared, but to give partner his choice. Slam is doubtful, since you have only 3 honor tricks and partner about 3½. The pass gives partner a chance to double or go on.

24. 3 Hearts. This bid serves a dual purpose. If partner has Spades stopped and elects to bid 3 No Trump you will be satisfied. If partner elects to go out slamming you have the necessary ingredients, with first-round control in Hearts and Clubs and second-round control in Spades. Partner's free rebid of 3 Diamonds shows a very fine hand.

25. 1 Diamond. This bid is not made in an effort to be fancy. It is simply that there is no satisfactory response and a temporary bid is recommended. The hand is too good for a raise to 2 Clubs and not good enough for a jump to three. No matter what partner does over the Diamond bid you will not be embarrassed.

26. Pass. This is not a very good hand. At the most liberal estimate it will produce only three tricks for partner, and this does not constitute a strong raise. Beware of the 4-3-3-3 hand. It's a wolf in sheep's clothing. It's never quite as good as it looks. I make it a practice to mentally subtract a King from my hand when I hold one of this distribution. Underbid rather than overbid evenly balanced hands.

27. Pass. Partner's previous pass makes game out of the question. Don't rebid Spades; partner might not like that suit at all.

28. Double. A pass by you at this point would be a slight inducement to partner to go on to 5 Spades, which it is doubtful that partner can make unless he elects to bid it in spite of your double of 5 Hearts. He must realize from the bidding that you are not doubling on Heart strength.

29. Redouble. East must have stepped out of line. Remember, partner has opened the bidding and jumped. But for the misfit, you would surely think of a slam. Even though the Hearts are badly banked it is inconceivable that the opposition will take more than three tricks.

30. 2 Hearts. Your hand is not strong enough to make two bids. If you should respond with 1 Spade you would not then be in a position to raise Hearts.

THE INTERNATIONAL CODE

THE LAWS OF
CONTRACT BRIDGE
1948

AS PROMULGATED IN THE WESTERN HEMISPHERE BY
THE NATIONAL LAWS COMMISSION

AMERICAN EDITION
Effective October 1, 1948

PROMULGATING BODIES

THE NATIONAL LAWS COMMISSION

HAROLD S. VANDERBILT, GEOFFREY MOTT-SMITH, *Chairmen*

R. J. BALDWIN
WALTER BEINECKE
MAJ. GEN. ALFRED M. GRUENTHER U. S. A.
LEE HAZEN

ALBERT H. MOREHEAD
HAROLD C. RICHARD
A. M. SOBEL
WALDEMAR VON ZEDTWITZ

RUBBER BRIDGE COMMITTEE FOR THE PROMULGATION OF THE AMERICAN EDITION

HAROLD S. VANDERBILT
WALTER BEINECKE
HAROLD C. RICHARD

WALDEMAR VON ZEDTWITZ
LEE HAZEN
GEOFFREY MOTT-SMITH

MAJ. GEN. ALFRED M. GRUENTHEP U. S. A.

CARD COMMITTEE OF THE PORTLAND CLUB

SIR A. NOEL MOBBS, K.C.V.O., O.B.E. *Chairman*

LT. COL. J. C. CRAIGIE, M.C.
DR. N. WOOD HILL
ARNOLD WARD
K. HURST-BROWN
SIR GUY DOMVILLE, BT.

H. H. RENSHAW
J. O. HASTIE
F. E. PERRY
GEOFFREY BUTLER
COL. G. G. J. WALSHE

BARON R. DE NEXON

EXECUTIVE COMMITTEE OF THE EUROPEAN BRIDGE LEAGUE

SIR A. NOEL MOBBS, K.C.V.O., O.B.E.
   (President and Chairman)

GREAT BRITAIN

BARON R. DE NEXON
EMILE HENRIQUES
J. ODRY
H. DEDICHEN (Honorary Secretary)

FRANCE
SWEDEN
BELGIUM
DENMARK

284

PREFACE TO THE AMERICAN EDITION

The new International Laws of Contract Bridge, effective as of October 1, 1948, replace the 1943 American edition of the Laws.

The first International Laws of Contract Bridge were promulgated in 1932 by The Whist Club, New York, the Portland Club, London, and the Commission Française du Bridge, Paris, and, in 1935, the same clubs issued a revised edition. In 1943 this code was replaced, in America, by a code promulgated jointly by The Whist Club and the National Laws Commission of the American Contract Bridge League.

By an agreement made in 1947 between The Whist Club and the American Contract Bridge League, the National Laws Commission, to whom The Whist Club delegated its title to prepare and publish the code presented herein, becomes the sole promulgating body of that code for America. The Portland Club and the European Bridge League have joined in the preparation and promulgation of the new International Code, temporarily suspended in 1943 owing to the war.

The National Laws Commission elected to its membership three members of The Whist Club committee on laws nominated by The Whist Club.

The Laws of Contract Bridge as presented in this book apply only to Rubber Bridge. Duplicate Bridge is governed by a separate International Code, also promulgated by the National Laws Commission. However, the two codes are identical in substance so far as the nature of the respective games makes it possible. When the 1948 edition of the Duplicate Bridge Laws is not available to a duplicate director he should follow the provisions of this book wherever they may apply, rather than any previous edition of the Duplicate Bridge Laws.

The National Laws Commission wishes to acknowledge the valuable contributions made in the preparation of the 1948 Laws by William E. McKenney, its chairman until 1948.

THE SCOPE OF THE LAWS

The Laws are designed to define correct procedure and to provide an adequate remedy in all cases where a player accidentally, carelessly or inadvertently disturbs the proper course of the game, or gains an unintentional but nevertheless unfair advantage. An offending player should be ready to pay a prescribed penalty graciously.

The Laws are not designed to prevent dishonorable practices and there are no penalties to cover intentional violations. In the absence of penalty, moral obligations are strongest. Ostracism is the ultimate remedy for intentional offenses.

The object of the Proprieties is twofold: to familiarize players with the customs and etiquette of the game, generally accepted over a long period of years; and to enlighten those who might otherwise fail to appreciate when or how they are improperly conveying information to their partners —often a far more reprehensible offense than a violation of a law.

When these principles are appreciated, arguments are avoided and the pleasure which the game offers is materially enhanced.

PART I

DEFINITIONS

THE PLAYERS—

PARTNER—The player with whom one plays as a SIDE against the other two. He occupies the opposite seat at the table.

OPPONENT—A player of the other side.

DECLARER—The player who for his side first bid the denomination named in the contract.

DUMMY—Declarer's partner.

CONTRACTOR—Declarer or dummy.

DEFENDER—An opponent of declarer.

HONOR—Any Ace, King, Queen, Jack or ten.

HAND—The cards originally dealt to a player or the remaining portion thereof.

ROTATION—The order of progression applying in the game, which is from player to player clockwise.

DENOMINATION—The suit or no-trump named in a bid.

ODD TRICK—A trick won by declarer in excess of six.

CALL—A comprehensive term applicable to a bid, a double, a redouble or a pass.

BID—An offer to contract to win at least a specified number of odd tricks in a specified denomination.

PASS—A call signifying that a player does not, on that occasion, elect to bid, double or redouble.

PLAY—To contribute a card to a trick, including the first card which is the LEAD.

TRUMP—Each card of the suit, if any, named in the contract.

FOLLOW SUIT—To play a card of the suit led.

REVOKE—To play a card of another suit when able to follow suit.

OVERTRICK—A trick won by declarer in excess of his contract.

UNDERTRICK—A trick by which declarer falls short of his contract.

SLAMS: Grand Slam—the winning of thirteen tricks by one side; Little Slam—the winning of twelve tricks by one side.

VULNERABLE—Having won a game toward rubber.

The meaning of the following terms is clarified in the laws: Pack, section 1; Deal, section 8; Contract, section 22-b; Sufficient Bid, Insufficient Bid, section 23; Double and Redouble, sections 24 and 25; Trick, section 47; Penalty Card, sections 67, 68 and 69; Game, section 94; Rubber, section 95.

PART II

THE DRAW, THE SHUFFLE, THE CUT, THE DEAL

THE PACK—RANK OF CARDS AND SUITS

1. Contract Bridge is played by four players with a pack of 52 cards, comprising 13 cards in each of 4 suits. The suits rank downwards in the order—Spades (♠), Hearts (♥), Diamonds (♦), Clubs (♣). The cards of each suit rank downwards in the order—Ace, King, Queen, Jack, 10, 9, 8, 7, 6, 5, 4, 3, 2. When practicable, two packs with distinguishable backs are used.

THE DRAW[1]

2. Before every rubber, each player draws a card from a shuffled pack spread face downwards on the table. A drawn card should not be exposed until all players have drawn. If a player exposes more than one card, or draws one of the four cards at either end of the pack, or draws a card from the other pack, he must draw again. In drawing, equal cards rank according to suit.

PARTNERSHIPS

3. The two players who draw the highest cards play as partners against the other two. The player with the highest card deals first and has the right to choose his seat and the pack with which he will deal. He may consult his partner but, having announced his decision, must abide by it. His partner sits opposite him. Thereafter, the opponents may, after consultation, determine their respective occupancy of the two remaining seats.

THE SHUFFLE

4. The pack for each deal is prepared by the player on the left of its dealer, if practicable while the other pack is being dealt. Preparing a pack consists of collecting the cards, shuffling them, and placing the shuffled pack face downwards on the left of the next dealer. The cards should be shuffled thoroughly and in full view of all players, but without exposing the face of any card.

5. A properly prepared pack should not be disturbed until its dealer picks it up for his deal, at which time he is entitled to the final shuffle. No player may shuffle a pack other than its dealer and the player on his left.

THE CUT

6. A pack must always be cut immediately before it is dealt. The

[1]If more than four persons desire to play, it is customary to follow the Rules for Club Procedure (at end of Laws section) to determine which of them shall have the right to play.

dealer presents it to the player on his right, who lifts off a portion and places it on the table toward the dealer beside the bottom portion. Each portion must contain at least four cards. The dealer completes the cut by placing the bottom portion uppermost.

NEW SHUFFLE—NEW CUT

7. Before the first card is dealt, any player may demand a new shuffle or a new cut. There must be a new shuffle and cut if a card is faced in cutting, or if there is a redeal. When there is a new shuffle, only the dealer may shuffle.

THE DEAL

8. The dealer must deal the cards face downwards, one at a time in rotation into four separate hands of 13 cards each, the first card to the player on his left and the last card to himself. If he deals two cards simultaneously or consecutively to the same player, he may rectify the error, provided he does so promptly and to the satisfaction of his opponents.

9. The dealer must not allow the face of any card to be seen while he is dealing. Until the deal is completed, no player may look at the face of any card, and no one but the dealer may touch any card except to correct or preclude an irregularity.

CHANGING THE DEALER

10. The turn to deal passes in rotation unless there is a redeal, in which case the same dealer redeals.

CHANGING THE PACK

11. The packs should be used alternately unless there is a redeal. The pack originally belonging to a side must be restored if reclaimed, but a deal may not be stopped to restore a pack. A pack containing a distinguishable damaged card must be replaced.

PART III

GENERAL LAWS COVERING IRREGULARITIES

REDEAL

12. There must be a redeal:

(a) If, before the last card is dealt, a redeal is demanded because a player is dealing out of turn or with an uncut pack.

(b) If it is ascertained before the last card is dealt that the cards have not been dealt correctly, or that a card is faced in the pack or elsewhere.

(c) If it is ascertained before the first call is duly made that a player has picked up another player's hand and seen a card in it.

(d) If it is ascertained before the cards have been mixed together that one player has picked up too many cards, another too few; or that the pack, when the deal began, did not conform in every respect to the requirements of section 1.

(e) If the players have allowed their hands to be mixed together before finding a missing card, or in the belief that a redeal is in order.

There may not be a redeal except as provided above.

MISSING CARD

13. A missing card, when found, is deemed to belong to the deficient hand.

When clause (d) or (e) of section 12 applies, there must be a redeal.

When neither clause applies, the deal stands, and, if the missing card was found in a trick, the defective trick law (section 80 or 81) applies. The missing card may become a penalty card under section 26 or 67, or failure to have played it may constitute a revoke. It must be placed in the deficient hand unless it becomes a penalty card or is found in a trick that stands as played.

SURPLUS CARD

14. If a player has too many cards, there must be a redeal unless he has omitted to play to a trick, in which case the defective trick law (section 80 or 81) applies.

DRAWING ATTENTION TO AN IRREGULARITY

15. When an irregularity is committed, any player (except dummy if he has looked at another player's hand) may draw attention to it and give or obtain information as to the law covering it. The fact that the offending side draws attention to its own irregularity does not in any way affect the rights of the opponents.

ENFORCEMENT OF A PENALTY

16. Either opponent individually (but not dummy) may select or enforce a penalty. If the opponents consult as to penalty selection or enforcement, or if either opponent waives the penalty; the right to penalize is cancelled, but the rectification provisions (if any) of the applicable section still apply.

17. After attention has been called to an irregularity, no player may call or play until all questions in regard to rectification and penalty enforcement have been determined.

18. The penalty provisions of the laws apply only after agreement on the fact that an irregularity has been committed, and after specific statement of the penalty to be applied.

19. All questions as to what course to follow must be settled by the players before the game continues. A penalty once paid or other action once taken stands, even though at some later time it is discovered to have been incorrect.

IMPROPER REMARKS AND GESTURES

20. If by a remark or unmistakable gesture a player other than declarer: discloses his intentions or desires, or the nature of an unfaced hand, or the presence or absence of a card in an unfaced hand; or improperly suggests a lead, play, or line of play; or improperly directs attention to the cards on a trick to which his partner has yet to play:

(a) If the offense occurred before the auction closed, (penalty) either opponent may require the offending side to pass whenever it is its turn to call; and if the offending side become defenders, declarer may require or forbid the opening lead of a specified suit.

(b) If the offense occurred after the auction closed, (penalty) declarer or either defender, as the case may be, may require the offender's partner to withdraw any lead or play which may have been suggested by the improper remark or gesture, and to substitute a card which does not conform to the improper suggestion. This penalty may be exacted on any trick subsequent to the offense but only on one such trick. The offender's partner may not be required to withdraw his card from a trick to which an opponent has played after him. Before this penalty may be enforced, a majority of the players must agree as to what lead, play or line of play has been improperly suggested.

PART IV

THE AUCTION

DURATION OF AUCTION

21. The auction begins when the last card of a correct deal has been placed on the table. The dealer makes the first call, and thereafter each player calls in rotation. After the first call has been made, the auction continues until three players have passed in rotation. This closes the auction.

PROCEDURE AFTER AUCTION IS CLOSED

22. After the auction is closed:

(a) If no player has bid, the hands are abandoned and the turn to deal passes in rotation.

(b) If any player has bid, the last bid becomes the contract and the play begins.

BIDS

23. Each bid must name a number of odd tricks, from one to seven, and a denomination, and must supersede any previous bid by naming either a greater number of odd tricks or the same number in a higher denomination. A bid that supersedes the previous bid is sufficient; one that does not is insufficient. The denominations rank downwards in order: No Trump, Spades, Hearts, Diamonds, Clubs.

DOUBLES AND REDOUBLES

24. A player may double only if the last preceding bid was made by an opponent and no call other than a pass has intervened. A player may redouble only if the last preceding call other than a pass was a double by an opponent.

25. All doubles and redoubles are nullified by a proper subsequent bid. If there is no subsequent bid, the scoring value of the contract is increased as provided in section 98.

CARD EXPOSED DURING THE AUCTION

26. If during the auction a player faces a card on the table, or sees the face of a card belonging to his partner:

(a) If an Ace, King, Queen or Jack, or a lower card prematurely led, or more than one card;[1] (penalty) the owner's partner must pass when next it is his turn to call. Every such card must be left face up on the table until the auction closes; and if its owner is then a defender, it becomes a penalty card.

(b) If a single card, lower than a Jack and not prematurely led, there is no penalty.

IMPROPER CALLS[2]

IMPROPER CALL PREMATURELY OVERCALLED IN ROTATION

27. If a player calls before the penalty for an improper call by his right-hand opponent has been enforced (see section 17), the auction proceeds as though it had been a proper call; except that if the improper call was a bid of more than seven, or a double or redouble made when only a pass or bid could be a proper call, the auction proceeds as though the improper call had been a pass.

[1] If two (or more) cards are faced or seen at different times, clause (a) applies to both of them even though one has been picked up as provided in clause (b).

[2] All possible improper calls are listed under this heading. Calls not recognized by nor dealt with in these laws are merely improper remarks. The auction proceeds as if an improper remark had not been made, unless the remark is sufficiently informative to warrant the imposition of a penalty under section 20 (a).

CHANGING A CALL

28. If a player changes a call in any way and does so practically in the same breath, his last call stands. There is no penalty unless he has changed to an improper call, in which case the appropriate "improper calls" section applies.

29. If a player changes a call in any way, and does not do so practically in the same breath, the change of call is void, and:

(a) If the first call was improper, the appropriate "improper calls" section applies.

(b) If the first call was a proper call, either the offender must allow his first call to stand, in which case (penalty) his partner must pass when next it is his turn to call; or the offender must substitute any other proper call, in which case (penalty) his partner must pass whenever it is his turn to call.

INSUFFICIENT BID

30. If a player makes an insufficient bid, he must substitute either a sufficient bid or a pass.[8] If he substitutes—

(a) The lowest sufficient bid in the same denomination, there is no penalty.

(b) Any other bid, (penalty) the offender's partner must pass whenever it is his turn to call.

(c) A pass, (penalty) the offender's partner must pass whenever it is his turn to call; and if the offending side become the defenders, declarer may require or forbid the opening lead of a specified suit.

CALL OUT OF ROTATION

31. A call out of rotation is void. The auction reverts to the player whose turn it is to call; and—

(a) If a player has passed out of rotation before any player has bid, or when it was the turn of the opponent on his right to call, (penalty) the offender must pass when next it is his turn to call.[4]

(b) If a player has made any call out of rotation other than a pass listed in (a), (penalty) the offender's partner must pass whenever it is his turn to call.[5]

[8]As provided in section 18, a player is entitled to select his substituted call after the applicable penalties have been stated. Any call he may have substituted previously is void, unless his left-hand opponent has overcalled it, in which case section 27 applies.

[4]Example: North (dealer) 1 Heart, South pass. The pass is void, and the auction reverts to East. After East has called, South must pass. Thereafter, North and South may in rotation make any proper call.

[5]Example: North (dealer) 1 Heart, South 1 Spade. The 1-Spade bid is void, and the auction reverts to East. After East has called, South may make any proper call. Thereafter, North must pass whenever it is his turn to call, but South may make any proper call whenever it is his turn to call.

32. A call is not out of rotation when made without waiting for the right-hand opponent to pass, if he is required to pass because of a law infringement.

33. If a player, whose turn it was to call, calls before attention has been drawn to a call out of rotation by his left-hand opponent, the auction proceeds as though that opponent had not called.

SIMULTANEOUS CALLS

34. A call made simultaneously with another player's proper call is deemed to be a subsequent call.

NAMING BID INCORRECTLY IN DOUBLING[6]

35. If a player in doubling or redoubling names an incorrect number of tricks or a wrong denomination, he is deemed to have doubled or redoubled the bid as made.

DOUBLING WHEN THE ONLY PROPER CALL IS A PASS OR BID

36. If a player doubles or redoubles a bid which his side has already doubled or redoubled, (penalty) he must substitute any proper call, and his partner must pass whenever it is his turn to call. In addition, if the offender elects to pass, either opponent may cancel all previous doubles and redoubles.

37. If a player doubles his partner's bid, redoubles an undoubled bid, or doubles or redoubles when there has been no bid, (penalty) the offender must substitute any proper call, and his partner must pass whenever it is his turn to call.

BID, DOUBLE OR REDOUBLE WHEN REQUIRED TO PASS
BID OF MORE THAN SEVEN

38. If a player bids more than seven, or bids, doubles or redoubles when required by law to pass; the offender is deemed to have passed, and (penalty) the offending side must pass whenever it is its turn to call, and if the offender becomes a defender, declarer may require or forbid the opening lead of a specified suit.

DOUBLY IMPROPER CALL

39. If a player makes a call subject to penalty under two or more "improper calls" sections, either section may be applied but not both.

CALL AFTER THE AUCTION IS CLOSED

40. A call made after the auction is closed is cancelled. If it is a pass by a defender, or any call by a contractor, there is no penalty. If it is a

---

[6] It is improper to state the number of tricks or the denomination in doubling.

bid, double or redouble by a defender, (penalty) declarer may require or forbid the other defender to lead a specified suit when first it is the latter's turn to lead.

REVIEWING THE AUCTION

41. A player who does not hear a call distinctly may forthwith require it to be repeated. There is no redress for a call based on a misunderstanding or on misinformation.

42. A player is entitled to have previous calls restated either when it is his turn to call, or after the auction closes but before the opening lead has been duly made. His request should be responded to only by an opponent. Dummy, or a player required by law to pass, should not ask to have calls restated, but may review the auction at an opponent's request and should correct errors in restatement.

43. After the opening lead, calls may not be restated, but declarer or a defender is entitled to be informed what the contract is and whether, but not by whom, it was doubled or redoubled.

PART V

THE PLAY

COMMENCEMENT OF PLAY

44. After the auction closes, the defender on declarer's left makes the opening lead. After the opening lead dummy spreads his hand in front of him on the table, face up and grouped in suits with the trumps on his right. Declarer plays both of the contractors' hands.

DUMMY'S RIGHTS

45. Dummy should refrain from all comment and from taking any active part in the play, except that he may:

(a) Give or obtain information as to fact or law.

(b) Question players regarding revokes as provided in section 71.

(c) Draw attention to an irregularity, or try to prevent one apparently about to be committed.[1]

Dummy forfeits these rights if he looks at a card in another player's hand.

DUMMY'S LIMITATIONS

46. Dummy should not exchange hands with declarer, lean over to see a defender's cards, leave his seat to watch declarer play, or, on his own initiative, look at the face of a card in any other player's hand. If

[1]Example: He may warn declarer against leading from the wrong hand, but only when it is apparent that declarer is about to do so.

dummy, as a result of any such act, sees a card in any other player's hand, and thereafter:

(a) Is the first to draw attention to a defender's irregularity, declarer may not enforce any penalty for the offense.

(b) Warns declarer not to lead from the wrong hand, (penalty) either defender may choose the hand from which declarer shall lead.

(c) Is the first to ask declarer if a play from his hand constitutes a revoke, and the revoke card is consequently withdrawn, (penalty) either defender may require declarer to substitute his highest or lowest correct card.

LEADS AND PLAYS

THE SEQUENCE AND PROCEDURE OF PLAY

47. The leader to a trick may play any card in his hand. After a lead, each other hand in rotation plays a card, and the four cards so played constitute a trick.

48. In playing to a trick, each player must if possible follow suit. This obligation overrides all other requirements of the laws. If unable to follow suit, a player may play any card.

49. A trick containing a trump is won by the hand playing the highest trump. A trick that does not contain a trump is won by the hand playing the highest card of the suit led. The hand winning a trick leads to the next trick.

PLAYED CARD

50. A card in any hand is played when named as the one a player proposes to play; but a player may change his designation if he does so practically in the same breath.

51. A card in any unfaced hand is played when it touches the table face upwards after being detached from the remaining cards with apparent intent to play; a defender's card so detached is also played as soon as his partner sees its face.

52. A card in dummy or any other faced hand is played when touched unless for a purpose other than play either manifest or mentioned.

TAKING BACK PLAYED CARD

53. A played card may not be withdrawn except:

(a) To comply with a penalty.

(b) To correct a revoke.

(c) To correct the error of playing more than one card to a trick.

(d) To substitute another card after an opponent has corrected either a revoke or a failure to comply with a lead or play penalty.

PREMATURE LEAD OR PLAY BY A DEFENDER

54. If a defender leads to the next trick before his partner has played to the current trick, or plays out of rotation before his partner has played, (penalty) declarer may require the offender's partner to play:

(a) His highest card of the suit led; or

(b) His lowest card of the suit led; or

(c) A card of another specified suit.

If declarer has played from both contractors' hands, a defender is not subject to penalty for playing before his partner.

LEAD OUT OF TURN

55. A lead out of turn may be treated as a correct lead. It must be so treated if the non-offending side plays a card before attention is drawn to the irregularity.[2]

56. If either defender requires declarer to retract his lead out of turn, the card wrongly led is replaced without penalty; and if declarer has led from the wrong hand, he must lead from the correct hand and (penalty), if he can, a card of the same suit. A defender's drawing attention to declarer's lead out of turn is equivalent to requiring its retraction.

57. If declarer requires a defender to retract his lead out of turn:

(a) If it was a contractor's turn to lead, declarer leads from the correct hand and the card led out of turn becomes a penalty card.

(b) If it was the other defender's turn to lead, (penalty) declarer may forbid the lead of that suit, in which case the card wrongly led is picked up; or may treat the card led out of turn as a penalty card, in which case any card may be led.

SIMULTANEOUS LEADS OR PLAYS

58. A lead or play made simultaneously with another player's proper lead or play is deemed to be subsequent to it. If a defender leads or plays two or more cards simultaneously, he may play either card, and the other card becomes a penalty card.

INABILITY TO LEAD OR PLAY AS REQUIRED

59. If a player is unable to lead or play as required to comply with a penalty, either because he has no card of the required suit or because of his obligation to follow suit, he may play any correct card. The penalty is satisfied, except in the case of a penalty card, which must be played at the first legal opportunity.

[2]If, after an opening lead by the wrong defender, declarer exposes his hand, see section 65.

PLAYING BEFORE PENALTY HAS BEEN ENFORCED

60. If declarer plays from either hand before enforcing a lead or play penalty, he is deemed to waive the penalty.

61. If a defender plays to a contractor's lead out of turn after declarer has been required to retract it, the defender's card becomes a penalty card.

62. A play by a member of the offending side, before a penalty has been enforced, does not affect the right of the non-offending side to enforce a penalty.

EXPOSED CARDS

DECLARER EXPOSING CARDS

63. Declarer is never subject to penalty for exposure of a card, and no card of declarer's ever becomes a penalty card.

64. If declarer plays more than one card he must designate which is his play, and must restore any other card to his hand.

65. If declarer exposes his hand after an opening lead by the wrong defender, and before dummy has spread any part of his hand, dummy becomes declarer.

66. If declarer intentionally exposes his hand otherwise than as provided in the preceding section, it is treated as a claim or concession of tricks and section 88 applies.

DEFENDER EXPOSING CARDS

67. If a defender faces a card on the table, or sees the face of a card belonging to his partner before he is entitled to see it in the normal course of play or penalty enforcement; any such card becomes a penalty card, except as otherwise provided in these laws.[8]

DISPOSITION OF A PENALTY CARD

68. A penalty card must be left face upward on the table until played. A defender should not pick up a penalty card and restore it to his hand; but if he does so, and if declarer plays from his own hand or dummy before requiring that the card be faced on the table again, such card ceases to be a penalty card.

69. A penalty card must be played at the first opportunity, whether in leading, following suit, discarding or trumping. The play of a penalty card is always subject to the obligation to follow suit, or to comply with

[8]Exceptions to section 67: A card led out of turn may be treated as a correct lead (section 55) or may be picked up (section 57-b). An exposed card may not be treated as a penalty card if dummy improperly (section 46-a) draws attention to it, or to the irregularity that caused its exposure.

a lead or play penalty. If a defender can play two or more penalty cards, declarer may designate which one is to be played.

DEFENDER IMPROPERLY EXPOSING HIS HAND

70. If a defender improperly exposes his remaining card or cards, declarer may treat the remaining cards of either defender as penalty cards. The hand of the other defender, if exposed, may be picked up.

THE REVOKE[4]

INQUIRIES REGARDING A REVOKE

71. Any player, including dummy, may ask a player who has failed to follow suit whether he has a card of the suit led, and may demand that an opponent correct his revoke.

CORRECTING A REVOKE

72. A player must correct his revoke—

(a) Made in any of the first eleven tricks, if aware of it before it becomes established.

(b) Made in the twelfth trick, if aware of it before the cards have been mixed together. There is no penalty for a revoke made in the twelfth trick and it never becomes established.

73. To correct a revoke, the offender withdraws the revoke card and follows suit with any card. A revoke card from a defender's unfaced hand becomes a penalty card; any other revoke card may be replaced without penalty. The non-offending side may withdraw any card it played after the revoke but before attention was drawn to it.

ACTS THAT ESTABLISH A REVOKE

74. A revoke in any of the first eleven tricks becomes established when the offender or his partner leads or plays to a subsequent trick or signifies his intention of doing so by naming a card, by claiming or conceding a trick, or by exposing a hand.

PROCEDURE WHEN A REVOKE IS ESTABLISHED

75. When a revoke is established, the revoke trick stands as played. It counts in transferring tricks as a trick won "after the revoke."

76. If a revoke becomes established, after play ceases two tricks are transferred to the non-offending side if the revoking side has won two or more tricks after the revoke. One trick only is transferred if the re-

[4] The penalty provisions of the revoke law are subject to section 46 if dummy has forfeited his rights. A claim of revoke does not warrant inspection of turned tricks except as permitted in sections 78 and 79.

voking side wins but one trick after the revoke. There is no penalty for an established revoke:

(a) If the revoking side wins no trick after the revoke.

(b) If it is a subsequent revoke in the same suit by the same player.

(c) If attention is first drawn to it after the cards have been mixed together.

(d) If it is made in failing to play any card faced on the table, including a card from dummy's hand or a penalty card.

TRICKS

GATHERING AND ARRANGING TRICKS

77. Each completed trick must be gathered and turned face down on the table by the side winning it. The cards of each turned trick should be kept together so that the trick can be readily identified. All the tricks taken by a side should be arranged together in front of declarer or of one defender in such manner that their number and sequence are apparent.

INSPECTING TRICKS
MIXING CARDS BEFORE A CLAIM IS SETTLED

78. Declarer or either defender may, until his side has led or played a card to the next trick, inspect a trick and inquire what card each hand has played to it. Except as above provided or to account for a surplus or missing card, turned tricks may be inspected before play ceases only with the other side's consent.

79. After play ceases, the tricks and unplayed cards may be inspected to settle a claim of a revoke or of honors, or the number of tricks won or lost. If, after such claim, an opponent so mixes the cards that the claim cannot be proved, it must be allowed.

DEFECTIVE TRICK

80. If a hand has played too many cards to a trick, or has omitted to play to it, and if attention is drawn to the irregularity before a player of each side has played to the next trick, the error must be rectified. A card withdrawn from a defective trick, if played from a defender's unfaced hand, becomes a penalty card.

81. If attention is drawn to a defective trick after a player of each side has played to the next trick, the defective trick stands as played, and:

(a) A hand with too few cards plays the hand out with fewer cards than the other hands, does not play to the final trick (or tricks), and if it wins a trick with its last card the lead passes in rotation.

(b) A hand with too many cards forthwith faces and adds to the defective trick (but without changing its ownership) a card it could properly have played to it.

TRICK APPROPRIATED IN ERROR

82. A trick appropriated by the wrong side must be restored on demand to the side that played the winning card, and, in any case, its scoring value must be credited to that side, subject to section 93.

FAILURE TO COMPLY WITH A LEAD OR PLAY PENALTY

83. If a player is able to lead or play a penalty card, or a card or suit specified by an opponent in conformity with an agreed penalty, but instead plays an incorrect card:

(a) The offender must correct his error if aware of it before he or his partner plays another card. If the incorrect card was played from a defender's unfaced hand, it becomes a penalty card. A card played from the hand on the offender's left may be withdrawn if it was played after the error and before attention was drawn to it.

(b) After the offender or his partner has played another card, the incorrect card may not be withdrawn. After play ceases, (penalty) there is a transfer of tricks to the non-offending side as though the offense were an established revoke (section 76).

CLAIMS AND CONCESSIONS

CONCESSION OF TRICK WHICH CANNOT BE LOST

84. The concession of a trick which cannot be lost by any play of the cards is void if attention is called to the error before the cards have been mixed together.

CONCESSION OF TRICK WHICH HAS BEEN WON

85. If a player concedes a trick he has in fact won (as by claiming nine tricks when his side has already won ten, or conceding defeat of a contract his side has fulfilled), the concession is void. If the score has been entered it may be corrected as provided in section 93.

DEFENDER CLAIMING OR CONCEDING TRICKS

86. A defender may show any or all of his remaining cards to declarer for the purpose of establishing a claim or concession. If a defender makes a claim or concession in any other manner, he may be liable to penalty under section 20.

87. A concession of tricks by a defender is not valid unless his partner accedes. This provision does not preclude the enforcement of a penalty for a defender's irregularity.

DECLARER CLAIMING OR CONCEDING TRICKS

88. If declarer intentionally exposes his hand, specifically claims or concedes one or more of the remaining tricks, or suggests that play may be curtailed, it is deemed to be a claim by declarer; and—

(a) Play should cease; and declarer should place and leave his hand face upwards on the table and forthwith make an adequate statement of his intended line of play.

(b) At any time after declarer's claim a defender may face his hand and may suggest a play to his partner. Declarer may not enforce any penalty for an irregularity committed by a defender whose hand is so faced.

(c) Declarer's claim must be allowed if both defenders accede to it, or if either defender allows his hand to be mixed with other cards.

(d) Either defender may require that play continue, in which case the section 89 applies.

89. If either defender requires that play continue after declarer's claim, declarer must play on, leaving his hand face upwards on the table. Declarer may make no play inconsistent with any statement he may have made. Unless declarer has stated his intention to do so at the time of making his claim—

(a) He may not lead a trump while either defender has a trump.

(b) He may not finesse either in the suit led or in trumping the suit led.

If declarer attempts to make a play prohibited by this section, either defender may require him to withdraw it, provided neither defender has played a card after it.

PART VI

THE SCORE

KEEPING SCORE

90. Each side has a trick score and a premium score. The scores of the respective sides for each rubber should be entered in two adjacent vertical columns, the trick points in descending order below a horizontal line separating the trick and premium scores, the premium points (i.e., all points other than trick points) in ascending order above this line. A scorer should enter scores made by his side in the left-hand column. Whenever a game is scored, a line should be drawn across the trick score of both sides and underneath all trick point entries made in that game, none of which carry over to the next game. Subsequent trick points should

be entered only below lines so drawn. Lines drawn prematurely should be forthwith erased.

RECORDING THE SCORE

91. When play ceases, all four players are equally responsible to see that the number of tricks won by each side is correctly determined, and that all scores are promptly and correctly entered in the score or scores, in accordance with the scoring table (section 98).

SCORING TRANSFERRED TRICKS

92. A transferred trick ranks for all scoring purposes as a trick won in play by the side receiving it.

CORRECTING THE SCORE

93. A proven or admitted error in any score may be corrected at any time before the rubber score is agreed, except that: If each player keeping score has made an error in entering or failing to enter a part score, or in omitting to score a game or in awarding one; such an error may not be corrected after the last card of the second succeeding correct deal has been dealt, unless a majority of the players consent.

A GAME—THE RUBBER

94. A game is won by the side which first scores a total of 100 or more trick points for odd tricks bid and won.

95. A rubber ends when a side has won two games, and the winners of the final game add to their score: 500 points if their opponents have won one game, 700 points if their opponents have not won a game. At the end of the rubber the trick and premium points of each side are added. The side with the larger total score wins the rubber, irrespective of the number of games (if any) which it has won. The difference between the two totals represents the number of points won.

EFFECT OF INCORRECT PACK

96. Scores made as a result of hands played with an incorrect pack are not affected by the discovery of the imperfection after the cards have been mixed together.

SCORING AN UNFINISHED RUBBER
PLAYER OBLIGED TO LEAVE

97. If for any reason a rubber is not finished, the score is computed as follows: If but one game has been completed, the winners of that game score 300 points; if but one side has a part score (or scores) in an unfinished game, that side scores 50 points; the trick and premium points of each side are added, and the side with the larger total score wins the difference between the two totals.

98. CONTRACT BRIDGE SCORING TABLE

			Undoubled	Doubled
TRICK POINTS FOR CONTRACTORS	Odd Tricks Bid and Won in			
	Clubs or Diamonds, each		20	40
	Hearts or Spades, each		30	60
	No Trump { first		40	80
	{ each subsequent		30	60

Redoubling doubles the doubled points for Odd Tricks.
Vulnerability does not affect points for Odd Tricks.
100 Trick Points constitute a game.

		Not Vulnerable	Vulnerable
PREMIUM POINTS FOR CONTRACTORS — DEFENDERS	Overtricks	Trick Value	Trick Value
	Undoubled, each	100	200
	Doubled, each		
	Making Doubled or Redoubled Contract }	50	50
	Undertricks		
	Undoubled, each	50	100
	Doubled { first	100	200
	{ each subsequent	200	300

Redoubling doubles the doubled points for Overtricks and Undertricks, but does not affect the points for making Doubled Contracts.

PREMIUM POINTS FOR CONTRACTORS — HOLDERS	Honors in One Hand {	4 Trump Honors	100
		5 Trump Honors or 4 Aces at No-Trump	150
	Slams Bid and Won {	Little, not vulnerable 500, vulnerable	750
		Grand, " " 1000, "	1500
	Rubber Points {	Two game	700
		Three game	500

Unfinished Rubber—Winners of one game score 300 points. If but one side has a part score in an unfinished game, it scores 50 points.
Doubling and Redoubling do not affect Honor, Slam, or Rubber points.
Vulnerability does not affect points for Honors.

THE PROPRIETIES

(1) It is reprehensible to profit by information gained as a result of an irregularity committed by one's own side for which no penalty, or a penalty incommensurate with the information gained, is prescribed.

(2) It is improper to infringe a law deliberately, as by making an insufficient bid, whether or not a penalty is prescribed.

(3) A player should refrain from—

a. Varying the formulae used in calling;[1]

b. Calling with special emphasis, inflection or intonation;

c. Passing or doubling with exceptional haste or reluctance;

d. Making a call with undue delay which may result in conveying improper information to partner;

e. Indicating in any way approval or disapproval of partner's call or play;

f. Giving by word, manner or gesture an indication of the nature of the hand held;

g. Making a remark or gesture or asking a question from which an inference may be drawn;

h. Giving unauthorized information as to an incident of the auction or play;

i. Volunteering information which should be given only in response to a question;

j. Requesting, except for his own benefit, a review of calls or a placing of cards played to a trick;

k. An unnecessary hesitation, remark or mannerism which may deceive the opponents;

l. Attracting attention to the score, except when necessary to do so for his own information;

m. Calling attention to the number of tricks needed to complete or defeat the contract or to the fact that it has already been fulfilled or defeated;

n. Playing a card with special emphasis;

[1]The recommended calling formulae are: "Pass" (avoid "I pass" or "no bid"); "1 heart" (avoid "I bid"); "1 no trump" (avoid "without" or "without a trump"); "double" (avoid stating the number of tricks or the denomination doubled); "6 spades" (avoid "little slam").

o. Playing with undue delay when the play does not need consideration;

p. Preparing to gather a trick before all four hands have played to it;

q. Detaching a card from his hand before it is his turn to lead or play;

r. Failing to keep the tricks in correct order and distinct from one another, or allowing some to be placed on the opposite side of the table;

s. Watching the place in a player's hand from which he draws a card, and drawing any inference therefrom;

t. Making gratuitous comments during the play as to the auction, the adequacy of the contract or the nature of the hand.

(4) It is improper to attempt to conceal a revoke by revoking again, or to conceal a revoke card if a hand is not played out, but there is no obligation to call attention to an established revoke or other irregularity committed by self or partner.

(5) It is improper to play out of turn, carelessly or otherwise.

(6) While it is reprehensible to allow partner's hesitation, remark or manner to influence a call, lead or play, it is proper to draw inferences from an opponent's gratuitous hesitation, remark or manner, but such inferences are drawn at one's own risk.

(7) It is proper to warn partner against infringing a law of the game (e.g., against revoking, or against calling, leading or playing out of turn).

(8) All four players are responsible to see that each hand plays a card, and but one, to each trick, and should forthwith correct such an irregularity.

(9) Declarer should play out all hands in which there is any doubt as to the eventual outcome.

(10) Bystanders or members not playing should refrain from making gratuitous remarks. They should not call attention to any irregularity or mistake, or speak on any question of fact or law except when requested to give an opinion.

(11) It is improper to employ, without explaining its meaning to the opponents, a convention in calling or an unusual convention in play, the significance of which may not be clear to them. When applied to a call, the term convention covers a call designed to convey an arbitrary or artificial meaning, or used by a player with the assurance that his partner will not accept it in its natural sense. Such a call is not subject to penalty as an improper remark. It is necessary that a convention so used should be fully understood by the other side, and players using conven-

tion calls should be ready to reply fully to a proper inquiry by an opponent as to their meaning or use. Should it be necessary to make such an inquiry during the auction, the partner of the player who has made the convention call should reply. The committee of any Association, Tournament or Club, or a group of persons playing Contract Bridge, may prohibit or restrict the use of conventions which are both generally unrecognized and sufficiently intricate to cause unreasonable delay.

RULES FOR CLUB PROCEDURE

The following rules, governing membership in new and existing tables, have proven satisfactory in club use over a long period of years.

DEFINITIONS

MEMBER—An applicant who has acquired the right to play at a table either immediately or in his turn.

COMPLETE TABLE—A Table with six members.

INCOMPLETE TABLE—A Table with four or five members.

TIME LIMIT ON RIGHT TO PLAY

A. An applicant may not play in a rubber, unless he has become a member of a table before a card is duly drawn for the selection of players or partners.

NEWLY FORMED TABLES

B. If there are more than six applicants, the six highest-ranking ones become members. The four highest-ranking members play the first rubber. Those who have not played, ranked in their order of entry into the room, take precedence over those who have played. The latter rank equally, except that players leaving existing tables to join the new table rank lowest.[1]

EXISTING TABLES

C. An application establishes membership in a table either forthwith or (if the table is complete) as soon as a vacancy occurs, unless applications in excess of the number required to complete a table are made at the same time, in which case precedence between applicants is established as in the preceding rule.

D. After each rubber place must be made, by the member who has played the greatest number of consecutive rubbers at that table,[1] for any member who did not play the last rubber, except that a member who

---

[1]Precedence between those of equal rank is determined by drawing cards, the drawer of the higher-ranking card obtaining precedence.

has left another existing table must draw cards for the right to play his first rubber with the member who would otherwise have played.

E. If a member breaks up a game by leaving three players at a table, he is not entitled to compete against them for entry at another table.

MEMBERSHIP LIMITED TO ONE TABLE

F. No one can be a member of more than one table at the same time, unless a member consents, on request, to make a fourth at another table and announces his intention of returning to his former table as soon as his place can be filled. Failure to announce such intention results in loss of membership at his former table.